POLES APART

Poles Apart

SOLIDARITY AND THE NEW POLAND

Jacqueline Hayden

IRISH ACADEMIC PRESS

FRANK CASS

This book was typeset
in 11.5 on 13.5 Ehrhardt by
Seton Music Graphics, Bantry and
first published in 1994 by:

in Ireland
IRISH ACADEMIC PRESS
Kill Lane, Blackrock, Co. Dublin, Ireland,

in Great Britain
Frank Cass and Company Ltd
Gainsborough House, 11 Gainsborough Road,
Leytonstone, London, E11

and in North America
IRISH ACADEMIC PRESS
c/o International Specialized Book Services,
5804 NE Hassalo Street, Portland, OR 97213.

© Jacqueline Hayden 1994

A catalogue record for this title
is available from the British Library.

Frank Cass ISBN
0-7146-4589-3 hbk; 0-7146-4121-9 pbk

Irish Academic Press ISBN
0-7165-2532-1 hbk; 0-7165-2533-X pbk

Printed in Ireland by
Betaprint of Dublin

For Jan and Krystyna Litynski

CONTENTS

ILLUSTRATIONS

Between pages 116 and 117

MAPS

PREFACE

I think that I should start by explaining why I had to write a book about Solidarity and the people that I met in Poland in the summer of 1980. I had gone there in July, well before news of the strikes had impinged on Western consciousness, for all the wrong reasons. I had become involved in a silly argument about latent censorship within the Irish media with a Dublin barrister who was convinced that nothing critical of left-wing governments would be published or broadcast in Ireland. As an eager young freelance I was very anxious to prove him wrong and even more anxious to accept his offer to pay for a flight to the Eastern European country of my choice. Having chosen Poland I found that editors were, perhaps predictably, interested in stories about the Catholic Church behind the Iron Curtain. And so with a brief which I realized in retrospect was somewhat narrow, I set off for Warsaw armed with the names of dissidents, writers and Church activists.

I had done my homework. I knew, or thought I knew, a little of Poland's sad history of partition and rebellion against its two imperialistic neighbours. I understood in a detached way the history of worker resistance to food price rises and wage freezes in Communist Poland. But nothing could have prepared me for the drama, excitement and passion of August 1980. Within hours of stepping off the plane in Warsaw, on that sunny day in July, I was listening to the excited explanations of one of Poland's leading dissidents, Jan Litynski. Sheer good fortune had brought me to the flat of Jan and Krystyna where foreign correspondents would later flock for information about the progress of the strikes across Poland. Jan and Krystyna changed my life. They brought me on a journey of discovery through the intellectual and dissident opposition movement and introduced me to the circle of workers, including Lech Walesa, who would literally change the course of Polish history; more than that, they accepted me as their friend and broadened my horizons by sharing their personal story with me.

On the night before the Gdansk shipyard strike began I sat with Lech Walesa and the rest of the strike committe as they discussed their plans. Later, in April 1981, when Walesa had become a household name around the world, he told me that I had been the first non-Polish journalist to interview him. Jan and Krystyna had given me a unique window of opportunity from which I could observe the 'Polish Revolution' as it evolved. In *Poles Apart* I am trying to tell the story of Poland's democratic transition through the personal stories of the men and women that I first met in 1980. I hope that by focusing on the experience of some of the key players I can expose aspects of the complex arguments surrounding controversial issues such as the imposition of martial law in 1981, the Round Table agreement between Solidarity and the Communist Party (which resulted in the first semi-free election in 1989) as well as examine the factors which precipitated the defeat of the post-Solidarity parties in the September 1993 election.

In order to get a sense of the story as it unfolded I returned to Poland many times between 1989 and 1993, gathering the political reaction and emotional response of those I had first met in 1980. I hope that in the following pages the reader will gain some insight into Solidarity's struggle, its victory and the factors that have led to the public's disenchantment and rejection of the Solidarity dream.

My debt of gratitude to Jan and Krystyna Litynski is enormous. When they took me into their home in July 1980 they offered both friendship and a window on the dramatic events which were unfolding in Poland that summer. It is impossible to thank them enough for the support and encouragement that they have given me. In dedicating *Poles Apart* to them I hope in some small way to acknowledge their contribution to my personal and intellectual development.

Poland's Ambassador to Ireland, Ernest Bryll, and his wife Malgosia saved *Poles Apart* from the dark corners of the bottom drawer. At a time when I was losing faith they injected their enthusiasm back into my project. I must sincerely thank both of them for reading and re-reading the text and for their comments, notes and helpful additions.

Ambassador Richard O'Brien in Warsaw has been a constant help in the compilation of *Poles Apart*. His advice and suggestions always proved helpful. I am greatly indebted to him for his consideration of the text. Without the hope of my numerous interviewees this book would not have been possible: I am very grateful to all of them.

Many people provided invaluable help in arranging interviews and organizing schedules during my many research trips to Poland. I would particularly like to thank Ms Joanna Lamprecht, Ms Ilonna Wroblewska, Ms Malgorzata Bernard and Ms Maghda Zorawska.

There is a great chasm between the seed of any idea and its ripening; for the day to day encouragement and support that brought *Poles Apart* to completion I owe much to my friend and partner, Frank Clarke.

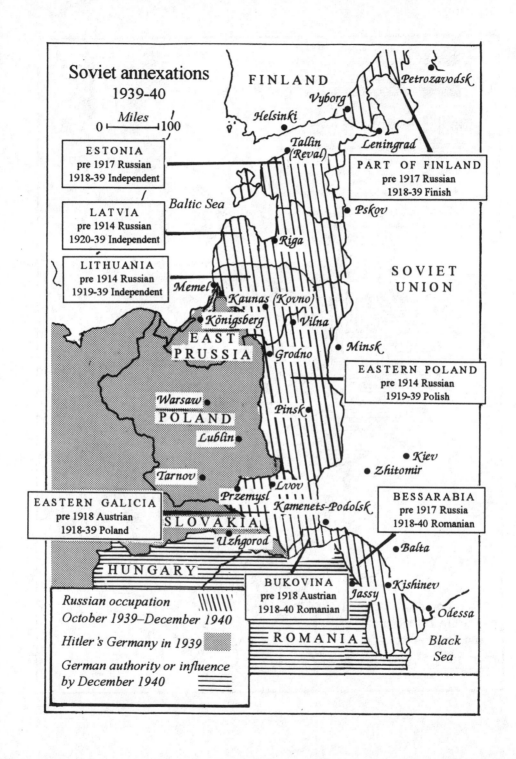

Soviet annexations
1939-40

Miles
0 ⊢————⊣ 100

FINLAND

Petrozavodsk

Vyborg

Helsinki

Tallin
(Reval)

Leningrad

ESTONIA
pre 1917 Russian
1918-39 Independent

PART OF FINLAND
pre 1917 Russian
1918-39 Finish

Baltic Sea

Pskov

LATVIA
pre 1914 Russian
1920-39 Independent

Riga

SOVIET
UNION

LITHUANIA
pre 1914 Russian
1919-39 Independent

Memel

Kaunas (Kovno)

Königsberg

Vilna

EAST
PRUSSIA

Grodno

Minsk

EASTERN POLAND
pre 1914 Russian
1919-39 Polish

Warsaw

POLAND

Pinsk

Lublin

Kiev

Zhitomir

Tarnov

Lvov

Przemysl

Kamenets-Podolsk

BESSARABIA
pre 1917 Russia
1918-40 Romanian

EASTERN GALICIA
pre 1918 Austrian
1918-39 Poland

SLOVAKIA

Balta

Uzhgorod

HUNGARY

BUKOVINA
pre 1918 Austrian
1918-40 Romanian

Kishinev

Jassy

Russian occupation
October 1939–December 1940

Hitler's Germany in 1939

German authority or influence
by December 1940

ROMANIA

Odessa

Black
Sea

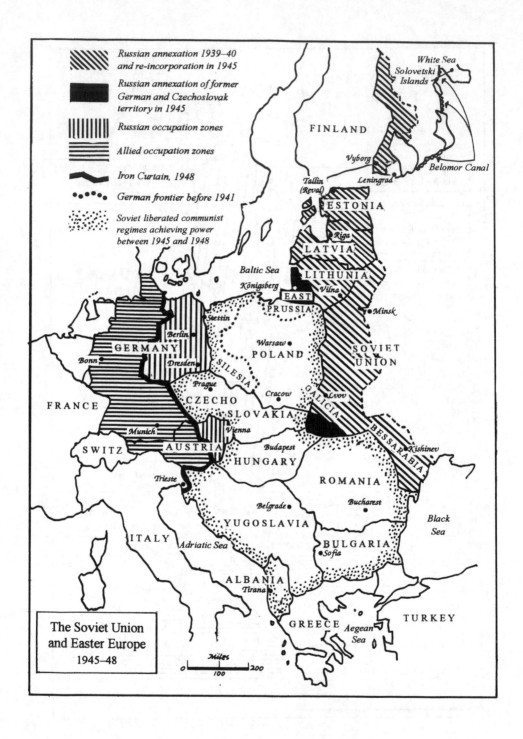

Russian annexation 1939–40 and re-incorporation in 1945

Russian annexation of former German and Czechoslovak territory in 1945

Russian occupation zones

Allied occupation zones

Iron Curtain, 1948

German frontier before 1941

Soviet liberated communist regimes achieving power between 1945 and 1948

White Sea
Solovetski Islands
FINLAND
Vyborg
Belomor Canal
Tallin (Reval)
Leningrad
ESTONIA
Riga
LATVIA
Baltic Sea
Königsberg
LITHUNIA
Vilna
EAST PRUSSIA
Minsk
Stettin
Berlin
POLAND
Warsaw
SOVIET UNION
GERMANY
Bonn
Dresden
SILESIA
Cracow
Lvov
GALICIA
Prague
CZECHO SLOVAKIA
FRANCE
Munich
Vienna
BESSARABIA
SWITZ
AUSTRIA
Budapest
Kishinev
HUNGARY
Trieste
ROMANIA
Bucharest
Belgrade
Black Sea
ITALY
YUGOSLAVIA
Adriatic Sea
BULGARIA
Sofia
ALBANIA
Tirana
GREECE
Aegean Sea
TURKEY

The Soviet Union and Easter Europe 1945–48

Miles
0   100   200

REGINA'S STORY

'At that time, a man was not a man for
these people: a man was just a thing.'

My most abiding memory of August 1980 is not of the moustached
figure of Lech Walesa jumping on to the Gdansk shipyard gates.
It is of the diminutive frame of a white-haired old lady, hunched over a
typewriter, puffing away on a cigarette, as she types up an underground
information bulletin edited by her son, the dissident Janek Litynski.
Completely absorbed, she was oblivious to the comings and goings of
the mighty men and women of the press, who unceremoniously poured
into the tiny flat in Warsaw's Wyzwolenia Street, looking for news of
strikes and arrests. Looking back now in 1994 I realize that Regina
Litynska is a key to an understanding of why what could have been just
another round of strikes became the Polish Revolution.

A former young communist with a Jewish background, Regina was
jailed before the War for her political activities. Her life mirrors the
gargantuan tragedy played on a stage largely ignored by the Western
Allies who abandoned Poland to its fate in Stalin's hands. Regarding
her communist past as her greatest mistake and shame, Regina is dismissive of her suffering in forced labour camps in the former Soviet
Union, not wishing to compare her pain with the magnitude of the
Holocaust, or the scale of Stalin's purges.

The significance of Regina's life is not in the jailing, the dislocation
and forced labour or in the loss of her baby and two husbands, for that
is almost normal in the Dantean conditions of post-war Poland. The
true significance of her story is that she retained her belief in the potential of Utopian communism even after she had seen the horror of the
'Promised Land'. Here she was not alone. General Wojciech Jaruzelski,
Poland's controversial hero or traitor, the man responsible for the introduction of martial law in December 1981, remained a loyal communist
despite his father's murder by the Soviets and his own abuse in a
Siberian labour camp. In Regina's progress towards her eventual renun-
ciation of communism one sees the repeatedly shattered hopes of a
society that was promised change, reform and hope as successive first

secretaries were sacked, or pensioned off, in ritual disgrace as a panacea for ills that would only be cured by the abolition of the system.

For the rest of Europe, 1968 was the year of student protests but for Poland it was also the year she became the last European country to target her Jewish population for persecution. Once again Jewish people were the scapegoats. This time they were caught up in a plan hatched by the Interior Minister, General Mieczyslaw Moczar, which was designed to discredit communist leader Wladyslaw Gomulka. For Regina it was the last straw. One of the many Jews who left Poland in 1968 was Regina's best friend, Nusia. As young girls they shared a prison cell on the Polish-Soviet border. Not only were her friends once again being persecuted but her son was arrested for his part in the student protests after the Soviet ambassador ordered the closure of Adam Mickiewicz's classic play, *Forefather's Eve*.

The March arrests were to play a key part in galvanizing the class of '68 into a generation of dissidents who would take a leading role in cementing the unique relationship of worker, Church and intellectual dissident. It was this relationship that broke the historical cycle of worker unrest which traditionally ended with the promise of reform and the disgrace of a party scapegoat. Back in 1968 the 'Polish August' was barely a dream but for Regina communism's promise of a vision of justice and liberty for all was irrevocably tarnished. 'I saw that the King had no clothes.'

At just over five foot one I stand head and shoulders above Regina Litynska. With her bone structure matching her height she would be almost oriental in her appearance were it not for her strong Polish face and straight silver hair. When I met Regina at the beginning of 1992 she looked exactly as I remembered her from our first meeting in 1980. In those days she shared her three-roomed flat on Wyzwolenia Street with her son Janek and his wife Krystyna. Many Eastern Europe correspondents will remember the apartment where Janek gave his informal briefings on the progress of the wave of strikes that hit Poland that July and August. Always doing two things at the one time Janek delivered the information in an excited and staccato style to the press corps for whom the briefings were a godsend. By 1980 Janek was a well known dissident with several periods in jail under his belt. He was a founder member of KOR, the Workers' Defence Committee, which had been set up in 1976 by a group of intellectuals to support workers facing trial after bloodily repressed strikes at Radom and at the Ursus plant near Warsaw.

Amidst the frenetic activity, the continuous rounds of lemon tea, the talk of possible arrests, the casual reference to past periods in jail, I will always remember Regina's back hunched over the typewriter in a booklined cubicle which served as her bedroom and the family's study. And of course the never-ending waft of smoke over her head as she resolutely and silently typed up her son's counter-revolutionary propaganda. Interested in who she was I was told that Regina had a story and that her life had been tragic. In a sense, I was told, her story is the story of Poland. Twelve years later I asked her to tell me that story.

Regina was the only child of her mother's second marriage. She never knew her father, who had died in the first war in 1917 when Regina was barely a year old. Her mother, who survived until Regina was just twelve, had four other children by her first husband. When Regina was born there, Lwow belonged to Poland, but the city (like Regina) had virtually no say in questions of destiny. Norman Davies' *God's Playground*, cites six alternative versions of the city's name indicating its Prussian, German, Austrian, Polish, Ukrainian and Soviet occupations. Between 1923 and 1945, Lwow and the rest of East Galicia was under Polish rule but after the war Stalin's 'Polish stooges' agreed to the imposition of Eastern borders as demanded by the Soviets. Winston Churchill told the representative of the Polish government-in-exile, in London, Stanislaw Mikolajczyk, that Poland was on the verge of annihilation: 'Unless you accept the frontier you are out of business forever. The Russians will sweep through your country and your people will be liquidated.'[1] Many years later Regina, who had rejoiced when she heard of her beloved Lwow's incorporation into the Soviet Union, proffered the view that it didn't make much difference to the ordinary citizen whether he was shunted backwards and forwards over frontiers in pursuit of the communist dream or some racial nightmare.

Regina's dream had been to go to medical college but a combination of a quota system which limited the number of Jewish people allowed enter certain schools at the university and the sheer impossibility of finding the money for the fees ensured that Regina's dream remained just that. So having left the aunt's house where she had lived for three years after her mother's death she took the familiar road for young women of good background and no money: she found employment as a live-in childminder. But it was when she got what she regarded a plum job, as a replacement bookkeeper at the largest chocolate factory in

Lwow, that she made the contacts that were to shape the rest of her life. That she so quickly met people active in the city's communist organizations is perhaps not unusual in a city that gave birth to the first-ever Polish trade union in 1870. In 1935 Regina joined the local branch of the young communist organization. 'Like many other Jews, I joined because it promised equality. I had a vision of justice and liberty for everyone.'

Polish communists found themselves between a rock and a hard place during the thirties. By the beginning of the forties Stalin had crushed the movement on the rock of deviationist tendencies. Regarded as traitors to the national cause at home, Polish communists faced jail in Poland while some 5,000 members were killed after Stalin ordered the liquidation of the party in 1938.[2] One historian has noted that only those fortunate enough to find themselves in Polish jails survived. One key Polish communist who was lucky enough to be in a jail in Lwow between 1938 and 1939 was Wladyslaw Gomulka. His earlier experience of the inhumanity of Soviet style communism convinced him that only a hard line form of the 'Polish Road to Socialism' would save the country from Soviet domination. Arrested for activities against the interest of the Polish state on 28 June 1938 Regina began her three and a half year sentence in Lwow prison. After the sentence was cut to two and a half years following an appeal she and the friend she had made during the trial were transferred to Fordon prison near Bydgoszcz. It was a month before the outbreak of the Second World War.

Looking back Regina is reticent about criticizing the prison conditions. 'We were trying to overthrow the state,' she quips. Despite her refusal to complain and her insistence that by comparison with German and Soviet camp standards they were treated well there is no doubt that conditions were rough. A cell designed for two was occupied by ten and provided with beds for four prisoners. There was no other furniture (no table, no chairs) and a bowl in the corner served as a lavatory. Prisoners were allowed out of their cell once a day for a walk and once to go to the toilet. However, prisoners never knew the timing of the trip to the lavatory. Years later, when her daughter-in-law Krystyna came out of prison after martial law, the two women agreed that one of the greatest pleasures of being released was being able to run in a straight line after being able to exercise only in a confined quadrangle.

Three days after the war officially started, Regina and her friend Nusia listened in their cell to the German bombardment of an important bridge nearby. On 3 September 1939, as the Germans drew closer, the prison authorities opened the cells of all of the inmates, with the exception of the political or communist prisoners. Hearing all the activity outside, the women knew that the Polish Army was retreating and that they had to get away or else face their fate at the hands of the Germans. With the warders gone one by one the cells emptied as inmates helped each other break down the doors and escape. Over the night and morning, some 250 women made their way out of Fordon. Because they were wearing what could have looked like an army uniform from the air, or from a distance, a passing Polish officer warned Regina and Nusia to change their clothes and disperse into small groups. He told them to try and make their way by night and to hide by day in the woods. Regina remembers that some of the soldiers, taking pity on them, threw them apples.

Having lost Nusia Regina began walking to Warsaw. Her march took about two weeks. But it was only with the help of a professional thief who brought her and a group of about eight other starving people to his house that she was able to penetrate what was by 14 September a city encircled by Germans. Abandoned by the Polish general staff and government, Warsaw was resisting against all odds. She was so exhausted that she says she cannot remember hearing the incessant bombardment of the city by the 2000 aircraft and 2600 tanks Hitler had deployed against Poland in the hope of overrunning the country rapidly.

After the capitulation of Warsaw on 27 September a German-Soviet convention was signed dividing the spoils along the line of the rivers Bug and San. Delighted at the news of the Red Army's late arrival on Polish soil on the 17th, Regina began the hazardous walk to Lwow to meet the reality of her dream of a Soviet and communist state: 'I was so stupid and idealistic that I remember crying after some drunken Red Army soldiers bothered me in Lwow. I couldn't imagine that there could be drunks in this ideal country.' Because of the secret protocol in the Molotov-Ribbentrop Pact neither Regina or indeed Churchill knew of the furtive plan to yet again obliterate Poland from the map of Europe. Rejoicing that at last she would take part in building Utopia, Regina looked for her job back at the chocolate factory: 'I just wanted to be a worker.' It was to be many years before the veil was lifted from Regina's eyes and she accepted the reality of her communist dream – the reality of the massive deportations in huge railway convoys to the furthest outposts of Soviet domination.

While Regina and many committed communists like her believed that they were building a new communist world with Soviet help, Stalin pursued his plan to destroy the possibility in any shape or form of an independent Poland.

One is never quite sure about what is fair and proper when as a journalist one asks about the intimate details of a person's life. Sometimes a request for the revelation of a name or parentage causes pain unanticipated by the interviewer. For whatever reason Regina did not want to tell me the last name of the man she married in Lwow in 1940. His first name was Henryk and like millions of others his hopes and plans fell victim to the intrigues of evil men. While Hitler's decision to cancel his non-aggression pact with Stalin saved Poland from annihilation, it shattered the fledgling life that Henryk was building with Regina. He was mobilized to the Red Army some months before Germany invaded the Soviet Union with the launch of 'Operation Barbarossa', leaving Regina behind expecting their baby. She never saw her husband again. 'I never knew what happened to him or whether he died. We simply never found each other after it was all over.' Regina's baby was born prematurely at the hospital in Lwow in May 1941. A little girl, the baby was weak and was placed in an oxygen tent. It had been a complicated delivery and difficult for Regina. But with no other means of support she had to return to work as soon as she was able, leaving the baby at the hospital.

On 22 June, the day the second front opened, soldiers arrived at the factory and told the employees that they were being taken to build trenches a short distance away just outside the city. The entire workforce was loaded onto trucks. 'Several kilometres outside Lwow, I began to realize that we weren't going to build trenches-that we were being taken away. I tried to jump out but I was pulled back. People around me knew that I wouldn't have been able to get away. It had been a very hard birth. My little girl was only five weeks old when I was taken. I never saw my baby again.' When I asked Regina to describe her feelings then and her feelings now about leaving the baby, she simply asked, 'Would you like me to do a vivisection?' I felt ashamed of my question.

As she was shunted deeper into the Soviet Union, the Germans moved closer and took Lwow. Regina was to remain in Kazakstan working on a series of collective farms until the Red Army crossed the river Bug in July 1944 when the eastern part of Poland, including

Lwow, was liberated. When she finally returned, after three years as a slave labourer, nobody at the hospital knew anything about the existence or whereabouts of her baby. Fifty-two years later Regina still has the same nightmare. She goes to Lwow to find her baby. Bombs are falling everywhere. Suddenly the baby is there, before her eyes. But she cannot reach her. She cannot touch her. Then she wakes up.

Regina's group were not taken straight to Kazakstan. She worked for over half a year in a cotton wool factory in Russia until she collapsed and had to have an operation. When she and her group were moved, she was simply told that they were going. She never had any sense of who was in charge of running her life: 'People just did as they were told. We weren't taken there as enemies of the system. This was the way they treated normal people. Many Poles were sent to Russia simply because they (the Russians) killed their enemies.' At that time, 'a man was not a man for these people: a man was just a thing.'

The journey to Kazakstan took over a month and Regina remembers that their transport was a train meant for livestock. Later her group crossed the Volga river on barges. She worked on a number of different collective farms. Conditions were generally the same, varying only in their harshness. Regina is reticent about how she survived. Her daughter-in law Krystyna tells of meeting one of the women who shared a dormitory with her. She told Krystyna that she had only survived the horrific conditions because Regina had made her drink her own milk ration. There were worms in the flour, lice in the bedding and hunger everywhere. Regina somewhat euphemistically sighed that 'anything you wanted was there'. Even the piglet she and her four friends bought from their rations, in the hope that it would provide them with meat, ate its fill and promptly died of tuberculosis.

Her acute sense of being just a thing, a mere workhorse, came home to me particularly as a woman when she described the treatment she received from a Soviet doctor when she stopped menstruating. At a hospital near the camp she was asked her age: 'How old are you? Twenty-eight? So it's all over for you, Regina. What are you worried about?' It was one of the few times that she wept, not least for her one and only lost child.

Listening to Regina I had to constantly remind myself that she was not a prisoner, that she was not being punished and that she accepted her conditions as part of some necessary toll on the road to

Utopia: 'We had no books, no movies, no access to radio or newspapers. There was absolutely no provision for a personal life. We just worked and slept.' But how did she rationalize such treatment from the representatives of a society and system that she hoped would one day be universal? 'I thought that because it was wartime that the proper, the true communists, were away at the front. I thought that only the crap stayed behind.'

Still retaining a dry sense of humour Regina explains how she got away from the collective: 'I didn't think that the war could be won without my cooperation and participation. I wanted to fight.' She first wrote to General Wladyslaw Anders who commanded the Polish Army in the East which had been raised after 1941. It was largely formed from Polish deportees. Because of his allegiance to the government-in-exile in London, General Anders' relationship with Stalin did not last long and so, having left Soviet territory, his army was eventually incorporated into the British Eighth Army. Having had no luck with General Anders, Regina wrote to the Polish Army (AP) under the command of General Zygmunt Berling. Completely subordinate to the Soviet Command, it was established by Stalin as part of his post-Molotov-Ribbentrop programme for Poland. After an exchange of letters Regina was allowed to go to Moscow, where, having learned to type, she got a job with the Union of Polish Patriots, an organization set up by Polish communists with the connivance of the Soviets. Apart from exercising political control over Berling's army, it was the nucleus of the group that was to take control of the first post-war government – the Polish Committee of National Liberation.

Knowing that by the summer of 1944 Lwow and much of eastern Poland had been liberated, Regina ran away from Moscow. She wanted to go home to find her baby. Her flight was in vain.

Regina's second husband Ryszard was a journalist in the Polish Army and like her was a member of the young communist movement. She had first met him while travelling between her first point of deportation, the cotton wool factory on the river Volga, and Kazakstan in 1941. She was to meet him again through Berling's army a couple of years later though it wasn't until 1945 that they married. On 18 January 1946 Regina gave birth to a son. It was a moment when the shadows lifted. But not for long. Ryszard died of tuberculosis just a year after his son was born. At thirty-one, Regina was twice widowed, had lost her baby girl and along with the rest of the exhausted remains of the

Polish population she had to set about trying to earn a living in a country that was both morally and physically devastated.

Her first job after the war was with the Main Office for the Control of Press, Publications and Public Spectacles. By her own admission, it was an important job and involved her deciding what had to be removed from newspapers before publication. Regina is obviously uncomfortable talking about this period in her life, but is emphatic that the job did not involve any privileged treatment. One of the key issues in post-communist Poland is the degree of Polish participation in, and connivance with, the establishment of the one-party state. In that context the extent of an individual's knowledge of the massively repressive measures meted out to the Polish wartime resistance is the subject of much dissimulation. Effectively, the resistance was offered a stark choice between absorption into Soviet Army formations and liquidation.

In her book *Oni* (Them), Teresa Toranska vividly explores the self-exculpatory themes employed by leading Polish communists to explain how the end justified the means. Though he was the second in command in the Polish United Workers Party, Jacub Berman denied any knowledge of the extent of the repression against anti-communist groups right up to his death in 1984. He maintained that assertion despite his undoubted overview of the activities of the internal security operations. Poland's top communist between 1944 and 1956, Boleslaw Bierut, actually maintained that he knew nothing about the fate of Poland's pre-war leaders most of whom had been eliminated on Stalin's orders. Sixteen of those leaders including the vice-premier of the government-in-exile in London and the last commander of the Home Army were actually sentenced by a Moscow court in June 1945 as 'saboteurs and subversionist bandits'.[3] At one point the Soviets used a former Nazi concentration camp at Majdanek to intern members of the Polish Home Army who had fought alongside the Soviets against the Germans.

But what did a member of the censor's office know of the activities of the Ministry of the Interior? 'I didn't know that people were tortured. I didn't see things. Now I know that people from the Home Army were tortured. I didn't know about the arrests of anti-communists. In my stupidity I wanted to be a communist. I didn't see things or didn't want to see things. I didn't see my narrow-mindedness.'

In perhaps the most searing analysis of the psychological predicament of the individual under Stalin, in Czeslaw Milosz's *The Captive*

Mind, the author draws this picture of a fervent believer. 'He has served perhaps three years behind the walls of prisons or slave labour camps there. He was not broken, he did not lose his faith. Wherever trees are being chopped down, splinters must fall. The fact that he and many of his fellow inmates were innocent, proves nothing. It is better to condemn twenty innocent people than to release a single evil doer. To endure this trial successfully is a source of moral strength for him, and of esteem from his comrades in the Party. Having learned the workings of the machinery behind the scene, he knows the country of socialism to be a vale of tears and of gnashing of teeth. Nevertheless, the belief in historical necessity and the vision of the fruits of tomorrow, persuade him that the harsh reality of the present – even extended over many years – is unimportant.'[4]

In simple terms, as Regina puts it, 'People believed that it was going to be better.' What sustained that belief was a series of factors linked to the concept of the Polish Road to Socialism. At its crudest level the view was that Poland would make a better fist of implementing real communism than her traditional enemies would. The effect on those Poles who saw the enormity, the barbarity, the determination and the sheer vastness of Stalin's apparatus, either while interned for imaginary crimes in the Gulags, or while jailed as slave labourers, was complex. It was not simply one of revulsion as one might naively imagine. It is a theme we will be returning to in other chapters, in particular when we examine the role of General Wojciech Jaruzelski.

Stefan Staszewski became a communist when he was fourteen years of age. His brother was killed during the great purge in the USSR in 1937. He served seven years in Kolyma labour camp after his party card was withdrawn. Following his release he returned to Poland and was Warsaw Communist Party boss until 1957. Describing the camp to Teresa Toranska, Staszewski said it was a place where 'corpses were laid out between the barbed wire like logs of wood, incredible amounts of frozen corpses, and where out of each truckload of twenty four people going from Magadan to the Taiga, two survived the winter.' So how could Staszewski return home a communist? How could his faith survive? 'I returned to Poland convinced that here, we would not have the same thing as in the Soviet Union, because we were different. Different in culture and customs and raised in a tradition of private and public life. I returned convinced that we would create a new model in principle, of course, a common and related one, but different nonetheless.'[5]

By the mid fifties Regina was feeling 'uncomfortable with the practice of communism', though she was still ideologically committed. She says that she still 'didn't think that there was anything fundamentally wrong at that stage'. But things were wrong enough to make her leave the censors' office and take a job in the administrative end of children's radio. As one historian has remarked there was no taking of power by the communists in Poland as all opposition had been well and truly crushed. The communists within Poland simply handed it over to the Soviets on a plate. The real struggle had occurred in the period prior to the establishment of the Polish United Workers Party in December 1948 when Wladislaw Gomulka lost his job as general secretary of the old Polish Workers Party. Branded a national deviationist by Moscow his eventual rehabilitation in 1956 after the 'Bread and Freedom' protests at Poznan was the occasion of renewed hope and a wave of optimism that things would really change. Like many Poles, Regina mistook Gomulka's 'Polish' tendencies for liberalism. It was wrongly thought that his opposition to the inhuman methods employed by the Soviets in the collectivization programme implied a lot more about his ideas for Polish communism than it actually did. The out-ward appearance of a Polish victory perceived in Gomulka's election as the party's first secretary hid the traditional method of dealing with unrest; the regime simply changed its leader and claimed that what went before was a deviation or error. His return on what was mistakenly perceived by many Poles, as an anti-Stalinist ticket, was confirmed by Krushchev after a rancorous meeting during the Polish party plenum in October 1956. Earlier that year, in February, Krush-chev gave his secret speech to the twentieth congress of the Soviet Communist Party, which began the process of reevaluation and condemnation of Stalin's crimes.

In return for Krushchev's acceptance of Poland's peculiar conditions and the need for a Polish Road to Socialism, Gomulka moved quickly to kill the power of the workers' councils which had emerged during the so-called 'Polish October' and reasserted the authority of the censors' office. Because Gomulka had been one of Stalin's victims Regina and many others like her failed to see that he was in fact an orthodox Stalinist with a small s. Here was no revisionist, but a true believer whose traditional anti-Russian and Polish nationalism was being confused with liberal thinking. The effect of this sham change was massive disillusionment. That, combined with huge increases in the price of food in December 1970, led to a confrontation between the government and the workers in Gdansk, which left many dead after Gomulka ordered the counter revolution to be put down.

The irony of the man who symbolised opposition and resistance to Soviet methods ordering the Polish Army to fire on Polish workers was not lost. The myth of the 1970 martyrs was a key factor in the making of the Polish Revolution in August 1980. But for Regina Litynska the break came two years earlier. While 1970 was the symbolic year for the workers, the student arrests and anti-Jewish purges of 1968 had a profound effect on the intelligentsia. In 1980 it was the coming together of the workers, the intelligentsia and the Church that for the first time seriously threatened the Party's dominance.

'Gomulka, instead of concerning himself with the country's fundamental problems, had already, a year before, begun to ferret out fascist slogans and to scream about how Poland was being threatened by Zionism, by a Fifth Column, and how he wouldn't stand for it.'[6]

Edward Ochab was perhaps the most senior communist to take a stand against the anti-Jewish campaign that was orchestrated by the Interior Minister, General Mieczyslaw Moczar, in the spring of 1968. As an obedient party man, he had even given up his position as first secretary (March–October 1956) to clear the way for the rehabilitation of Gomulka. But in 1968 he resigned all his posts in protest at what he called the campaign being waged by the 'dark forces'. While the degree of Gomulka's involvement in initiating the campaign is much debated, that campaign certainly deflected attention away from the rising social discontent within Poland and for this, if for no other reason, he was slow to denounce the 'superpatriots' who were behind the anti-Jewish activity. One-time Warsaw party boss, Stefan Staszewski, who described himself to Teresa Toranska as a Jew and a revisionist, was in no doubt that Gomulka played the anti-Jewish card in explaining Poland's deteriorating economic situation: 'People were seeing the Soviet Union as the cause, so what could be better than giving them Jews as the cause: indeed, there was an abundant tradition of this: when something is wrong blame the Jews'.[7]

Regina never felt Jewish. She didn't practise her religion: 'I never felt separate. I'm Polish but one is Jewish because other people know it.' She emphasizes that she was not picked out: 'I didn't suffer. I was not persecuted.' But many of her friends did lose their jobs or felt sufficiently threatened to leave Poland. It is estimated that some 25,000 Jews left following Gomulka's decision to issue them with exit visas. It had all started with the Israeli victory in the Six Day War in 1967. Generally Poles celebrated the victory of 'our Jews' over 'their Arabs'. However, the Soviet and Polish governments supported the Arab side. And so an unfortunate link was made between Jewishness, anti-Soviet sympathy and dissidence.

For Regina the whole experience was very painful: 'Now communism was associated with anti-Zionism. All my previous doubts came to a head. It was the final straw for me. Central to my ideas of what communism was about was that it centred on liberty and on justice. I had a beautiful idea of internationalism. But then it turns out you can be persecuted because you are a Jew – or maybe a gypsy. It turns out to be a very nationalistic thing.' But Regina didn't turn in her party card straight away: 'I was completely disillusioned but I took an opportunistic approach. I didn't want it to be harder for Janek.'

With or without Regina's help, it was going to get harder for her son who, along with over a thousand students, was arrested after the Forefather's Eve protest. The play written by Adam Mickiewicz included anti-Russian references which were cheered by the audience. After the Soviet ambassador objected (although the Soviet embassy always denied any involvement), the play was closed. When the students took to the streets, General Moczar sent in the ORMO (Volunteer Reserve of the Citizens' Militia) and pitched battles ensued, with much unnecessary violence meted out by both the militia and the police. The whole affair was used by the general to support his claims of a massive Zionist conspiracy. It was claimed that the student ringleaders were all Jews. In fact the purge was used not just to attack Jews, as it was also a ploy to clear the universities and institutions of liberal reformist elements in general. Apart from the oft-repeated feature of Polish history of resorting to a scapegoat to deflect attention from real issues, the anti-Semitic campaign seems mainly to have been aimed at embarrassing Gomulka and at placing Moczar in the role of Poland's saviour. The more important long-term effect, however, was to help mould a generation of questioning intellectuals (some of whom were of Jewish background but who saw themselves simply as Poles) into a band of dissidents who were to eventually establish an open opposition to the 'power'.

Whatever Regina's reason for holding on to her party card, her fate was sealed by her son's arrest. She was sacked from her job in children's radio. She was, however, in typical Polish communist practice, not shoved right over the precipice. She was demoted to the administrative section where she held a job as a typist until retirement age. 'I changed my political views and it was not just because of my son.' Regina is adamant that her transformation from ardent communist to opposition supporter was a gradual response to her own disillusionment with the reality of the Utopian promise. It was not just the Jewish issue or the arrest of her son. A phrase she often uses – the King had no clothes – is for her a metaphor for the empty cup communism offered to the Polish people. Regina's repoliticization was hastened not only by her association with Janek's dissident friends but by contact with their mothers and fathers when the 'boys' were arrested. She argues that being involved with food parcels, finding lawyers etc., was not for her a political gesture. Perhaps she found it easier to perceive it as families helping their own but in the context any act of support was, of course, political or at least regarded as such by the authorities.

The essence of the movement which Regina found herself passively supporting was its determination to function openly. KOR (Workers' Defence Committee) was initially established in September 1976 by a wide ranging group of intellectuals, including Jan Litynski, to help the workers facing trial after the savage suppression of the strikes and protests at Radom and the Ursus plant near Warsaw. Nationwide strikes had followed sudden and massive food price rises which had been introduced that June without any warning. By supporting the workers the intellectual dissidents began the process of crossing the social divide which eventually led to the flowering of a mass movement of opposition. KOR brought together old-style socialists, former communists, Catholic intellectuals and the 'class of '68'. Its philosophy was at heart simple. Change, it was argued, could be brought about from below by ordinary people organizing themselves in social groups which operated outside the structures of the party and the state. 'Civil society' was simply the opposite of the state as defined by the Party. To achieve this 'civil society', KOR argued, Poles had to talk, write and act as if they were in a free country. The revolution it proposed was evolutionary. What it demanded from people was the abandonment of the practice of 'doublethink' and doublespeak'. Czeslaw Milosz described the practice in *The Captive Mind* as the 'art of *Ketman*'. Essentially *Ketman* was the art of survival under the oriental despotism of the shah in feudal Persia or, as Milosz argues, the art of survival under Stalin: 'Officially, contradictions do not exist in the minds of the citizens in the people's democracies. Nobody dares to reveal them publicly. And yet the question of how to deal with them, is posed in real life. More than others, the members of the elite are aware of this problem. They solve it by becoming actors.'[8]

And so the evolutionary revolution began with a commitment to telling the truth. KOR was committing the greatest crime of opposition: its members ceased to be schizophrenic. They took off their actors' make-up and like the children in 'The Emperor's New Clothes' they told the truth.

Telling the truth was the first step, printing it was the next. In September 1977 a group of KOR activists, most of whom had just been released from jail after an amnesty, founded an unofficial newspaper called *Robotnik* (The Worker). Aimed at raising the political consciousness of the workers, its purpose was to provide them with information and editorials about past strikes as well as outlining practical ways to organize themselves. In 1980 *Robotnik* was to play a key role in disseminating information about the progress of the wave of strikes across Poland. While the paper's editor was Jan Litynski, it was Regina who did much of the typing.

What appeared to me to be an incredible leap from committed young communist and censor to unofficial typist for an opposition, underground newspaper was perhaps not so dramatic in a country where the 'art of *Ketman*' and outward acquiescence vied with tremendous courage and dignified resistance for the hearts of the people. Perhaps one of the key factors in the making of Solidarity was the participation of people from all walks of life including, most especially, former communists like Regina.

The image of Regina at her typewriter smoking her cigarette always conjured up for me a sense of what August 1980 was all about. It was about thousands of people all over Poland, writing, typing, meeting openly and apparently, if not in reality, fearlessly. 'I was never afraid for myself. I was only afraid for Janek. Afraid that when he was underground that I would bring the police to him if I managed to see him.' Regina was fearless because the whole of the Soviet apparatus had worked for years to instil terror into the minds of the people. They were successful. How could anyone with Regina's background fear going to jail?

When I spoke to Regina about her feelings about Solidarity in early 1992 she used the same phrase she had used about her youthful perception of communism. 'Solidarity was a kind of dream. Now the dream is not coming true. The in-fighting for power is ugly.' Solidarity, the story of a movement of mass opposition, is a happy story. However, the story of the birth of democracy and real politics in Poland is not without pain. It is a story we will be hearing from others in later chapters. But in what Solidarity's *anciens combattants* call Poland's 'new reality', Regina is very proud of her son, who is now an MP and a leading member of the post-Solidarity party, The Democratic Union. But she's pessimistic about the future: 'People are worried and there are so many unemployed. On the one hand unemployment is a necessary evil but people have no reserves to live on. I would like to see a stable government. People should stop seeking their own private interest. I know sacrifices are necessary but they should be more evenly distributed. No one should starve. I want Poland to be a real part of Europe, in every sense, and have full shops like they do. But I also want people to have the money to be able to buy in them.'

Looking at the reality of everyday life Regina, rather sadly, concludes that the struggle may not have been worth it: 'I doubt it more and more. We're finding the transition to capitalism so hard. I don't see any solutions. The economic problems are so great. Even when I was a communist, I thought that the worst thing it had done was to destroy the morale of the people. Now they're gone and our morale is still broken. Maybe we're not mature enough to make the break with the past and make the necessary changes.'

At 78, Regina is still working. She has a job at the travel office in the Catholic Intellectuals' Club. When I put it to her that by any standard she had had a sad and difficult existence she was, as always, reticent about overstating the harshness of her life. When I asked her if she had been happy it was only after a long pause that she said, 'Not too much.' Had she ever felt deep joy? 'When my son was born.'

THE STRIKERS

'When the events and heroes of current history fail to conform exactly to the desired or expected pattern, the only wise solution is to seek the reason why and try if possible to influence the shape of things. Getting cross with history and withdrawing, cursing under the tent will lead us nowhere.'[1]

When I began writing about the Gdansk strike on my return to Ireland at the end of August 1980 I was repeatedly asked by editors, as well as friends and colleagues, whether Solidarity was left or right, anti-Soviet, anti-Stalinist, Trotskyite or syndicalist. My answer seemed to please nobody. Solidarity posed a major problem because it did not fit into a neat pattern of opposition acceptable to Western governments, the media, human rights groups, or peace campaigners. Solidarity forced all sorts of traditional opponents on to the same side. On the left it challenged those who still revered the Soviet Union as the home of the Revolution, while the right found itself celebrating a workers' revolution. The role of the Church posed a problem for those who refused to see its influence as anything other than reactionary and regressive. Thrown into the melting pot was talk of anti-Semitic and nationalist tendencies within the movement. The truth was that there was no single voice, no dominant aim or goal. Of course, groups like KOR wanted to prise power away from the Party, but it was not regarded as an immediate or realizable goal in August 1980. Even leaving aside the fact that KOR and the intellectual groupings were far from being homogeneous, it must be remembered that they were just one element in the matrix.

The fact that great historical moments are a combination of sheer chance, unleashed charisma and prolonged plotting was perhaps nowhere so obviously proven as in Gdansk. On a personal level that truism, at least in so far as it related to the combination of chance and plotting, can be applied to my good fortune in being in Gdansk at the right time. However, I can only claim to having realized in retrospect that I was a witness to the beginning of one of history's great moments.

Sitting in Anna Walentynowicz's flat with Lech Walesa and the other members of the Founding Committee of Free Trades Unions of the Coast, on the night before the strike, I sensed no air of impending confrontation. I got no hint that the action planned for the next day was to be more special than the strikes which had been breaking out all over Poland during that summer.

I had arrived in Gdansk from Warsaw on the overnight train on Tuesday 12 August. I was hoping to meet Anna Walentynowicz, the woman crane driver who had just been dismissed by the management at the Lenin Shipyard. The omens for the trip had been good. Exhausted, having stood for most of the five-hour journey in the corridor of the packed train, I had literally been picked up by a middle-aged woman who would not hear of me doing anything other than go home with her to sleep and eat. Missing my Western comforts I was washed out, having slept on floors and in cramped train compartments over the previous few weeks as I travelled around Poland with Jan Litynski while he advised and exhorted the strike makers. I will never forget the starched white sheets and the feeling of security as I awoke in Pani Boroch's apartment to the sight and smell of soft-boiled eggs, sliced smoked fish, cheese, wonderfully fresh black bread and hot chocolate. How, I thought, could I repay her hospitality? How much of this family's rations was I ravenously consuming? But she would countenance no contorted gesticulations of gratitude. She seemed to get immense pleasure from simply watching me eat. When eventually the son whose bed I had purloined returned, I began to try and explain that the purpose of my trip to Gdansk might be harmful or dangerous for them. In American and broken English, he told me that he would help me to find the members of the Free Trades Unions of the Coast. And of course, he said, everyone knew Anna Walentynowicz.

Looking back, the preparedness of ordinary people to help a stranger make contact with a group who were under constant surveillance and threat of imprisonment says much about the spirit that pervaded in Gdansk. It was that spirit that prompted many commentators to maintain retrospectively that Solidarity could not have been born in any other part of Poland. However, what struck me most about Pani Boroch's son as he helped me travel across Gdansk to meet Anna was that like many young people in Poland his mind was not cluttered with ideological problems. He simply wanted an American lifestyle. Democracy meant dollars, Coke and Levi's. Twelve years later the reality that threatens Poland's emerging democracy is that Poles are now painfully aware that democracy is not a free ticket to the consumer society.

Grunwaldzka street is about five minutes by car from the centre of Gdansk. It is a wide road and one of the few remaining areas with any hint of elegance. Some pre-war buildings have survived, leaving an impression of tatty refinement, very unlike the grey Stalinist tower blocks which are unfortunately more the norm in this levelled country. Given the heightened tension in Gdansk over the previous few days, there was nothing subtle about the police surveillance outside Anna's flat when I arrived with my teenage guide and his young companion. The two boys apologized for not waiting for me and reluctantly left explaining that they did not wish to bring attention on their families. Relieved by their going, I knew enough to realize that even what they had done could result in expulsion from school or unwanted visits from the police.

Though my invitation to Anna's flat had been arranged by the Litynskis, I had no idea who would be there or that I would sit in on the last meeting of the Free Trades Unions group before the occupation-strike that was to begin the next day at the Lenin Shipyard. Amazingly my presence did not seem to cause a problem for anyone as the group assembled. Jan Litynski's word guaranteed my bona fides and the reports and planning went ahead as normal amid offers of lemon tea and poppyseed cake from Anna.

Often the individual histories and motivation of the men and women who become the spearhead of revolution cease to be relevant as events supersede the original spark. That is not the case with the birth of Solidarity for at least two reasons. Though Lech Walesa's name became synonymous with Solidarity and indeed Poland in the eyes of the world, and though he might have leapt centre-stage when he addressed the workers at that crucial moment at the shipyard gates, he did not get there alone. Leaving aside, for the moment, the role of the intellectual 'experts' who played a major part in the negotiations with the government, one cannot underestimate the role played by strike committee members like Alina Pienkowska who actually prevented the sit-in collapsing early on. The debate about Lech Walesa's fitness to be President and the nature of his influence on the development of democratic politics in Poland goes back to the perception of how he behaved during those heady days in August and after. It is also the case that within the polarity of opinion and motivation to

be found among the other strike makers, one can identify the seeds of
the political fragmentation that was to devastate Solidarity ten years
later when Lech Walesa declared the 'War at the Top'. In declaring
the war Walesa destroyed Solidarity as a mass movement. The effect of
that, whether Walesa intended it or not, has been the emergence of a
huge range of political parties in post-communist Poland. Many of the
post-Solidarity parties trace their roots to the 'class of '68', the Catholic
intellectual groups and the dissidents. Others, and most particularly
those parties who regard themselves as representing the trades union
voice within the parliament and senate trace their roots to the big industrial enterprises including the Gdansk shipyard where initially a mixum
gatherum of worker control, a sort of syndicalist variant, appears to
have been the predominant political aim. However, one has only to
listen to the story told by the men and women who gathered in Anna's
flat to appreciate that being suppressed, illegal and underground probably helped save Solidarity from premature self-destruction. There are
of course many others whose personal stories foretell the eventual destruction of Solidarity and the disenchantment (to put it at its mildest)
with Lech Walesa, but for the moment let us stay with those who
planned and plotted with him during that momentous summer of 1980.

So, who are the seven people who met at Anna's flat on the evening
before Solidarity was born? *Bogdan Borusewicz*, a KOR activist, had
been an important influence on the decision to establish the Founding
Committee of Free Trades Unions of the Coast in Gdansk in 1978.
After martial law he was to play a key role in running Solidarity from
the underground. He is now a member of parliament while his wife
Alina Pienkowska, the nurse who helped save the strike from an early
collapse, was until 1993 a member of the senate. *Bogdan Lis*, another
famous underground activist, was a member of the senate but did not
run in the elections in November 1991. He is now concentrating on his
business activities. *Andrzej Gwiazda*, regarded as the leader of the
group at the beginning, has now completely broken with his former
comrades. Both he and his wife *Joanna* and *Anna Walentynowicz* have
denounced one of the other conspirators present as a communist
puppet. That other conspirator was *Lech Walesa*.

The Crusaders: Andrzej and Joanna Gwiazda

Andrzej Gwiazda looks like the angry God I had heard about at
national school. If, instead of his worker's check shirt and jeans, he

had worn something more celestial, the image would have been complete. The intensity seemed almost to burst out of his prominent veins and his staring, serious eyes. Andrzej dominated the small gathering at Anna's flat, and years later it was his presence in the room rather than Lech Walesa's which dominated my memories. His style was the antithesis of Walesa's volatile, cute, pragmatic and almost comic image. If Walesa appeared to bob about, making jokes while strutting around peacock-like, Gwiazda's energies imploded, leaving an impression of someone who was just about controlling the forces within him. When he smiled, it was as if the fuse had been pulled out but, in his eyes, one saw through the laughter something caged, angry and in pain.

Though born in Pinczow in central Poland in 1935, Andrzej's family were living near the Soviet border in 1939. Like the rest of his generation he vividly remembers 17 September, the day the Soviets invaded eastern Poland. His father, an army reserve officer, had been conscripted before the outbreak of war, so whatever horrors he had to suffer he did not witness the deportation of his wife and family to Siberia. Andrzej was five years old when his family, including his grandmother, made the forced journey to the labour camp. Of his six years in Siberia and of his feelings about Soviet communism, he simply says that 'there were some things to settle after that'. The next piece of information that Andrzej chose to impart during an interview early in 1992 was that he had kept 160 kilos of TNT in storage in a garage in Gdansk as a young man: 'I'm sorry that I did not collect printing machines instead. But I never expected that the war with the communists would be fought with paper.' 'Fortunately,' he added, 'we only used the explosives for training.'

Andrzej had moved to Gdansk in 1948 when he was in the final year of primary school. He trained as a technical engineer and like his wife Joanna was to find work in one of the shipyard's auxiliary companies. She worked at a shipbuilding research and design centre and had come to Gdansk to study. Born in November 1939, Joanna's flat face and strong features betray her Ukrainian origins. Always vocal, Joanna possessed a good grasp of political tactics, a facility, it would be later argued, Andrzej had little acquaintance with.

There were three members of the Founding Committee of Free Trades Unions of the Coast and one of them was Andrzej Gwiazda. The announcement was made in *Robotnik*, the underground paper edited by KOR-member, Jan Litynski. Later in 1978 the Gdansk group, emulating the intellectual dissidents in Warsaw, were to produce their own paper, the *Coastal Worker*. Bogdan Borusewicz, an out-of-work activist and intellectual, was not formally a member of the committee. And though he was the link between the Gdansk group and Warsaw, and had made contact with them in 1976 after the Radom repression, it was regarded as vital by KOR that the workers themselves take the initiative.

Looking back twelve years later over my notes and published material I was struck by how absolutely clear this group was about its aims. Bearing in mind that they were performing a complicated balancing act in trying to force the system to its limit without slipping over the precipice, their collective political guile is breathtaking in retrospect.

'When asked for the reason behind the group the whole committee replied that the immediate aim was the creation of a free independent trade union.'[2] Sitting in their crammed eleventh floor flat, early in 1992, Joanna explained their tactics: 'The activity was a tool for implementing change. Our success in small areas drew people's attention to the possibility of greater demands.' Then and now political definitions were resisted and with good reason: 'We did not use the term 'anti-communist'. We were trying not to be defined. Even though we did not believe that the system could be reformed, in our propaganda and activities we did not put so much stress on it because we were aware that many people thought that reform was still possible. Trade union activity was not felt to be restrictive because taking part in it did not imply any particular attitude to the state . . . Trade union activity allowed us to demand improvements without supporting the system.' There was one difficulty, however, as Andrzej pointed out: 'The only weakness of the trade union concept of our activity was that if the system was able to change and improve the working conditions and life of the people then there would not be any need to abolish the system. However, our official line was that if the system was able to ensure human rights and proper living standards, then our role would end. We knew, of course, that if we did not abolish the system it would abolish us. Unlike many people who supported us, we knew that our trade union activity was dangerous, it was not safe. We were attacking the very heart of communism, the financial base of the system.'

Jerzy Wiatr is professor of political sociology at Warsaw University. He was a communist party member and is now a leading member of the SdRP (Social Democracy of the Republic of Poland). He argues that the key to the massive impact of Solidarity, as a mass movement, on the communist apparatus lies in the concept of the worker in both communist and Solidarity populist political culture. In both dogmas the worker had been elevated as the epitome of the highest moral standard: 'The intellectuals could be wrong but never the worker. The Party could have stomached a confrontation with the intellectuals but when they found themselves in conflict with the workers, the house of mental cards collapsed.' So while on the one hand Joanna and Andrzej and the others were excluding any mention of a political perspective and were cloaking their activities in purely trade union clothing, in reality they were hitting at the heart of the political *raison d'être* of communism. They were attacking the Party's monopolistic claims to be the sole and true representative of the workers' interest. Later we shall see that the post-Solidarity political parties are paying a high price for the movement's glorification of the worker. For while the worker played a radical role as the instrument that struck at the heart of the old system, he was the first to pay the price and the first to resist the massive post-communist economic restructuring.

As I have already said there was no indication that something cataclysmic was going to happen as I sat in Anna's flat on the night before the strike began. As recently as the previous month an attempt to organize an anti-price rise strike had failed. However, on 7 August the authorities threw a match into the tinder box when they sacked the well known and much liked crane driver, Anna Walentynowicz. Thinking they were neutralizing a troublesome and persistent activist the shipyard management handed the Free Trades Union Committee the cause they had been looking for. It was a crucial mistake. For Anna was something of a heroine, both in her personal life and by the terms of the communist order under which she had worked for just under thirty years. She had won three medals for her fifteen years uninterrupted work at the Lenin Shipyard and, believing as a young girl in the true goals of communism, she had been a diligent and hard worker. Sacking her, just weeks before she reached her thirtieth year of service would make her ineligible for pension. Here indeed was a cause.

I do not intend to detail here the blow by blow and day-by-day development of the strike itself. That story has been well related elsewhere.³ What I am concerned with are the issues and events which highlight the seeds of later divisions within Solidarity and the conflicts which foreshadow the debate over Lech Walesa's fitness to be President of Poland. But there is one key event which occurred very early on in the strike which could have been the end of it had it not been for the quick thinking of three women. The event is also significant for those who question Lech Walesa's judgement and grasp of what was going on, while for Joanna, Andrzej and Anna it is the first and most tangible proof of their allegation that Lech Walesa was and is a communist agent.

The strike had begun early on Thursday 14 August, when a number of young men raised banners inside the shipyard protesting against Anna's sacking. Later in the morning, when the crowd had grown, Walesa made a dramatic entry to the yard. Jumping on to a large mechanical digger near the main gate, he declared the sit-in strike. Responding quickly and realizing the seriousness of the situation, the shipyard director agreed to negotiations and arranged for Anna to be chauffeured from Grunwaldzka Street. At this stage there were five demands: the reinstatement of Anna and Lech, a pay rise, security from reprisals, an increase in family allowances and the erection of a monument to those killed during the food price rise protests in December 1970. (December 1970 is a key moment in the psyche of Polish worker resistance. The unthinkable had happened that December: Pole had killed Pole.)

Oddly for a system obsessed with secrecy and security, the authorities agreed to the entire negotiations being transmitted over the works radio network. To an outsider it looked as if all one knew about the Iron Curtain was being turned on its head. And it was. Here was the principle of the dictatorship of the proletariat being applied with the I's dotted and T's crossed. As a factor in the making of an historical moment it is impossible to overestimate the importance and power of the microphone in the making of the Polish August. One thing is certain: it was the making of Lech Walesa.

Over the next couple of days the more the authorities conceded the more confident Walesa and the crowd grew. Sympathy strikes were gathering momentum in nearby Gdynia and Sopot, while other yards had come out in Gdansk itself. Playing a clever dividing game, the Lenin management offered three quarters of the pay rise demanded by the strike committee, in the hope that they had split the workers. It was here that, in the language of the Passion, Walesa fell for the first time. Unable to deal with the enlarged strike committee, some of whom were happy to settle for money, he effectively declared the strike over on Saturday afternoon. And so came Alina Pienkowska's finest hour. Realizing that in accepting management's terms the Lenin Shipyard was abandoning the workers from the enterprises who had come out in support, she mounted a barrel, forget about her shyness and begged the strikers not to go home. While Alina, Anna and another woman, Ewa Ossowska, were attempting to galvanize the Lenin workers, Joanna and Adnrzej Gwiazda siezed a truck and rushed off to 'Elmore', their own workplace, afraid that workers there, hearing that the Lenin had gone back to work, would do the same. With their purloined 'Elmore' truck they made a tour of striking enterprises, telling them to join an Inter-factory Strike Committee (MKS): 'We told them that if we got together we'd be strong enough to carry on.' And so as Joanna and Andrzej tried to put the actual mechanisms for an inter-factory accord in place. Walesa back at the Lenin put his finger to the wind and announced a Solidarity strike.

I cannot overstate the shock it was to hear Joanna and Andrzej Gwiazda describe Walesa as a communist infiltrator. And not just because it seems unimaginable that the man who is credited with precipitating the collapse of communism in Eastern Europe could in reality be a sham. I was shocked and saddened because in a naive and perhaps immature way the men and women whom I met in Anna's flat were, for me, symbols of a fervour and heroic commitment that seemed sadly lacking in the greedy West whence I had come. As I sat listening to them I could not help but think that they had somehow been petrified in time. Unable to cope with the enormity of the events that they had helped to trigger, events which very quickly grew beyond their control, they simply rejected the new reality and in so doing rejected the new Poland. And in denying the reality of the collapse of the communist party it was also necessary to question the integrity of those who conspired with them to bring about that collapse, and on a wider stage to deny the reality of the collapse of the entire Soviet system. For Joanna and Andrzej and indeed for Anna Walentynowicz, their belief that Walesa tried to stop the strike that Saturday afternoon is proof of his treachery. 'Did he go over?' I asked. 'The fact that he stopped the strike means that he was always there,' answered Joanna.

Ludka Wujec, now a prominent member of the post-Solidarity party, the Democratic Union, was in regular contact with the Gdansk group during 1980, through her work with Jan Litynski on *Robotnik*. She sees the conflict as having arisen out of very human factors: 'In my opinion the conflict between Gwiazda's group and Walesa started because they knew him from everyday life. They knew all his strengths and weaknesses, and all of a sudden he became a national hero. Cooperating with him during the strike, they had saved him so many times but they didn't share the same extent of public praise. He became a cult figure and the more praise was heaped on him the more frustrated they became because they felt they had organized it all. Gdansk became a Mecca. Everyone wanted to meet him, all the intellectuals, all the international media. They found they couldn't moderate him anymore. Perhaps someone with more natural modesty would have been able to take criticism, but not Lech.' Ludka argues that for the people advising the Gdansk committee from Warsaw, there was no doubt that Andrzej was regarded as the leader up to the start of the strike: 'Our view was that Gwiazda was the leader: Lech was a kind of clever guy but with a very good relationship with the crowd; then we did not know he was charismatic. Andrzej's contribution to the strike on the coast was enormous. He was the one in control.' There was more than one key moment or move in the cycle of events in August, but the decision to found the Inter-factory Strike Committee is definitely one of them. But having achieved that the next hurdle was the modification of the plethora of strike demands that came in from the various enterprises. Andrzej did have help, not least from Bogdan Borusewicz of KOR and Bogdan Lis, but there does seem to be a consensus that he had a major input into their presentation and sequence. Eventually twenty-one carefully worded demands were presented to the authorities.

But as the strike moved into its second stage there were two distinct but interlocking elements. There were the long, exhausting and mostly public negotiations handled by the strike committee and by the 'experts' who had been invited in by the Solidarity side and the government team. Meanwhile, inside and outside the shipyard negotiating room Walesa was bringing the battle to the whole of Poland and the world. A star was born.

Ludka Wujec argues that it was not a complete coincidence that Walesa emerged as the leader. He was remembered for his role during the 1970 repression in Gdansk. He was on the strike committee then and he had done his time in jail. But most importantly he seized the moment. 'The man who becomes the leader is the one who can handle the microphone.' No matter how much Andrzej wanted to lead, he was missing one vital qualification. He was an engineer. 'It had to be a worker, a blue collar worker, who led the strike. Besides, Andrzej was philosophical. To be a strike leader one has to be good with the crowd.' Ludka Wujec also points out that it was not just Walesa's pragmatism: 'He was disciplined and industrious. Andrzej lacked political timing.' Jan Litynski emphasizes the difference in style between the two men: 'Walesa welcomed the "experts" including Poland's future first post-communist prime minister Tadeusz Mazowiecki and historian Bronislaw Geremek, who came to Gdansk to help with the negotiations. According to Litynski they were impressed not only by the organization of the strike itself but by Walesa's ability to stir the crowd, and they admired his negotiating skills. The experts found it less easy to do business with the more combative and fundamentalist Gwiazda. In Walesa they iden-tified a real politician.

Of course, it was these very qualities that were to incense the Gwiaz-das: 'His policies were not consistent. When he meets a radical crowd he wants to lead it. He doesn't try and convince people: he joins them. Then when he meets the authorities he's immediately on their side.' Andrzej adds that when Walesa 'wants to show the Reds that he's a good partner in negotiations he tells them they've conceded too much when our side is winning something.'

Questions concerning Walesa's style, however, are not the essence of the Gwiazda allegations. He claims that Walesa 'was supported by very powerful forces in this country – by the Church and by the Communist Party, who did not see an enemy in him and by the secret police, with whom he was in touch. We would stress that a big role was played by Western opinion. We blame Western jour-nalists. Poles looked to the West for hope. For the West, Solidarity was Walesa. They thought he was great. People here were helpless against such argument and opinions.' The Gwiazdas claim that Walesa's treach-ery goes back to 1970, that he admitted to them in 1978 that he informed the secret police about his friends who were active during the riots. It is claimed that he admitted identifying rioters from pol-ice film of the events. Unfortunately, according to the Gwiazdas, the tape on which the admission was recorded is now lost. So, how, I asked, could he have been allowed to join the Free Trades Union

Committee and play so prominent a role? Their answer was that it was at the suggestion of Bogdan Borusewicz, someone else who is now regarded in a treacherous light, who argued that Lech should play a role because, like Anna Walentynowicz, he had been sacked from the yard.

For Jan Litynski the conflict within the Gdansk group started because of differences of style and because of simple personal conflict. It is hard to imagine two individuals less alike than Adrzej Gwiazda and Lech Walesa. If one is reminiscent of an angry God, the other plays an excellent grinning devil. But this personal conflict was only a microcosm of the bigger conflict over democracy within the union. It came to a head in March 1981 after what came to be known as the 'Bydgoszcz Affair'. From then on the allegations about Walesa's dictatorial tendencies were out in the open and Andrzej Gwiazda was not the only person making the accusations.

The early part of 1981 had been very tense in Poland. In February General Wojciech Jaruzelski had taken over as prime minister and the Party reformer and editor of *Polityka*, Mieczyslaw Rakowski, was to head a permanent committee to deal with government–trade union relations. Solidarity was pleased and hoped that they had be able to do business with the new regime. Moscow, however, was not pleased at all. The Polish leaders were called to the Kremlin, where the Politburo's anger was vented. There followed a series of events including harassment of Solidarity activists by police, unprovoked assaults on persons and places displaying Solidarity flags and badges, and sackings. Then, on the day that Walesa was to meet with the new prime minister, an elderly KOR activist had his pelvis shattered when a weapon known to be exclusively used by the police was used on him in a Warsaw street. Earlier on the morning after the 'High Noon' in Moscow, one of Poland's most famous opposition activists, Jacek Kuron, was detained, while a day or so later it was the turn of another key dissident, Adam Michnik. With tension high, a Solidarity bulletin published a leaked tape recording of a speech given by a Polish politburo member to security chiefs in which he advised them on how to fragment and destroy Solidarity from within.

Amid claims of massive provocation by the hardliners, orchestrated both from within and without Poland, Solidarity's advisers urged caution. Walesa was coming under intense pressure to react and retrospectively it seems difficult not to conclude that there were elements within the Party who were determined to manufacture the confrontation that would justify a massive repression against the union.

At the centre of the 'Bydgoszcz Affair' was the beating up of a Regional Solidarity leader, Jan Rulewski. He had gone to the region to help local Rural Solidarity activists who were looking for recognition for their union. After the local group had occupied the offices of the United Peasants Party (part of the so-called government coalition) they were invited to attend a local council meeting. However, very early on in the proceedings a large contingent of police arrived and, after a sit-in had been declared, the group was forcibly removed. Afterwards it was discovered that several people including Rulewski had been badly beaten up.

Hot on the heels of the previous provocations there was an explosion of anger within Solidarity. It was only after excruciating debate that Walesa managed to prevent an immediate general strike, getting reluctant agreement for a four hour nationwide warning stoppage for Friday, 27 March. A general strike was planned for the following Tuesday if an agreement was not reached with the government. With all sorts of conflicting advice and demands ringing in his ears, Walesa spent much of the weekend before the planned general strike closeted with Deputy Prime Minister Mieczyslaw Rakowski trying to hammer out a deal. Certainly he was under no illusions about what the Church or the intellectual advisers thought. Both Bronislaw Geremek and Tadeusz Mazowiecki saw civil war on the horizon, while it can only be guessed what horrific picture of Soviet retribution Rakowski was painting for the exhausted Walesa.

When the capitulation was announced on television, Poland was stunned. Cunningly Walesa managed to get Andrzej Gwiazda to make the announcement. For Walesa the decision not to go ahead with the strike was ironically based on the same reasoning that would later be used by General Wojciech Jaruzelski to justify his decision to implement martial law. Both men argued that the risk of bloodshed was too great. The outflowing of accusations of connivance with the government, of cowardice, of a lack of democratic procedures and of outright dictatorial tendencies against 'King Lech' given vent at the National Commission meeting that followed was to tarnish irrevocably the image of the union as a totally united mass movement.

Whether or not Bydgoszcz was planned in particular, or whether it occurred out of a general atmosphere of contempt within the security services, is debatable; but what is clear is that it was a watershed for Solidarity on a number of levels. Firstly, because the union drew back from the abyss; secondly, because it brought into the open the opposition to Walesa's style of leadership and the question of how the union should operate; and, thirdly, because it copper-fastened the concept of the 'self-limiting' revolution which was to be the union's key strategy right up to the Round Table talks in 1989 when Solidarity peacefully convinced the Party to hand over the reins of power.

Andrzej Gwiazda offered his resignation at the National Commission and in true Stalinist style denounced himself, accusing himself, among other things, of failing to uphold the cherished principle of democratic procedures. Now, he says, Bydgoszcz was the turning point, the moment when the union went irrevocably down the wrong road: 'Then the anti-democratic and conciliatory wing gained the upper hand.' According to Joanna, Solidarity's internal elections which followed Bydgoszcz elevated the wrong element within the union. She says that the call for people with organizational talents meant that 'career-minded people' gained the high ground. She claims that from then on the strugglers, fighters and hardliners were discouraged and that what she calls people with a 'clerk' mentality rose to prominence. What of course was happening in reality was a straightforward struggle for power within the union. It was a struggle that the Gwiazdas and their faction were to lose. But though Lech Walesa was elected chairman of the National Commission at the Congress in October there was a sizeable vote against him. For some who voted for the other three candidates it was simply a tactic to keep Walesa under check. Jan Litynski was a tactical voter: 'I did not like Walesa. Of course, it was obvious that he was a real leader. Gwiazda's idea to be chairman was ridiculous. But I liked him, so I voted for him: he had no chance. I thought it was a necessary show of opposition to Walesa. But there was a much deeper conflict going on between the democratic tendencies and the "True Poles", that is, between our stream [the post-KOR stream] and this group who were the nucleus of what would later become the Christian National Union (in post-communist Poland). Ideologically they were right wing and opposed to our liberal, secular approach. They supported Walesa and here, Gwiazda played an important role against this tendency. But for Gwiazda it was just a fight against Walesa.'

Of course, the dividing line between the various streams within the movement was not a fixed one. But in the three most identifiable streams one sees the nuclei of the main post-Solidarity political parties. Apart from the Christian National Union (ZChN), which was formally established in 1990, the Confederation for an Independent Poland (KPN) also drew its support from the nationalist and populist end of Solidarity. In simple terms this grouping demanded an independent and free Poland placing national sovereignty and free elections at the top of the political agenda. As we will see later, however, the xenophobic, fiercely Catholic and almost messianic interpretation of the right road for Poland is still being voiced in various guises by these post-communist, post-Solidarity parties. KPN, for instance, argues that the Round Table talks were a sell-out and that communism could have been toppled in Poland had Solidarity continued to use its main weapon – the strike.

Today the second tendency within Solidarity has found its political voice in the mainly social democrat parties such as the Labour Union and the Solidarity Parliamentary Club. (The latter failed to make the five per cent threshold in the September 1993 post-communist landslide.) Central to this tendency was the 'self-government' notion of worker control of the workplace. In essence the idea was to give the worker real control over production and distribution and in that way prise away the reins of economic power from the communists. The 'self-government' idea was linked to decentralization. Today, among other things, its adherents talk of a strong regional policy, as well as the provision of financial and other credits which would allow workers buy a stake in the state enterprises currently being privatized.

It is from the third group that Poland has mainly drawn its post-Solidarity political leadership. This group included the dissidents, the 'class of '68' and pragmatists who saw the future in terms of compromise with the Party. Lech Walesa was the first among this group, as were most of his advisers. After Walesa declared the 'War at the Top' in the spring of 1990, this wing broke into several tendencies which would later become political parties. In crude terms most of the old KOR dissidents formed the liberal and mainly secular Democratic Union, while the pro-Walesa and more populist elements formed the Centrum Alliance. But, as we will see later, the lines between the post-Solidarity parties are fluid. In the main that is because the parties fragmented on the basis of personalities rather than programmes.

For Joanna and Andrzej Gwiazda speculation about the shape of Poland's political parties is futile. Their feeling that Solidarity had been somehow hijacked had become a conviction by the time they were released from prison after martial law (introduced on 13 December 1981). Joanna was released in July 1982 after the general amnesty for women, while Andrzej was released in July 1984, re-arrested and finally released in May 1985. Joanna says that she 'found it very difficult to convince people that our work should be carried on without the knowledge of Walesa, Borusewicz [who had escaped arrest and was a key architect of underground Solidarity], the Church and the police. People said we were crazy.' The couple claim that the Walesa faction bought support with American dollars and that money donated from abroad to help what they describe as the independent opposition never reached them. They concede that not all the Solidarity supporters were bought over by Walesa: 'Not everybody. Not the lower ranks, who did not realize what was going on. Some don't even realize now. We saw the documents when we were in the United States. We saw the papers allocating money for various regional groups. We checked when we came back. The money never reached those people.' So I asked them if they were alleging that Walesa had acted fraudulently? Both said that they did not know what Walesa had done with the allegedly missing funds, but that Father Jankowski, a Gdansk priest and one of Walesa's advisers, had said that everything was okay.

Joanna and Andrzej live alone in a tiny flat on Zabianka Street some ten or fifteen minutes' drive from the centre of Gdansk. It is a huge typically Stalinist tower block just like all the others, grey, with broken pavements, broken window panes and poor lighting. Stacked on top of each other like battery hens, the men and women who exist here were meant to have but one purpose – work. Somehow, I thought, there is even a message in the size of the lifts, which barely fit three people. Walking into their home my eyes were assaulted by the sight of a million tiny objects. There was not an inch of free, clear space. Everywhere there were pieces of equipment, machines, nuts and bolts, radio and recording parts, half-completed wooden things, books, paper, insignia, rosary beads, holy pictures, local and ethnic wooden art; and all of the time Andrzej fidgeted with some little gadget as we talked. Had it not been for the barren and stark ugliness of the landscape, it was as if I had joined a pair of magpies in their nest high above in the branches of some ancient tree.

As our interview proceeded, I had sensed a growing tension as Andrzej stirred his tea incessantly. But when I asked for their views on the collapse of communism, I felt as if there had been a controlled explosion in Andrzej's head: 'First of all, communism has not collapsed. Maybe it's now reclining in a more comfortable position. I can assure you that the Round Table talks made a much more comfortable bed for communism. Talking about the collapse of communism is repeating irrational and absolutely senseless propaganda.' But how, I asked, could most of the opposition have taken part in it. Were they all fools? 'The Round Table talks were theatre, a spectacular show and not just for the Polish people. It's Polish *perestroika*. The whole thing was a political sham. It was prepared and created by the communists, who decided which of the opposition activists should take part. The real negotiations had been underway since the beginning of martial law. Look: it would have been impossible for the communists to introduce Perestroika alone. The fact that the changes were made under the name of Walesa resulted in the disappearance of any resistance. Now people realize that they have been cheated.'

Essentially the Gwiazdas argue that under the guise of economic reform Poland's assets are being sold abroad to line the pockets of the new alliance between the communists and the opposition: 'The behaviour of the United States shows that there was a conspiracy between the Americans and the Soviets to introduce Perestroika here.' Joanna adds that 'the Yanks are just stupid. They're afraid of nationalism here. They say openly they had prefer to deal with just one opponent on the nuclear issue. The Yanks are afraid of true freedom being won by the countries in Eastern Europe. They're also afraid of the expansion of Poland's economy. We're a threat to Western Europe. The West wants production restricted here. It's obvious with recession everywhere, they don't want competition from us.'

When I asked what could be done to save Poland from this huge conspiracy, the Gwiazdas came full circle: 'We must establish free trades unions. We must stop the destruction and liquidation of our state enterprises. People have been fooled by this capitalist propaganda. Joint ventures have been created from abroad to stop our home production. Look at Poland. The communists destroyed the economy in the name of one ideology. Now the so-called post-communists are destroying the economy for the sake of capitalist ideology. Now we've got central planning by another name.'

And so, I asked gingerly, was life better now that they were free from the harassment of secret police? Free from arrest and imprisonment? Somehow they seemed unsure about what they should say. Hesitantly Joanna said that when they had what she described as 'improper' telephone conversations the line was cut: 'Sometimes they follow us in their cars. They don't imprison us. But I think our conversation now is being recorded.' Both laughed nervously. Somehow I felt they had said what they thought I wanted to hear, not really knowing if they believed it themselves.

Just after the September 1993 election I again visited Gdansk to meet Joanna and Andrjej. He had run in the election but had not been successful. Joanna explained that it was impossible for them to get publicity for their campaign because even shopkeepers were too afraid to put up their posters. Andrzej had run on a three-point programme. He called for the 'disposal of Lech Walesa as President', the introduction of a majority system as opposed to the newly introduced proportional representation system, and action to stop Poland being turned into a 'Euro region'.

As I had foreseen, the landslide victory of the SLD and the PSL, which were the direct descendants of the old Communist Party and the former ZSL (United Peasant Party), left the Gwiazdas even more convinced that a great conspiracy had taken place in Poland. Joanna pointed out that 'the only permanent ideology in the Communist Party was that it had to stay in power. In its old form it was doubtful if the Party could retain power so they changed the form. This post-revolutionary form of Party is difficult even for the members. But if communism means that people cannot decide their fate and don't have influence, and if the economy is centralized, then this has not changed. But what's true is that the Marxist ideology has been done away with. But as you see the former communists still have power. They are now leading businessmen.'

I left Zabianka Street knowing that there was more than a grain of truth in what they had said.

Pani Ania: Anna Walentynowicz

Anna Walentynowicz is the personification of the Stalinist female heroine. Hewn in grey concrete slabs, these Mother Earth figures display but one female physical and psychological characteristic. With their gigantic breasts firmly fixed above solid hips and square legs they proclaim their role as suckler of the nation. Were it not for the unfortunate state of her political views Anna would have been any good communist's dream. Anna believed in the worker state and Anna believed in justice and a fair deal for workers, but unlike the Party she really believed it. It was not for Anna some Utopian goal or mumbo jumbo to be ritualistically mouthed. Until 1968 she had been a member of the official trade union at the Lenin Shipyard. But when she exposed a scandal among union members who had misappropriated a union poverty fund she was sacked. After protests from her fellow workers Anna was allowed return to work but not in her old job. By the time I met Anna she was a well known and popular figure at the yard. The protest against her dismissal planned for 14 August was nothing unusual for her: she was almost a veteran when it came to being sacked. And so she had as much time for me that afternoon and evening at her flat in Gdansk as if she was a carefree granny, with just another kid turning up for tea.

If Anna had been born a day earlier her birthday would have coincided with the birth of Solidarity. She had been born in 1929 in Wolyn, now part of Russia, and had lost both her father and mother during the war. Her only brother had been shipped, like so many others, to a labour camp somewhere in the old Soviet Union. She was never to see him again. Anna says that she came to Gdansk in 1945 'with strangers' who settled themselves on a farm formerly owned by German people. Though she is reticent, it still obviously hurts her that she was treated as a 'free servant'. She remained on the farm until she was twenty-one, when she got a job at the shipyard. After what she describes as 'an unhappy love', she had a son. It is perhaps an interesting reflection on the kind of woman Anna is that, despite an offer of marriage from a man who was not the father of her future child, she decided to go it alone: 'I felt I had to bear the consequences of my actions alone.' Nine years later, in 1964, she changed her mind and married Kazimierz, who had worked with her for over ten years in the same brigade at the yard: 'I had him for seven years and fourteen days. But he gave me so much love I don't feel like a widow. It's just as if he's gone away on a trip and that he'll be back soon. My husband gave me some recompense for all the bad things I have suffered, all the bad things that were said of me as a single mother. But then in God's plan it must have been that I was meant to be alone.'

For Anna the feeling that the events of her life were meant to be, goes beyond a mere faith in the omniscient influence of the Almighty. Like many fundamentalist Poles who believe in their country's messianic role, Anna has a sense that she was destined and picked out to play an important part in Poland's struggle: 'I am going to tell you about a dream. When I was very young, I dreamed that I saw an apparition in the back yard of the house. I saw the bust of a man in a purple robe. In his left hand he was holding an open book while in his right he had a quill. Now while I was sure that the figure was only a statue the eyes were alive. He had living blue eyes. As a child, I often wondered how half a man can be living. But I was never afraid of the image, and I never forgot it. Then when I came to this area in 1951 I saw the same bust in the form of a relief near the altar in the Church. There were four elements to the relief. The priest explained to me that they represented the four Evangelists and that the one that I had described was St Luke. Thirty years later after the strike, after we'd got our monument [to the dead of 1970; the monument was one of the original demands of the strikers], another priest, Father Adam Skwarczewski, told me that Solidarity would die. How could this happen, I said, now that we have our monument honouring our dead? I did not believe him. But he said that Solidarity would die but that it would be reborn and give new life. He said it would bear fruit a thousandfold. When he said all this, I asked him if he was charismatic and told him about my dream. He then asked me what connections I had with the church where I saw the relief. I remembered that it was the church where I had my son baptized, where I was married, where I buried my husband and where I had hidden in August 1980 to avoid arrest. Father Adam then told me that God had plans for me. Then I thought how I had been the one with cancer five years before Kazimierz died. He had thought that I was going to die and yet I am still alive.'

It was after Anna was told that she had five years to live following surgery for cancer that she decided she had 'to do something': 'I wanted to live. I was determined to use those years. They wanted to pension me off at the shipyard. My job as a welder was very heavy but I went on a three-month training course to be a crane operator and passed. Then I started trying to help poorer people.'

But it was after Anna's contact with KOR and attendance at Flying University lectures that a sense of wanting to do 'good' was transformed into something more concrete. This network of lectures and seminars held unofficially brought diverse elements of Poland's intelligentsia and worker activists together and was to be another factor in the politicization and socialization of the rainbow coalition which nurtured Solidarity. Ludka Wujec, in whose flat many Flying University lectures were held, remembers Anna as 'very warm-hearted. She provided real care for the group in Gdansk. She was not a leader but she was very well known in the yard. Sacking her was the spark. It was the beginning of the whole strike. I felt that she had an inborn sense of justice. She was an extremely honest person and very courageous.'

Years after my first meeting with Anna it was this image of a woman with a straightforward desire to improve the lives of those around her that dominated my thoughts. A woman not really political, but a woman who knew that real change meant something political. So why did she get involved in the Free Trades Union group? 'I wanted to help people – but through political changes. To give clothes or bread is only help for one day. To help someone for the future, for the long-term needs political change. I wanted to tell people to stop feeling afraid and feel free and at home in their own country.'

But what was the factor that drew together the goodwill of people such as Anna, that gave people like her the courage and will to act? What was it that turned the slow process of the coming together of the worker and the intellectual into a vibrant force for change? Sociology professor Edmund Wnuk-Lipinski is not alone when he argues that the catalyst for the momentous events of August 1980 was the visit of the Polish Pope, John Paul II, in 1979: 'It was the crucial moment when the control of public language by the state was broken and the social isolation of the people was ended. Society had been atomized. People tended to see society as an alien environment. And all of a sudden people saw that it's not only me or my friends but millions of people who think this way. It was a cognitive shock for Polish society.' Jan Litynski puts it another way: 'People felt the passion of the people, saw that people could organize themselves. There was a great feeling of oneness. That one is not just an individual, but that one is part of a great body. I wrote an article after the visit saying how alienated the government was from the people. For the first time people saw how small "they" [the Party] were. And not just small, farcical. A new category of people was discovered.

Suddenly there was "us".' For Anna it was much simpler: 'After the election of a Polish Pope and the papal visit, people got closer to each other. We became braver and we were nicer to each other.'

Discovering that an individual from one's past is not the person one thought can be very self-revealing. It hurt to find out that a woman who had been my heroine was anti–Semitic and xenophobic. I wanted a pure flame, a true and simple champion of the people, the embodiment of Solidarnosc, brothers and sisters on the barricades together. My stomach heaved the moment I heard it coming. 'I must add something. The minorities should be treated properly in this country, but they should not occupy important posts and they shouldn't govern us. The government should consist of Poles. I am talking about people like Geremek [Bronislaw Geremek, former adviser to Walesa, former Speaker of parliament, and now the leader of the Democratic Union], Michnik [Adam Michnik, leading dissident, now editor of *Gazeta Wyborcza*], and several others. Let them live, but they shouldn't be governing and deciding my fate.' But why? What had they done? 'They are Jews' was her terse reply. Naïvely I asked how she could dismiss Bronislaw Geremek like that. Hadn't he, along with Mazowiecki and others, played such an important part in helping the strikers negotiate the Gdansk agreement? 'Seemingly yes – but they did not help at all. It was only after martial law that I learned that these experts had been sent to us by the communists. They made us lessen our demands. We had to win over our own advisers before we could sit down at the negotiating table. They had their plan A and plan B and their variants. We had our twenty-one demands. And we won even though we were threatened with another World War.'

Sadly the outrageous claims made against the experts probably stems from simple resentment that the control of the strike slipped out of the hands of the original committee. Both Anna and Joanna Gwiazda were upset when Geremek ignored their instruction to leave the meeting of the strike committee when the settlement was reached. 'You are only our adviser,' they told him. 'Leave and wait and then if we need you, we'll call.' This treatment for one of Europe's best known medieval historians.

Like the Gwiazdas, Anna believes that there has been a massive conspiracy which robbed Solidarity of true victory in the guise of the sham collapse of communism, engineered by the communists with the help of Walesa and many other so-called puppets: 'Up until the Round

Table communism was a decaying corpse, but the corpse dictated conditions to those who thought they owned Solidarity. Now the communists have just changed their name to Solidarity. Now they're more perfidious and clever than ever. They're worse than the old communists use to be. At least they never took pensions from anyone. In the past everything was controlled by the Soviet Union; now Poland's economic plans are decided in Washington.'

But at the heart of this outpouring of paranoia and behind this need to find a scapegoat is the simple fact that Lech Walesa deprived Anna Walentynowicz of her role in the union. From the beginning Walesa showed his killer instincts as a politician. And when Anna became a problem he made sure that she was not selected as a delegate to Solidarity's National Congress in July 1981. And so in Anna's eyes Walesa became a demon: 'He was the King. He used the workers to throw me out. Walesa was prepared by the communists just in case something like August happened. The communists ordered people to join the union at the beginning. They were fighting against us from the inside. But they did not completely succeed and that's why they had to introduce martial law.' Then as an afterthought Anna adds that her one-time friends and fellow conspirators, Bogdan Lis and Bogdan Borusewicz, had also been double agents. But surely not Alina Pienkowska, the nurse who saved the strike? 'Of course she's in it. It's time for purges. We cannot blindly trust all those who used to be our friends. Now they are our enemies.' My heart sank.

And so, I wondered, what were Anna's goals or aims now? 'My dream is to live in an independent Poland. There is still hope. We must get rid of this government. They've no mandate. We cannot follow the United States or the Soviet model. We must create our own model. The people must create our own government and constitution. But they must only have one year's trial period, and if they betray people they must be replaced immediately and they must pay for what they've done. We have to make a revolution. But not of arms or knives. Not bloody. A revolution like our Polish August. But this time, without the services of the Geremeks or Mazowieckis. Nothing's been won, none of our twenty-one demands, except the monument in Gdansk, and that's only propaganda.'

Time had frozen for Anna. It was as if Lech Walesa had never jumped up on to the shipyard wall.

Exposing the Fiction: Alina Pienkowska and Bogdan Borusewicz

How close did Lech Walesa come to aborting Solidarity? His premature announcement that all the shipyard workers' demands had been
met could have had catastrophic historical consequences. But then of
course we would not have known it. Happily the Solidarity baby was
saved because of the quick-footed response of an adept nurse, Alina
Pienkowska. Who knows whether Alina looked at Walesa's gaffe in
strategic terms or whether she simply saw that he was betraying the
workers from all of the other factories who had come out in support of
the Lenin yard. One way or another her spontaneous show of loyalty
was crucial. Professor Wnuk-Lipinski argues that the real beginning of
Solidarity was not the original strike but Walesa's announcement of a
solidarity strike after Alina's intervention: 'Hers was the dramatic moment. That moment changed everything. Before it was particular, but
after that it was universal.'

In the underground marriage of Alina Pienkowska and Bogdan
Borusweicz there was a coming together of two of the three elements
that transformed the August strikes into a revolution. With their secret
church wedding after martial law, two separate political traditions were
united. Alina was twenty-eight, widowed and the mother of a five-year-
old son when I met her in Anna's flat. I liked her instantly. She was
very open, extraordinarily active and struck me as an extremely warm
woman. Born into a highly political family in a country where being
politically involved almost automatically ensured terms of imprisonment, Alina grew up understanding the price of opposition. Her
grandfather had been an active supporter of the peasant leader,
Wincenty Witos, who, apart from serving three times as prime minister
in the Second Republic, was one of the focal points of opposition to
Marshal Josef Pilsudski's dictatorship.[4] Alina remembers her own father
telling her that along with his sisters he was barred from even entering
the polling booth during the 1947 elections. Though coming from a
strongly political background Alina is cautious about describing her
own politics: 'I don't feel, even now when I am a Senator, that I am
political. I reacted against social injustice. Just working in the shipyard
I saw how helpless the workers were. They had no influence on anything. Officially we had trade unions and organizations to help us but it
was pure fiction. I just thought that I had to change the fiction in this
very shipyard. I saw how censorship worked in ordinary life. There

were so many things that the shipyard paper did not talk about. If there were industrial accidents it was always the workers' fault. In those days I just wanted to stop the lies. I really hadn't political ideas but I was against totalitarianism more than I was against communism.'

If Alina Pienkowska finds it hard to describe herself in political terms, her partner and co-conspirator Bogdan Borusewicz is from head to toe the archetypal politician. 'My family,' he explains, 'came from an area occupied by the Soviets before 1940. So I knew all about what went on. We had to leave home when I was three years old and we ended up in Gdansk. There was a strong independence tradition on my mother's side. My uncles were in the Polish Army before the war, and my cousins were in the unofficial underground army which fought the Germans. My father was imprisoned and badly wounded by Lithuanian police who were collaborating with Germany when he was in the Home Army. My father, who was a teacher and farmer, left us, so my mother brought the three of us up. I could do as I liked. That's how I ended up in the opposition. I went to prison for the first time in 1968 during the student demonstrations. I was convicted of printing and distributing subversive information and served a year and a half, of a three-year sentence. While I was in prison my teachers helped me with my studies, so I ended up only losing one grade. That really annoyed the secret police, who thought that people like me should be punished. I went to the Catholic University of Lublin because I thought it was the only University likely to take me with my political record. While there I began to get involved in semi-legal activities like church and scientific organizations. Then in 1976 I went to Radom. During that time I met lots of opposition people including the people who founded KOR. But I am a man of action. There was a lot of talking going on. I finally got tired listening to talk about cooperating with the workers. I thought that Radom and Ursus might be the place to start but they were poles apart. The Gdansk workers were far more politicized after the events of 1970. They were bitterly disillusioned by Gierek's promises.'[5]

In fact Borusewicz played a key role in establishing the Founding Committee of Free Trades Unions in Gdansk and forged the links between the worker activists there, KOR and organizations such as the Young Poland movement and the human rights organization, ROPCiO. So while Alina and probably most of her fellow worker activists thought in terms of local reform in the late seventies,

Borusewicz was a convinced proponent of what came to be known as
the 'evolutionary revolution': 'I took a broader political view. It was
not a case of just local goals. I was aware that whatever we did it
would have an influence on the long-term political situation. What
we did in Gdansk was the outcome of KOR's analysis. Central to it
was Kuron's idea of a civil society. That is, setting up alternative
structures to the state. But the changes we wanted could only come
about with the cooperation of the workers.'

Borusewicz was not just a clever operator himself; he recognized
political ability in others and was the one to encourage the participation
of Lech Walesa. However, he was also one of the first to dispas-
sionately recognize the problems created for the union by the style of
leadership engaged in by Walesa.

By early 1981 he says he was 'concerned about the situation as it
was developing. Things were getting out of control in Solidarity. I
was worried about the autocratic tendency of the union – and I don't
mean just Walesa. It was obvious in the attitude of some of the
regional leaders as well.'

Alina resigned from Solidarity's Regional Board along with Andrzej
Gwiazda and Anna Walentynowicz because 'Walesa had become too
dictatorial. Perhaps that's too big a word – but we were not being con-
sulted.' For Alina, Walesa is 'a very important symbol. Undoubtedly
Walesa made mistakes as the leader of the trade union and now as
President. But when one evaluates him, it must be remembered that he
led the country to free elections.' Alina is convinced that Walesa's role
during martial law was crucial. Had he behaved differently, signed
anything, things could have been very different.'

Like thousands of other Solidarity activists, Alina was arrested on 13
December 1981 when General Wojciech Jaruzelski decided to introduce
martial law. The union was winding up a two-day national convention
in Gdansk when the general struck. Like sitting ducks many people
were asleep in hotel rooms or staying with friends in very unsafe
houses: 'I was arrested from Bogdan's house. He was not there but I'd
gone to warn him.' In fact Borusewicz saw that something was wrong
and made his escape, avoiding police who were shooting at the locks
on his apartment door.

And so began four and a half years of constant movement, fake
documents and never-ending conspiracy in the underground movement
that he helped to establish. When I asked him what effect that four and

a half years had had on him, Borusewicz quipped that it had been very positive: 'I got married. I was thirty-seven years of age. It was the only chance I had to get married without all the fuss and bother of organizing a wedding.' His answer highlights a reticence among former activists in relation to the opposition years. Many *anciens combattants* want to put those years behind them, sensing that people in post-communist Poland are resentful of what they perceive as a new 'nomenclatura' or inner circle who are being repaid with government jobs for their periods in jail or underground activities. Looking back Bogdan is unwilling to romanticize the period: 'The first months were very difficult. Then people either got used to the life or they went crazy or quit. After that the next question was – what next? How long am I going to stay underground. What's the purpose – what's the future political development? In the first months one thinks it's going to last half a year. Then after two years once starts to ask – could it be six or eight years? But they solved the problem for me. They arrested me on 9 January 1986.'

Alina was taken to Fordon prison after her arrest but was later moved to Goldalp near the Polish-Russian border. Goldalp was a makeshift internment centre and was before martial law the summer retreat for the employees of Polish Radio. 'For me and my friends the worst thing about being in jail was not the conditions. It was being deprived of our children. At Goldalp the women warders had their children staying with them. I remember looking out on to the grass one day and hearing a child call 'Mama'. I thought for a moment it was my Sebastian calling me. Even today when I hear a child call 'Mama' I immediately think of jail.'

Alina looks on her period in detention positively: 'We were never bored. We organized our time so well. There was never any fear of us breaking down. There were 300 women in the one place coming from all sorts of different backgrounds. There were actresses rubbing shoulders with women from textile factories. All human life was there. We had all kinds of classes, language classes and plays. I think that in sociological terms this experience would make great research.'

When she was released after ten months Alina went to work at the Lenin Shipyard's health centre. Seeing up to 150 people a day at the surgery facilitated her double life as a day-time nurse and night-time underground supporter. 'The secret police were almost helpless where I was concerned. Any one of the hundreds of people I saw each week could bring a letter or help me in some way. I arranged safe flats, organized cars and was in touch with the Solidarity health service for people in hiding. I had to be careful when I went to see Bogdan. The main thing was to lose the tail. But that's easier for a woman. There was one rule. Always start by going to an institution where there was lots of traffic. A hospital during visiting hours, for instance. I'd go in wearing a long skirt and blonde hair. But I'd come out with a short dark wig and a leather mini and tight leather jacket. I managed to see him about once every three months but we'd normally be able to stay together for a week or so.' On a personal level the underground period was a rewarding one for the couple. They were married and their daughter Kinga was born. Opinions vary about the importance of the underground years but Alina feels that the period was significant: 'I think that what did have an important influence on the downfall of communism was the fact that people organized themselves in underground structures which were completely separate from the system, the state.' But the legacy of the raids, the arrests and the searches on this very strong woman is that she's still afraid to be at home alone.

But what of Poland's present and indeed its future? After the union split in 1990 both Alina and Bogdan chose to remain loyal to what they perceived then as Solidarity's original aims. Both were members of NSZZ 'Solidarnosc', one of the more prominent parties who claimed to be the legitimate heir to the Solidarity mantle. Their 'Klub '(as parties are sometimes called in Poland) was abstentionist in the sense that while it participated in parliament and in the senate, the Klub was not prepared to take part in forming a government: 'We want to influence policy so that not only economic values are taken into account: we want to keep social values on the agenda as well.' Borusewicz was adamant that the party played a positive role and rejected suggestions that a group representing a trade union but unwilling to participate in government was in an incongruous position. Alina argued that they were there to highlight the social consequences of the massive economic reconstruction that had been going on in Poland since the end of 1989: 'We are there so that certain limits are not exceeded. It would be disastrous if there was nobody to raise the social issues in the debates. Two years ago I was in favour of a very fast transformation of our economy. It did not happen. Now the economic situation is very bad. The situation of the people is bad, in fact it's dangerous. To be a welfare state is not a good solution, but the recession is frightening, and unless the people are convinced that entrepreneurial activity is going to take off, they'll demand more social supports. If I am not convinced that the economy is going to take off, then I'll be demanding more social welfare.' That was early 1992. Then both Alina and Bogdan were highly critical of the pace of the reforms. He argued that while the battle against inflation was handled effectively by the first post-communist government of Tadeusz Mazowiecki, the industrial transformation of the country simply has not happened. Alina was particularly critical of what she claimed was the failure to implement social welfare, health and educa-tion reforms: 'Money is wasted if it's spent on these areas at the moment. Taxes and customs and other duties are not being properly administered. There's a danger of financial anarchy. If people see that private companies are not paying their taxes, are falling into debt, maybe soon ordinary citizens will stop paying their rents. Look: there is no way out. We can't just look at the financial situation: we have to take into account the ability of the people to survive. We can't just go down the social or the fiscal road alone. That's leading nowhere. That's why Solidarity is in parliament – not to block changes but to find a balance.'

With their emphasis on decentralization, strong local self-govern-ment and an industrial policy aimed at strengthening ties with the other former Eastern bloc countries, Alina and Bogdan trace their poli-tical roots to the self-governmentalist wing of Solidarity, but they've at least one leg between them in the fundamentalist, nationalist tradi-tion. Conscious that political activity was taking its first shaky steps in post-communist Poland, Alina Pienkowska stayed until late 1993 with what she knew and understood. 'My opinion is that the parties now are based on personalities – not on programmes. When that's resolved I'll think about what party I am going to join.'

The political crunch for both Bogdan and Alina came when NSZZ 'Solidarnosc' played a key role in the dissolution of Hanna Suchocka's government in the summer of 1993. Bogdan left the Klub after 'the no confidence vote. I realized that such a decision without deep thinking was a great mistake.' Having turned down an invitation from President Lech Walesa to join the newly formed BBWR (Nonpartisan Reform Support Bloc), a populist pro-Walesa grouping, Borusewicz joined forces with the depleted Democratic Union in the new parliament. He argues that there is no ideological contradiction in him supporting a party which places priority on the completion of the transformation process rather than on the social consequences of the reforms: 'Now the new post-communist government and the Labour Union emphasize the importance of social security and the support that's needed for the old and for workers. So now there is a need for parties like the Democratic Union [UD or Unia for short] who emphasize the need to complete the transformation to a market economy. Now a counterbalance is needed in parliament. Otherwise the reforms might be lost. I have always been a centrist and a pragmatist so I have no problem with Unia's liberal programme.'

Despite the rout suffered by the post-Solidarity parties Borusewicz says that he is a happy man: 'I'll stay in politics. I am happy. We've abolished communism and there's no going back now.'

For Alina the experience of political life has been different: 'I worked very hard in the Senate and did my best. I expected support and I did not always get it. I decided not to run in the election though I was asked by several parties including the Democratic Union. I don't even know whether to remain in the Solidarity trade union or not. I was very disappointed when the union became involved in the dissolution of parliament. That was a very negative act. The whole credibility of political activity is in question over the last couple of years. Much of what has been called politics has been simply primitive. All of this quarrelling between the parties has happened because for forty years people were not able to mature politically. Now you can see the result. A lot depends now on political maturity. I don't like the result of the election but it is democracy and that is what we fought for. Things are very complex here now. On the one hand people want money but they also want stability and they don't want revolution.' Alina appears very relieved to be leaving active political life: 'I have never been good for politics but I have had to be involved. Women are indispensable in political life. But I wanted to go back to humanitarian work. So I went back to work at the medical centre at the shipyard. I have several ideas on how to live my life. There's lots of opportunities to earn a living and still be involved with humanitarian and charitable causes.'

The New Entrepreneur: Bogdan Lis

Despite his father's best efforts to stop him, Bogdan Lis normally managed to sneak in and listen to Radio Free Europe when he tuned in at night. Lis says that there was an historical background to his later political views but that his father tried to steer the the family away from it. Though Bogdan was born in Gdansk in 1952, the Lis family were originally from Grodno, which up until 1945 had been part of Poland. After the war, as a part of Bylorussia, it became incorporated into the Soviet Union. 'Because of where we'd lived, we knew what the Russians were at.' That was a shorthand phrase I was to hear many times in Poland from people whose past sat heavily on their shoulders. Lis is tall and thin and now clean-shaven and more relaxed than I remembered him in 1980. In fact the streak of steely humour I saw in his eyes must have buoyed him as a child because he sounds as if he was a gutsy kid: 'I had some problems when I was in school, particularly in history class. I remember once putting up my hand and asking the teacher about the Katyn massacre. When the teacher told me that the Germans were responsible for the deaths of the 15,000 Polish officers, I said that the Russians had killed them. I remember the moment so well. The teacher did not argue but he said things were not so clear.'

Lis describes himself as generally active and perhaps wanting to draw a veil over his membership of the Party, which lasted right up until the birth of Solidarity, he explains that there was only one way to be active in Poland in the sixties and seventies and that was through official organizations. His activity landed him in jail for six months after the 1970 workers' revolt in Gdansk. 'We were treated like criminals. But I hesitated when Gierek came here and promised changes. But I was young then and susceptible to influence. But I never really changed my opinions.'

Lis remained a member of the old communist trade union even after he had secretly joined the Free Trades Union group in 1978: 'I worked at Elmore with Gwiazda. We were producing electronic steering instruments for ships. I worked in the mechanical production part of the process. Together with eight others we successfully took over the official trade union there. By the spring of 1980, we had won 14 out of 20 places at elections to the union committee. I did not even dream of creating any movement on a national or regional scale but I saw a chance to take over the official unions and act through those structures.' But martial law swept aside the cautious with the bold, the reformer and the 'evolutionary revolutionary': 'I don't think that martial law put down people's aspirations, it did not change people's opposition to communism. In many cases, it turned a simple non-acceptance of communism into hatred. People might have felt helpless, but Solidarity had left an awareness that one can be free, that it was possible to live differently. It had allowed people to get off their knees: it was tangible. It was like a glimpse of freedom.'

Bogdan Lis was close to Lech Walesa from the beginning, but was never afraid to disagree with him. He tried to maintain a diplomatic role between Walesa and the Gwiazda faction when the problems began to arise: 'I resigned along with the others from cooperating with Walesa in April 1981 (after the Bydgoszcz affair) because in that conflict he was wrong. But later, in other rows, ambition played a bigger role than any real problems. Though I shared the doubts about Walesa's merits, I knew that his role and function was bigger than the man. I thought Gwiazda was wrong. Even though I was critical of Walesa I never expressed it publicly. Walesa listened when I spoke to him personally.' Lis thinks that there were several reasons for the bloody rupture between Walesa and Gwiazda: 'Gwiazda was very idealistic; there was a real clash with reality there. He had a completely different understanding of what democracy meant. But in the end it was a clear fight for power. It caused a great shock to them all, to Anna, Alina, both the Gwiazdas when they were beaten. It resulted in a hurt that has lasted until today.'

Lis was lucky on 13 December. A friend got to him before the militia did and he got away. He did not go underground straightaway. At first he wanted to go to the shipyard, to the scene of former glory, but again friends warned him that there was no point. The yard was beaten. Lis was not the only senior Solidarity figure operating in this half-underground world in the immediate aftermath of martial law. With so many of the leadership in Gdansk for the Congress, the bulk of the nationwide arrests were concentrated there. But fortunately for Solidarity a handful of its key strategists and activists escaped – among them, the Mazowsze (Warsaw) regional boss, Zbigniew Bujak, Aleksander Hall, a member of the Young Poland movement, and, as we've already heard, Bogdan Borusewicz.

It was February before Lis managed to arrange a meeting between himself, Borusewicz and Hall. They met in Sopot, the seaside town near Gdansk, where they set about trying to set up an effective underground structure. While simply being free was a major propaganda exercise, the goal was to establish links between the leaders and the covert Solidarity membership in the factories and enterprises. Needless to say, much of the activity surrounded the procurement of flats and the organization of security procedures. Lis avoided arrest for two and a half years but was caught about sixty kilometres from Gdansk on his way to a meeting after he was denounced by a spy. From prison he managed to get a message to Borusewicz warning him to stay away from the meeting place. While free Lis had set up and was responsible for the underground's international support and contacts.

A good indication of how the government dealt with these 'criminals and hooligans' was the use of amnesties throughout the period. Because it was desperately trying to avoid the creation of a band of martyrs, even the ringleaders could expect to be let free within weeks or months of release. Lis was arrested a couple of weeks before the 1984 July amnesty and charged with treason. That charge made him ineligible for the amnesty, so the authorities conveniently reduced the charge the following December. Free for a couple of months Lis was again arrested in February 1985, this time in the exalted company of KOR theorist Adam Michnik, and Wroclaw's Solidarity boss Wladislaw Frasyniuk. Lis maintains that the underground was a success on a number of levels. But perhaps on a very simple level the government became used to the notion of an opposition, albeit, an underground one. It also got used to the idea of concession and conciliation, recognizing that the persecution of Solidarity's heroes simply strengthened the movement.

Looking back at Solidarity's early days and at the underground period, Lis says it was all so much simpler: 'There was only one enemy, one goal. Things were more honest, it was easier to trust each other. Now it's the same people but it's a political game. It was obvious that it had to end. I think I expected a split but I had hoped that there would be fewer examples of slippery business. What I really regret is that the divisions within the movement after communism ended did not happen on political lines; what's happened is based on personal conflicts. You can see what I mean when you look at the unlikely coalitions within parliament. If you compare programmes, some of the coalitions seem impossible but if you look at who is involved, it makes sense.'

Of all of the original Gdansk conspirators, Lis stands out as the one who has managed to distance himself from an over personal view of the union's controversial moments. He offers what he believes is a dispassionate analysis of why the War at the Top happened: 'I do understand what Walesa was trying to do. At that time in late 1989 after Tadeusz Mazowiecki became prime minister and in early 1990 we tend to forget that the Communist Party did not exist. Political life was dominated by Solidarity. But that did not allow for normal political development. There were parties but no political scene. It was obvious that if that was allowed to continue that Solidarity would become a power without an election. It was impossible to see the difference between the trade union and the government. But the union found it difficult to challenge the new government because it had no desire for it to fall. Though it was not directly participating in government Solidarity was taking all the responsibility for the tough measures which were being introduced to start the economic transformation. From Walesa's point of view the situation was difficult. He was explaining to the people what Mazowiecki's government was trying to achieve but he was not actually participating in political life. In other words Walesa found himself taking the rap. He saw the need for an opposition.'

Lis argues against blaming any one person for the breakup of Solidarity, but his interpretation is hotly disputed by many members of Poland's political élites: 'I don't think we can restrict the problem to just one person, however, far-reaching mistakes were made by three people. Firstly, Walesa wanted to remove all the old guard, the people with whom he had worked over the years. He did not just want to get rid of them from the political life. He did not want them near him in his personal life either. Secondly, I blame Adam Michnik who wrongly estimated Walesa's power after the communists fell and Mazowiecki took over. I talked to him in August '89. Michnik thought Walesa was a spent force.' And as editor of *Gazeta Wyborcza* he did his best to bury him: 'Instead of trying to influence Walesa, they left him to himself. The consequences of that was that Walesa was left without good advisers. He was surrounded by nondescript people. Walesa thought he was playing a big game but in reality he was the one who was being played with. Of course he won't admit that.' Lis also finds fault with the intellectual advisers around Walesa. He says that they failed to respond quickly enough to a political scene that was changing rapidly in the weeks and months after Solidarity's landslide election victory in June 1989: 'In particular Bronislaw Geremek noticed too late that the situation was changing. He did not notice that the way of taking decisions would have to change. The old opposition was too narrow. He did not see that only a very small elite had access to power and information in the new regime, in the new government. Geremek wanted to stay on good terms with Walesa but he was not prepared to get involved in rows with him.'

At the end of 1991 Bogdan Lis resigned from active participation in the union and he did not run for the senate in the November elections. 'I am not active in Solidarity any more. Political ambitions can only be realized in politics. Being a politician and a trade unionist is a problem, it's a contradiction. A politician is in parliament to protect the interest of the state. If he's also a trade unionist, he will not be able to fulfil his promises if he acts responsibly. The union should have a voice in parliament but it should take the form of a lobby. It should be represented by politicians who have roots in the trade union movement.' Lis moved away from Solidarity because he felt that it did not have a direct role to play in parliament. He sees the union's dilemma in terms of its inability so far to find a role for itself. In fact, having been the major player in the political transformation of Poland, the union and its political allies played a conservative restraining role, often espousing views it would have at one time denounced as communist.

Lis sees the irony in the fact that so many trade union activists are now becoming activists of another kind altogether, and that in their new business roles, former union people find themselves supporting pro-business and anti-worker agendas: 'Social welfare problems cannot be solved without dealing with the economic problems first. Look: I am in business. Most companies don't pay their taxes. They would go bankrupt if they did. It's profitable to cheat and smuggle.' Lis argues that communist economic dogma has been replaced with a liberal dogma: 'Economic policy should be flexible. I don't see any future in our current taxation and credit policy. It kills enterprise which means less money goes to the Exchequer.' He agrees that the strong emphasis on anti-inflationary measures which underpined Deputy Prime Minister and Finance Minister Leszek Balcerowicz's first post-communist economic programme were vital for the first period of the transformation. However, Lis feels the measures should have been limited to about six months: 'Now I think we should fight the recession by decreasing taxation, even at the cost of reducing revenue. It might even be necessary to print more money; otherwise the economy will be killed. It needs a kick start which will boost the development of enterprises. That in turn will mean more money, more employment. That way, there will be more money for the budget.'

Given the scale of the recession Poland faced between the middle of 1990 and the middle of 1992 when the economic indicators picked up, it is not surprising that many politicians suggested quick-fix methods of making money flow once more. But one senses a certain lack of reality when it comes to what is expected from the West. 'The European Community should support a protectionist policy in Poland. We need tough customs control of imports. We need to protect our own markets. For instance, there should be heavy duties imposed on imports of drugs. We have our own drugs industry. But there shouldn't be duty on the component parts we need for the manufacturing side of the drugs industry.' Listening to Bogdan Lis it is hard to differentiate what he is saying from the economic policies espoused by the Democratic Left Alliance (post-communist grouping made up of former Party members) during the September '93 election campaign.

At the beginning of this chapter I mentioned the discomfort experienced by both Left and Right-wing politicians and groups all over the world who found themselves supporting a movement which crossed over almost all the normal political barriers. Quite simply that was because as a mass movement of opposition to totalitarianism Solidarity was literally all things to all men (and women). On one level there are, for instance, huge differences between the way Alina Pienkowska and Bogdan Lis think about the political scene in Poland today. In a country where Left and Right is now upside down, she would be regarded as a conservative because of her views on social policy, while Bogdan would probably be seen as more progressive; that is, if one leaves aside his populist approach to generating the money flow. Whatever their differences, Alina and Bogdan mirror the pragmatic approach which was predominant in Solidarity. In early 1992 they worked together on a joint venture to set up a Polish-British Health Foundation to train doctors for private work in Poland. Lis runs his own importation business now, and when I met him he was anxiously trying to conclude a deal to export Polish kettles to Italy.

3

RELUCTANT HEROISM

JAN AND KRYSTYNA LITYNSKI

K rystyna Litynska is always quick to point out that she was interned for ten weeks after martial law while many of her friends
served much lengthier sentences. But though the duration was shorter
the long-term effects of that two-and-a-half month incarceration have
remained with her to this day. The 13th of December 1981 was bitterly
cold, like any other winter night in Warsaw. It was not a night to
huddle in a freezing cold barracks with no blankets, running water,
light or heating. Unwilling to glorify her experience, Krystyna is almost
matter-of-fact in her description of the tuberculosis she contracted as a
result of her period in Olszynka women's prison. Perhaps one side-
effect of the mass communication of the horrors of war and torture is
to lessen the impact of the withdrawal of basic human rights, wrongful
imprisonment and non-violent inhuman treatment. It appears to make
even the victims unwilling to complain lest it appear that they seek to
compare their treatment with that meted out by more gruesome or
brutal regimes.

The night of 13 December is in the same category as the day of the
assassination of President John F. Kennedy for most Poles. Everyone
remembers where they were and what they were doing. Rumours of a
possible Soviet intervention or military clamp-down had been circulating on and off since the strikes began in July and August 1980.
Tensions rose and eased, hopes ran high, and then low. But in a
country where people had grown used to living on a knife edge and
where people had begun to regard Solidarity's power as real rather than
symbolic the coup d'etat in the end came as a surprise.

By the autumn of 1981 Krystyna and Jan had moved from his
mother's apartment into a rented flat in a housing scheme, built for
army and police families, on the outskirts of Warsaw. Given their
political activity, the occupation of most of their neighbours was a
bit unfortunate. The couple's relations with the secret policeman who
lived opposite were not good. They had deteriorated rapidly after he

stuffed their keyhole with a sealing agent in protest at the cater-
wauling of their dog, Pilsudski (named after Marshall Josef Pilsudski,
because of the dog's likeness to the controversial dictator).

In recalling the events of 13 December, Krystyna remembers hurling
abuse at the secret policeman as she was led past him on her way to
the police car. In retrospect she felt she had been unfair because he had
had the courage to confront the arresting officers. Neighbours told her
that he had called after them: 'So now you're taking women.' Later,
she found out that his son-in-law, like many other sons and daughters,
was active in Solidarity.

The first inkling Krystyna and Jan had that something was wrong
was when they tried to telephone a cab for a friend who was about to
leave their flat. It is not unusual, even today, to have difficulty phoning
from one side of Warsaw to another. So, when neither his own nor a
neighbour's phone upstairs worked, Jan left the building and went to
another block in the hope that he could make the connection through a
different exchange network. By the time it dawned on him that the
phones were not working anywhere, the police were already knocking
on their door. When Krystyna opened it, she was grabbed by the
throat and pushed inside. In the struggle that ensued, she asked for a
search warrant. 'This time,' the secret policeman told her politely, 'we
will not be searching your flat. Pack your bags, Pani Krystyna and wear
something warm. It is very cold out tonight.' It was only when he
entered the hallway of his own apartment block that Jan saw what was
happening. He ran upstairs to a third-floor flat where some friends
lived, but before he was able to jump out of the window the door was
bashed in by a crowbar and he was nabbed before he could escape.
Hearing the shouting upstairs, Krystyna ran up to find Jan being
pulled downstairs by the police, who were so angry about their near
miss that they were going to take him away wearing only his shirt and
slippers. In the mêlée that followed Krystyna remembers being pulled
off Jan by a 'huge Ubek [policeman] with flat eyes'. It was then that
she broke her golden rule of not reacting or showing emotion in the
presence of 'them'. So, as she shouted to all around her that they were
'sons of bitches', she was nearly strangled by the furious Ubek with the
funny eyes.

Eventually they packed their bags in peace. The police tried to
remain polite and kept a decent distance while the neighbours hung
around the landings so as to get a good view of the goings on. Both

remember being more worried about what would happen to their dog than about what the night held in store for them. In a country where queueing for food was the most important daily chore, Jan remembers how awful it was to have to leave behind them a five-pound tin of ham which he had been given as a present. There was no bread in the house so they couldn't even make sandwiches.

Krystyna remembers how strange the atmosphere was when they arrived at Wilcza Street police station. The place was packed with all their friends who were greeting each other. 'The whole thing was very dramatic but in a serious way.' The first group she saw included a famous theatre director who was handcuffed to his son. At about five in the morning the first transport of women left the station en route to the women's prison. Looking out of the window of the police van, Krystyna saw a huge phalanx of ZOMO (riot police) guarding Solidarity headquarters in the centre of Warsaw. It is an image that is indelibly printed on her memory. Later, as the van moved towards the outskirts of the city, she watched as column after column of tanks slowly lumbered snake-like towards Warsaw, intent on strangling Solidarity's newly won freedom.

When her group reached the prison, it was obvious that the women guards did not know how to act towards the rather cosmopolitan and unusual batch of newly arrived prisoners. For a start they seemed unsure about how they should address them. 'Pani' is a term of politeness not normally afforded the criminal community in Poland, so the guards avoided direct references altogether at first. The scene degenerated into complete farce when it was realized that one of Poland's most famous stage and film actresses, Halina Mikolajska, was about to be incarcerated in a barracks with no heat, window panes, water, blankets or light. As the revered actress was being led down to her new accommodation, an enthralled warder urged her to mind the icy steps as well as enthusiastically telling Ms Mikolajska how delighted she was to meet her and how much she admired her work. In fact the actress was made of stern stuff. Since she had first became involved in KOR in 1977, she had grown used to being the victim of the secret police's dirty tricks department. She often found the keyholes in her apartment blocked with glue or her car sprayed with noxious chemicals. And of course she had suffered the hardest cut of all; she had on occasion been banned from working. Krystyna remembers her with great affection as a 'real', as opposed to a political, Catholic. She was a believer in the fullest sense.

Olszynka prison had until the previous March been used as a barracks. Since then it had been left vacant and ready but without running water, heating or light. When the women arrived, there was dust and dirt everywhere. There were seven bunk beds in their room. There was no blankets despite the freezing weather, so on that first night the women huddled under filthy mattresses to try and keep warm. It took three days for the prison authorities to organize a water supply. While Krystyna and her thirteen companions waited for the authorities to get organized, they gathered snow to flush the toilet which was behind a screen in the corner of the room. Slowly over the following days, lights and blankets began to appear.

As they tried to pass the early hours of 14 December, Krystyna remembers one woman in particular. She was divorced but because of the housing problem in Poland she was still living with her husband who had been diagnosed as clinically mad. When she was taken by the police she had been forced to leave her two children with her lunatic husband who, she said, regularly chased people with knives and pokers. She did not cry or become hysterical. She just lay down on her bunk staring rigidly at the ceiling. It was at least two weeks, as Krystyna remembers, before the woman's mother managed to get a message to her saying the children were safe and well.

Krystyna refers to Olszynka prison as the 'health farm.' When she was released, having been diagnosed as suffering from tuberculosis, she weighed forty-five kilos. 'There was no temptation to eat. Breakfast and supper were the same, with bread, margarine and fifth grade jam which came off a block. Dinner or lunch was either pea, cabbage or Scotch broth. Sometimes the barley stew had fragments of bacon in it with tufts of hair stuck to it. You can imagine the effect on our stomachs.'

Given the nature of the women involved it is not surprising that many ex-internees shrug off the experience. Krystyna's cell adopted a non-conformist approach to dealing with the prison authorities. 'If you rebel, you automatically acknowledge their power and authority. If you ignore them you win.' So, roll-call, where the warders tried to impose some sort of military regime, became hysterical, with women shouting out that nobody had escaped that night. Like Alina Pienkowska and many other women who were interned or jailed, Krystyna's memories are of the camaraderie and spirit that developed between the women. Perhaps it was fortuitous that Christmas followed less than two weeks after the mass arrests.

The Christmas holiday is celebrated with particular emphasis on tradition in Poland. After the fast on Christmas Eve, families start their festivities when the first star appears in the sky with a meal that has come from the sea, the woods, the mountains and the fields. Presents are then exchanged after midnight Mass. But on Christmas Eve 1981, Krystyna and her cell mates had what she describes as 'a very elegant supper' of boiled eggs. Because it is regarded as a potential narcotic, prisoners are not normally allowed tea, but Regina Litynska, Krystyna's mother in-law, had sent in a parcel with tea, sardines and a jumper. So, that night, the women celebrated by drinking, what the authorities judged to be a terribly dangerous brew.

Behaving and acting normally was the essence of the KOR philosophy of opposition. Celebrating Christmas as best they could, was much more than an attempt to keep their spirits high: the women were defying, by ignoring it, the attempt to crush their spirit of opposition. They even managed to adorn their quarters with a symbolic Christmas tree. On one of the daily walks around the quadrangle one of the women found a spiky twig which she brought back with her. And with great ingenuity they used the cotton wool from some Red Cross sanitary towels and some silver paper from their cigarette allowance to decorate their little bare twig. Then by 'recycling' the packaging and the tinsel paper from their 'Cosmos' cigarettes, Krystyna's adept colleagues made themselves a set of playing cards using the rocket on the back as the standard image and drawing the faces of the cards on the front: 'We drew our King to look like Jaruzelski. I remember that we played a lot of Patience.'

On New Year's Eve, they were allowed a great privilege. The lights, which normally went out at nine o'clock were left on until ten. Krystyna remembers it as being a funny night: 'We had three liqueur chocolates between seven of us. The next day was my birthday. I actually got presents. A Solidarity badge and ring were smuggled into the prison. I was delighted.'

Coming out of jail or any confinement can be a frightening experience. It was doubly so in Krystyna's case. Her husband was still interned as were many of her friends. She knew she was blacklisted and would be unable to get a job. She was not even sure where she could stay: 'Inside the rules were clear cut. Outside there was a world without a future for me.' Because she was ill, the authorities decided not to

transfer Krystyna to Rakowiecka Street prison. So without prior warning she found herself, along with two other women, free to leave.
Both her companions were seriously ill. One had cancer, while the
other had a heart condition and couldn't walk. And so a woman who
was less than seven stone and running a high temperature with suspected tuberculosis had to try and get them all home at a time of the
day when just about everyone seemed to be out or at work. In the
end she managed to contact Jan Litynski's first wife. She came to the
rescue in a taxi: 'I always remember that she came with chocolate. We
were in an awful state. The lady with the heart problem was really bad.
She needed to get to Lodz and with petrol rationed, and no money,
we didn't know how she would get there. First we went to my
mother in-law's, but she was not in. I was really upset, so we went
to another friend's house. Luckily they were in. After they welcomed us and we all kissed I just went into the bathroom and was
violently sick.'

For at least a year after her release, Krystyna had a large shadow on
her lung and was registering a high temperature every day. She was
receiving treatment for tuberculosis but nothing improved her condition. When after three months in Warsaw's respiratory hospital the
doctors decided to operate for suspected cancer, Krystyna thought
better of it and signed herself out. She is convinced that she took the
right decision.

Krystyna Litynska is an able and talented psychologist. Now that
Poland is free, she is much sought after and was at one point running
two separate psychiatric facilities. But from the time of her association
with Jan in 1975, she was blacklisted and found it very difficult to get
work officially after the middle of 1976. Following her release in March
1982 it took her over a year to find what she calls a 'real' job.

While she was imprisoned Krystyna received just two letters from
Jan. One had been brought to her by a priest, while his mother
brought another during a visit. Like so many other men grabbed in
the Warsaw region that apocryphal night Jan was taken to Bialolenka
internment camp just outside Warsaw. It was there that Krystyna
headed as soon as she was able after her own release. 'It was a Garden
of Eden,' Jan recalls, by comparison with the conditions he experienced later in Warsaw's main prison on Rakowiecka Street. There
is almost a nostalgia in his tone when he describes life at Bialolenka.
Because it was an internment camp the Bialolenka regime was less

harsh and provided reasonable library facilities for the inmates. Jan also remembers that the company was good. After all he was among friends. However, once he was served with a warrant charging him with treason in September 1982, Jan was moved to Rakowiecka Street, where life became much tougher on every level: 'It was far worse to be taken from Bialolenka to Rakowiecka than to be taken there from freedom.' For the first three months he was allowed no visits at all and received post only after seven weeks. Krystyna describes that period as 'very nasty: the minimum sentence he faced was five years and because he was charged with treason, the possibility of a death sentence was on our minds all of the time.'

For Krystyna, this period was one of constant organizing: 'It takes so much time when a person is in jail. First, letters have to be written to arrange visits and parcels. In the political cases the letters have to go to the censor so that takes even more time. Then, because he was trying to study, I had to ask the prosecutor for permission to get certain books in for him. The men were allowed a three-kilo parcel per month, so I had to try and get the best, the most nutritious food, into the parcels. That was not easy with all the shortages at the time. He was having a lot of problems with his teeth so I wanted to get him vitamins.'

With so many people interned or imprisoned, lots of families found themselves involved in organizing visits, petitions and food parcels. In fact it had the opposite effect to the one desired by the government. People who were not overtly political became part of a network of support activity which by its very nature had political overtones. So, while a clandestine underground was slowly establishing itself furtively, on the surface of Polish society, old ladies, brothers and sisters, fathers and mothers crossed backwards and forwards over cities and countryside carrying food parcels for the 'boys' (and girls). In their attempt to destroy Solidarity, the government gave the union what it needed to become invincible. It gave Solidarity a common mythology.

But, of course, while history tends to look at the political dimension of important events, for those involved there is also the very human reality of their experience. 'Jail cemented our relationship. It was Janek's fourth time inside. I felt he really needed me. I felt very responsible. When you're on the outside, you feel obliged to carry on, no matter what's going on inside oneself. You've got to provide comfort. Letters become very important for both people. I wrote a sort of diary for Janek. Love returns when people are in jail. During the Solidarity period [before martial law] we were ships in the night. Then there was a terrible longing.'

In June 1983, Jan's mother Regina went to see the Interior Minister, General Czeslaw Kiszczak, and asked him to allow her son to attend the First Holy Communion of his daughter, Basha: 'Basically the cops just arrived at the door and there was Janek. There were guests everywhere. All those people, it was quite frightening for someone who had been locked up for so long in a tiny cell. I hardly got a chance to talk to him.' Krystyna remembers that many of their friends were saying they would try and get him taken into hospital so that he would not have to go back to Rakowiecka. 'But in the end Janek said that it was up to me to decide whether he should go underground or not.'

When Jan disappeared there was a national alert and because his photograph was posted everywhere he had to change his appearance rapidly. That was actually quite difficult in his case. Jan Litynski is a slight man with very distinct mannerisms. In both his intensity and stature he is almost a male version of Edith Piaf. When he speaks, the thoughts and words shoot like bullets from a rapid fire machine gun. He never sits still. And in those rare moments when he does he is either chain smoking or repeatedly wrapping a lock of hair around his finger. He is just like a sprint athlete straining on the blocks in the excruciating moment before the starter pistol relieves the tension.

But with the aid of a beard, new glasses and a suit, something he was not used to, Jan took on a new persona. He was one of the most successful members of Solidarity's underground. He was never re-arrested and remained in hiding until September 1986, when after a general amnesty for political prisoners, he came out, along with the other last remaining underground activist, to a joint press conference of both groups. Nearly five years of his life had passed by since martial law.

The underground period has had important political ramifications. By its very existence it maintained a beacon of hope but, more importantly, its existence eventually forced the one-party state into a position where it tacitly accepted the reality of an opposition.'

For Krystyna Litynska it was not a very happy time: 'I very rarely met Janek. It was too dangerous. I was watched all of the time. The arrangements to go and see him were incredible. I only saw him once or twice every three months or so. Before he came out I hadn't seen him for six months—that was from March to September. That was too long. Jail is much better for a relationship than being underground.

When one's husband is in jail, you still get to see him, even if it is through a glass window. But then you feel useful. You're participating and involved. The underground had a bad effect on marriages. One learns to live independently. One develops one's own life, has one's own responsibilities. If a person didn't detach a little they'd become psychologically unwell.'

Though Jan Litynski was a leader among activists, his road to internment and arrest after martial law mirrored that of many others of his generation. After he went to Warsaw University in 1963 to study mathematics he became involved in the numerous political discussion clubs that were springing up all over the place in those years. One of the most famous groups was organized by Adam Michnik (later an MP and editor of *Gazeta Wyborcza*). Its title translates into 'the club of the searchers for diversity'. Like Litynski, Michnik came from both a communist and Jewish background and was later to become one of the most important interpreters of modern Polish history. Ludka Wujec, now a prominent member of the Democratic Union, has known Jan since he was five: 'I suppose up to about 1968, perhaps it was earlier, Janek wanted to fix socialism. The word "reformer" is a difficult one here, but basically most of the people involved in those discussion groups were moving in the direction of rejecting the system. But at the time they perceived themselves as operating from within it.' The authorities dubbed them the 'March Commandos' and the name stuck.

Essentially the groups were made up in the main of young Marxist intellectuals who were struggling to find socialism in the so called socialist state in which they lived. Jan says that he was influenced by the thinking of October '56 when for a brief period it looked as if a brand of liberal communism was about to sweep through Poland. That short flirtation with worker's councils and talk of liberal economics ended with the rehabilitation of Gomulka, though it took a little while for Poles to realize that Wladyslaw Gomulka was not some great reforming knight in shining armour: 'I felt that there had never been real socialism in Poland because socialism was based on a combination of workers ruling and democracy. During 1964 and 1965 both Jacek Kuron and Karol Modzelewski had been jailed for their writing. We were studying their texts and believed in a society based on a series of links between between worker self-governing enterprises and democracy. The problem was that we had no contact with the workers, but we certainly had a lot of contact with the lack of democracy. It was a long process, but the more we read and the more we analyzed Marxism, the more we questioned why democracy had to be limited to the proletariat. When you're young and you've read right through Marxist literature and you've worked out that it doesn't hold water, you try and work out where the mistake happened. Then eventually you realize that the big mistake was at the beginning.'

Jan was twenty-two when he was arrested following the student protests after the closure of the play *Forefather's Eve*. Sentenced to two and a half years for supposedly setting up an illegal organization, Jan ended up serving a year and a half in Rakowiecka Street prison. The jailings and persecution of both the Jews and the intelligentsia in 1968 galvanized a whole network of people, including lecturers and students, into an opposition stance. It also provided those who were jailed with credibility in the eyes of people who might otherwise have been dismissive of the activities of young hothead students. It would, however, be difficult to be dismissive of one-, two- and three-year jail sentences.

Jan is quite philosophical about his experience of imprisonment: 'It either breaks you and your character is gone for the rest of your life or else you stick it out. I had known that I had taken a certain course in life. I knew what the risks were. I thought I was doing what was right and just. If your attitude is that going to jail is the end of your life, that you are losing today, tomorrow and the future, then you'll break down.' Jan quotes the robust and colourful Jacek Kuron, who was no stranger to Polish jails: 'When you get involved you have to measure your arse up to the accused's bench. If you think it fits, continue.'

From that point on, there was no doubt that Jan Litynski's posterior measured up. 'It is important to understand that what the government engaged in during 1968 was one of the nastiest campaigns against the Jews and against the intelligentsia in the history of Poland.' As someone who was a member of both groups, Jan was now clearly identified as being opposed to 'them'. Because he had been kicked out of the university in March, Jan had been unable to sit the exams in June. When he was released in 1969 he found work as a barman and as a metal grinder as well as working at a shoe factory. Eventually he was able to get a job more commensurate with his skills at a computer centre where he worked as a programmer.

Jan never thought of leaving Poland, but many others did. Those who stayed found that the base of opposition within which they operated was broadening. From the outside it looked as if two extremes had joined forces. In reality as long as there was just one foe there was little to separate the aims of the Catholic intellectuals who began to cooperate with the Marxist and former Marxist dissidents whose characters had been moulded by the '68 experience. It would, however, be the late seventies before this new rainbow coalition of thinkers was able to put its theories of worker support and stimulation into practice. In the meantime the martyred workers in Gdansk, bloodied but victorious after their opposition to the Christmas 1970 food price increases, were creating their own mythology of heroic resistance. And though the intellectuals played no role in Gdansk, it was, combined with the events of '68, the end for many of any residual belief that the system was reformable.

Looking back at the sequence of events one could be forgiven for thinking that the Party almost connived in the making of the opposition. In its proposed changes to the Constitution in 1975, the Party attempted to have its leading role and the special relationship with the Soviet Union formally enshrined. The move resulted in a series of protests against the changes. And, as Ludka Wujec points out, 'it had the effect of integrating a whole group of people. Up to then the various discussion clubs at the universities had been simply examining and studying the past. As a result of the proposals protests were organized and petitions were being signed. A wide group of people were making contact.' And so when, in June 1976, Edward Gierek decided that the Polish economy could not sustain the food price-freeze any longer, the workers once again resisted. This time however they did not have to fight alone.

Krystyna remembers the night the massive food hikes were announced very clearly: 'It was 24 June. Jan and I were on our way to the Presidential Ball. It was a great tradition that Jan Josef Lipski held a huge name-day party (Poles celebrate their name day as much as their birthday). It was hot and Midsummer's Eve and the city streets were deserted. Jan is a popular name so many people were having parties. The windows were open, so we could hear all the radios. The prime minister was making a speech announcing the huge increases. It was very dramatic, because they'd been frozen for so long. There had been gossip, but it was a shock. The next day the protests began at the Ursus factory. A big crowd marched off to the nearby railway lines and dug up the sleepers. It stopped the Paris–Moscow express. A wave of strikes followed. At Radom workers set fire to the local party head-quarters. After that it spread all over the country. The government reacted with incredible brutality. There were murders and terrible beatings. Workers were literally terrified. Many were made run through a "path of good health". That was two lines of truncheon-wielding cops. In Radom it was particularly bad. There was incredible terror there. People were being thrown out of their jobs under "paragraph 52" which allowed the authorities to sack a worker who was absent without leave.' What would later be known as an intervention com-mittee then became active on an *ad hoc* basis. In the beginning its activities were unstructured: 'It was all very spontaneous. It was an effort to help those who'd been imprisoned. Their families were nor-mally very afraid and didn't know what to do. Often they were even afraid to come forward when help was offered. Basically we started going to the places where there'd been trouble, to places where people had been sacked or beaten up and we tried to help. Janek went to Radom very early on. He gathered information about what was going on and tried to help get people out of jail. Then after there was a series of suspicious deaths at militia stations, he began writing articles based on the information he had gathered.' Ludka Wujec was with a group of intellectuals who attended the trials of those charged with offences after Ursus: 'When we saw how helpless the families were, how frightened they were, we just spontaneously approached them and raised money, there and then in the corridor at the court. There were no leaders at Ursus. These people had been picked out of the crowd for punish-ment. They were entitled to a state appointed defence lawyer, but we got our own lawyers to help on a voluntary basis. It was the beginning of an organized network of help. We learned a lot from the workers we met. We heard a lot about arrests, sackings and all kinds of illegal procedures.'

Very shortly after the protests Jan, along with several other activists, began publishing an information bulletin detailing what was happening, where, and to whom. That 'Information Bulletin' was probably the first of the literally hundreds of dirty grey sheets that would play a vital role in counteracting the government's disinformation activities. That the pen is mightier than the sword is a truism, but if it had ever required verification the period following Radom and Ursus which culminated in Solidarity's victory in August 1980 would surely be proof enough.

As the contacts were made and the truth was outed it became clear that spontaneous help was not enough. It needed an umbrella under which to operate. And so, in September, a diverse group of intellectuals got together calling themselves, at first the Workers' Defence Committee (later, the Social Self-Defence Committee). Well known and respected economists, writers, lecturers, former communists and former pre-war socialists headed the list of KOR's members in the hope that they would afford protection to the less well known activists who were working at the grassroots level to help the workers. However, it would soon become clear that no amount of moral authority would keep Adam Michnik, Jacek Kuron, Jan Litynski or indeed many other young KOR activists out of jail.

Krystyna remembers 1977 as a tragic year but Jan points out that it was also the year of KOR's first success: 'First of all Janek was sacked from his job at the computer centre in February. So from then on, I was trying to earn a living for both of us. It was not easy because I was blacklisted as well. On 12 March my mother died. On 14 May a student activist, Stanislaw Pyjas, was killed in a militia station in Cracow. They said he fell down the stairs, but they killed him. Then on the 19th, Janek was arrested. I think about fourteen other KOR members were arrested at the same time. From then on the searches at the flat were regular. They (the secret police) would often follow me. They'd walk just a couple of metres behind me.' But as Jan emphasizes, the year was not all bleak. On 22 July, Independence Day, the government announced an amnesty and thus avoided the embarrassment of a series of trials of martyrs.

Within a month of his release Jan was busy establishing *Robotnik* which as we have seen in an earlier chapter, played a key role in fostering self-organization among workers. Over the next few years he travelled all over Poland gathering information, giving information and forging contacts between the intellectuals and the rank-and-file factory workers. He was particularly involved in the mining towns of Silesia and was later to be one of Walbrzych's first freely elected members of parliament.

Meeting Jan and Krystyna Litynski was a milestone in my life. The meeting made me do what young people often don't have time to do. It made me stop and think. I had arrived at Warsaw's somewhat undistinguished airport on an afternoon in late July 1980. In my notebook I had what turned out to be a fairly comprehensive list of KOR's most famous members. That, as I remember, was about the height of my organization. Having got through the agony and fear of being identified as a journalist travelling on a visitor's visa, I was delighted at having crossed the first hurdle. Being a bit of a prude I was somewhat put out when I was informed at the student hostel where I was to stay that because they were full I would have to share the room with three men. There were not even curtains between the beds. In my confused expectations of the trip I had anticipated all sorts of cloak and dagger scenarios straight out of Freddie Forsyth. But none of his anti-heroes had to undress underneath a blanket. Having mumbled my goodbyes to my new Swedish room-mates I set off to find the great and famous Jacek Kuron. Needless to say KOR's ebullient guru was not at home. In his place I found an intense young German who announced himself to be in the middle of a major thesis on Polish dissidence. This young man, sensing that I was in a bit of a muddle, suggested that I go over and see Jan Litynski. More importantly, he added that I should meet his wife Krystyna, who spoke English.

Krystyna Litynska had the most open and warm smile I had ever seen. She was small, slight, red-haired and very feminine. Despite her youthful and sometimes vulnerable appearance she also radiated an enormous strength and motherliness. She made those around her feel safe. In my stupidity, she was, of course, a million miles away from what I imagined a 'dissident' would be like. That first evening, I sat on the bed-cum-settee in the corner of the sitting room on Wyzwolenia Street, sipping lemon tea and explaining who I was, and why I had come. Amid the constant interruption of the telephone and door bell I listened as Krystyna told me about the series of strikes which were breaking out all over Poland. As the hours passed I listened as she both received and passed on information about strikes, plans and meetings. By the time Jan returned to the flat, she had already promised me that I could travel with him wherever he went. What is more, she would not hear of me staying at the hostel. The offer of a corner on her floor was more wonderful than the promise of a four-poster bed. I was bowled over by their kindness. Over the next couple of weeks I travelled with Janek to the mining towns of Silesia for meetings with workers who were trying to set up alternative trade union structures, and to places like Cracow for secret meetings between intellectual activists and workers from the Nowa Huta steel works which is nearby. In Warsaw I was secretly introduced to worker leader Zbigniew Bujak in a safe flat. He was constantly on the move that July and August as the arrest and harassment of activists increased and the tension heightened. On and off over the period I became conscious of the presence of shadows when I moved around with Jan. In the days immediately before and of course after the Gdansk strike the secret police presence became frightening. For the Litynskis, it was part of their normal life experience. I am not ashamed to say that I was terrified.

I will never forget one day in particular. I was back in Warsaw having left Gdansk some days after the strikes had begun. As I left the flat with Jan to go and meet Jacek Kuron, four security police got out of the unmarked car which had been parked just outside the apartment. As we walked off in the direction of the church on the corner they began following us at just a pace away's distance. I remember thinking that they looked as if they had been hand-picked for parts as heavies in some Hollywood B movie. They were short, squat, ugly men with bulldog faces. Jan remarked quietly that this was not the normal type of tailing. It was very menacing. He told me that we were going to split up as he was afraid that if he was arrested that I would be nabbed too. I knew that I had already broken enough rules to justify incarceration, given that I had been constantly associating with 'undesirables', and had been operating as a journalist on a visitor's visa. He wanted to leave me in a public place where the police would find it difficult to harass me. So we headed for the Hotel Europejski, which was home to many of the more senior Eastern European correspondents. As I crossed the threshold, the secret policemen quickened their pace. I literally bolted up the grand staircase and rushed past the rotund lady whose job it was to watch the comings and goings of the foreign journalists. Breathless and with minimal introduction I ran into the arms of the correspondents from *The Times*, *Observer* and *Washington Post*. I remember trying to act casual lest I emphasise (not that it was not obvious) my rookie status. Everyone agreed that I should contact the British embassy. So having slipped out of the side entrance of the Europejski I went to the Hotel Bristol across the road to meet a Finnish journalist I'd arranged to see. I hoped that by remaining in the company of foreigners I would make it difficult for them to arrest me. The Finn, seeing that I was anxious, decided to have a look out of the bedroom window to assess the situation. He too became uneasy when he saw the arrival of two marked militia vans. I did not feel much better when I remembered that Jan had said that arrests were normally carried out by uniformed officers in marked vans or cars. It seemed like a good time to make contact with her Her Majesty's representatives in Poland. I can't think of a polite way to describe the conversation with the gentleman from the British embassy. Suffice it to say that he did not regard it as part of his duties to look after the interests of an Irish journalist who was breaking the terms of her visa.

So, realizing that I had better avoid at all costs getting picked up, I made a dash for Wyzwolenia Street, clutching on to my properly accredited Finnish colleague. By the time I got back to the flat, Krystyna, realizing the danger signals, had arranged for me to leave Warsaw for a few days in the company of a seasoned Dutch radio journalist. Dick Verkaijk was an East European specialist and had been with the first batch of American forces that liberated Auschwitz.

Within hours of our leaving Warsaw, Jan was arrested and held under the usual forty-eight hours terms. This time, however, he was repeatedly rearrested when the forty-eight hours was up and was only released as part of the conditions of the Gdansk strike settlement. Looking back I imagine that Jan and Krystyna's quick thinking had probably saved the unhappy soul at the British embassy a lot of work on behalf of his Irish neighbours.

Driving out of Warsaw on the road to Cracow, in the back of Dick's station-wagon, I felt ashamed of myself as I abandoned my two friends who had shown so much concern for my safety. Unlike me, I thought, they would never be able to escape.

What impressed me about Jan and Krystyna was the knowledge that they had never thought of leaving Poland. In a Western country this couple would have had a secure income and a good lifestyle. In Poland they lived with Jan's mother in a cramped flat. Though enormously talented they had difficulty getting suitable work because of their politics. When Krystyna did get a job, it was at a clinic two hours away from her home. And after all of that travelling she had to queue for basic food stuffs like countless other Polish women. Both were regularly harassed and intimidated. Their home was repeatedly searched. Jan, was, by then, very familiar with conditions in Polish jails. But never once had I heard them proffer information about their personal troubles and hardships. They certainly never moaned. Talking to them I realized that they were firmly focused on their political goals. Years later, when I talked to them about martial law, about jail and about the underground years, their attitude was still the same. Incredibly they simply weren't bitter.

Jan's attitude to 'them' (the Party) has more than likely kept him sane through many difficult experiences: 'I don't feel any bitterness. Why should I? All my life I've been a vulture on them. As a totality I can't tolerate them but I've rarely had a personal feeling of hate to any individual.' Jan explains that there was not any big decision to become political: 'Being a dissident is about the choice of a certain style of life. It does require courage but that was not a problem for me.'

Krystyna was twenty-five when she met Janek in 1974: 'I was bookish, but not sheltered. My family was too big and too poor for any of us to be sheltered. My sisters, my brothers, we saw how hard our parents worked. They fought hard for our existence. I met Janek at an important time in my life when I was deciding what I should do with myself. I was working out what I wanted from life. He stepped out of a different world. All his friends had been together since '68. I began to hear about anti-Semitism, about people who were leaving the country or had left. I began to meet people who were names from another world. I began to open my eyes and see and understand things completely differently.'

I remember being struck by how difficult it was to categorize Jan and Krystyna's politics. And, as I've mentioned earlier, that was a problem the whole world faced when Solidarity failed to fit into a neatly defined pigeonhole. In *The Captive Mind*, Czeslaw Milosz highlights the unreality of many western Marxists who refused, even at the height of Stalinism, to acknowledge that in practice the Marxist model was not working out in Eastern Europe. Jan and Krystyna were well used to meeting ardent young communists from the United States, Germany or Britain who had to perform mental cart-wheels in order to retain their belief following a visit to Poland.

Unlike many people in the west who took a political stand on places like Poland, Cambodia or Angola, politics was not an abstract, idealistic or doctrinaire thing for them. They were living the reality of Utopian socialism but were far too intelligent to think that its political opposite alone was the cure for Poland's ills. In a sense then it was impossible to politically define Jan and Krystyna and many people like them, because politics, as defined in terms of right and left did not come into the frame in pre-1989 Poland. For Krystyna, like Janek, the dissident road is a question of choice: 'If you looked at Radom, at Ursus and at what happened to people there. If you looked at their suffering and at how people lived, if you come from a poor family yourself and know how difficult life can be, and then if you look at "them", at the secret police and think of the obscenities they whisper in your ear, you have to turn. It is not a political thing, it is basically about human sensitivity. Things are either right or wrong. It starts as a moral thing but then one's actions become political. You've no choice.'

By 1978, Krystyna was well and truly aware of the consequences of her choice. She remembers that in one week their flat was searched twice: 'There was one day—a very important day for me. In many ways it was a milestone. The police arrived at about five-thirty or six in the morning. I was on the afternoon shift at the clinic which was outside of Warsaw. The job was very important to me, I really wanted to get there. Normally the men who searched were very polite. There were four or five of them this time. They searched our tiny flat for hours. I had just had a tooth removed and I was still bleeding. The police were drunk and unpleasant. I was nervous and upset. The older man, the one in charge of the search agreed in the end, to let me go to work. So he drove me to where I got the works' bus and waited until I'd got on. It is very hard to explain how I felt. Nobody would have understood my feelings. What could I have said had I not been able to get to work. With the secret police shadowing me, I felt as if I was in a ghetto. I was alone. It was so different after the strikes, after Solidarity and martial law. In 1982 people would have understood if I'd explained what had happened. But in 1978, if I'd said anything, people would have been too frightened to help me.'

While it might have been the Pope who began the breakdown of the sense of individual isolation in Polish society, and though it was Solidarnosc that gave birth to the individual's sense of power within a mass movement, it was 'they', the Party, with the introduction of martial law, who generalized the dissident experience. It was not a simple case of creating martyrs and heroes. Solidarity at its height had ten million members. That was nearly a third of the total population. By resorting to martial law in order to deal with a situation it felt it could no longer control, the Party declared war on a huge section of Polish society. In doing so it turned dissidence into a mass movement. Jan Litynski sees 13 December as 'a farce. Everything had been said and done, everything had changed and they were return- ing to their old ways.' And what for? Over the next five years the Polish economy continued to deteriorate while the Party exercised power for power's sake. Eventually with the threat of economic collapse looming, the Party chose to recognize the existence of an opposition, by offering to share responsibility if not power. Jaruzelski's *coup d'état* was eventually brought down by the sterility of the power it sought to maintain.

In 'the new reality', as Krystyna likes to call post-communist Poland, she has been busy working both in the field of psychiatric care as well as working for various academic institutions. Jan is an MP and chaired the important Parliamentary Commission on Social Policy until the return of the post-communist coalition government in September 1993. Both are acutely aware of the range of complex problems Poland now faces: 'In socialist countries in the past, there was secret police and harassment but there was also a funny sense of safety. Big Daddy was always there to look after you. With no official unemployment, people were always sure of being paid. Now everyone has to be his own Big Daddy. Today the enemy is gone and people aren't sure who the new enemy is. As a nation we're having to learn how to deal with different political views and to learn political language. People are having to learn how to relate to people that they disagree with politically. There are so many new questions and problems. In the past there was just one ideology. One was either for it or against it. Now we're trying to find out what we meant when we said that we wanted a "civil society". What does it mean? It is not just the economy that has to be built. We have to establish new health, education and social security structures. We have to decide what kind of political model we want to operate in Poland. Should we have a strong President? Should parliament play the role it has been playing since the first elections?'

But whatever the problems, Krystyna is sure that she now lives in a real world where people are responsible for themselves: 'Life is much safer in one way, but in another way people here are very afraid of the future. Now everything depends on oneself. For me personally things are better. We have more money. It is good to have a husband who is bringing in a salary. I'm not the only one respon- sible anymore. We have our own flat. It is not big, but we're not living with my mother-in-law. But the best thing of all is the knowledge that I can walk down the street and not be afraid of the secret police. I'm not afraid of searches anymore and of course it is like being in paradise to read a free press.'

In 1991 President Lech Walesa gave a speech to the European Parliament in which he virtually told the West that it had a moral obligation to financially support Poland because it had rid itself of its communist manacles. So what?, was the response from Western business interests who would have preferred to hear what Walesa had to say about the progress the country was making in completing the transformation of the economy. Jan Litynski feels that people find it difficult to move on and respond to the rapidly changing world in which the whole of Eastern Europe finds itself: 'People here saw communism as a sort of cancer. They thought that if you operated and removed it, that afterwards, everything would be okay.' Lech Walesa knows full well that the battle was only beginning when the communists fell, but in continuing the rhetoric, albeit abroad, of looking for adulation and support simply for removing communism, he is copperfastening a false expectation that the changes will be rapid and painless. Another side effect of seeing the future through the eyes of the past is to inhibit political development and growth.

Jan is no longer comfortable being described as a dissident. He wants to leave that old battle behind him and start building 'the new reality'. For him that means many things, including the view that anti-communist witch-hunting is divisive, and a diversion from real political progress. But it is not just the communist past that should be jettisoned according to this view. Jan knows that hankering after Solidarity's halcyon days is perverting the development of parliamentary democracy: 'Of course we all grew out of a movement of protest. But things are more complex now and some of us have moved on.' The split within Solidarity, as we shall see later, was a painful one. Jan now acknowledges that thinking that the union would remain undivided was probably naive. He now thinks that it was also wishful thinking to hope that post-communist political activity would develop through a social movement. He is critical of the role of the various Solidarity offshoots which entered parliament: 'In the past the workers, and, of course, Solidarity, were to the forefront in the call for change. Now they're a very conservative force. They're now the biggest obstacle on the road to change.' At the heart of what Jan is saying is the view that the political game must be played within parliament, that the players must

move in from the streets. 'It is more pleasant to be in a mass movement, to be without responsibility, than to have to deal with reality.
Fighting for power isn't nice but it is real.'

It is somewhat ironic that the political party which is loudest in its
opposition to what it regards as the diversionary rhetoric of decommunization is the one whose most prominent members were almost
martyred by the Party. Jan Litynski belongs to the secular and liberal
end of the Democratic Union. As we'll see later the party was born out
of the grouping which supported Poland's first non-communist premier, Tadeusz Mazowiecki, when he ran against Lech Walesa for the
Presidency. In crude terms, that battle was waged between populist and
sober politics: 'The party was created, it evolved around the defence of
the liberal changes that were introduced by Tadeusz Mazowiecki's first
government. In simple terms we backed Balcerowicz [Leszek Balcerowicz, deputy premier and architect of the first economic reform plan].
The best way to characterize the Democratic Union is to say that it has
a sober way of thinking. We're not populist. We believe in a step by
step evolutionary approach to the economy. We don't believe in short
cuts or miracles. There is no getting away from hardship during the
short term. We believe that the flow of money within the economy has
to be strictly controlled. Otherwise inflation is inevitable. On the other
hand, many of us would be Keynesian if the conditions existed.' In
other words Jan's wing of the party believes in a capitalist market
economy with a 'human face'.

With many of the most famous names from KOR and the Young
Poland Movement now involved in UD, it is largely a party of the
intelligentsia. It is going after the middle class voter, a category that
up until recently did not exist in Poland. The old school of secular
dissidents generally looked West rather than East for inspiration.
Today UD supports membership of the European Community and
shies away from nationalist or xenophobic rhetoric.

I visited Poland during the first, partially free, elections in 1989.
This was how I began one newspaper article: 'There are two gold
leaf invitations pinned to the kitchen door of the Litynski flat on
Filtrowa Street. One invites "Mr Jan Litynski MP and Mrs Litynski"
to meet the American Ambassador, while the other is from the
Indian Embassy. This would not be unusual were it not for the fact
that, as a dissident and founder of Solidarity, Jan Litynski spent the

years between 1981 and 1986 either in jail or in hiding.'² The invitation contrasted starkly with the dark days of martial law when
Krystyna had fashioned a Christmas tree from a fallen twig and the
cotton wool from a sanitary towel. The Litynskis had come in from
the cold.

4

PAPER RESISTANCE

ZBIGNIEW BUJAK AND THE UNDERGROUND

Though I knew that the famous underground leader, Zbigniew Bujak, had placed himself on the margin of Polish political life, I somehow still expected to see a metaphorical guiding star over his political stables. As we climbed the maze of stairs looking for his office on Grojecka Street in March 1992 my interpreter asked the way. 'Are you looking for that guy who was running from the cops for all those years?' was the amused and irreverent response from a passing young man. I was taken aback by the casual dismissal of Bujak's four and a half years as the unofficial leader of Solidarity's underground movement. He had after all been regarded by many as the only significant rival to Walesa for the leadership of the union. Though there was no great depth to the remark itself, it simply reflected how remote the heroic tales of underground resistance were from the reality of life in post-Balcerowicz Poland. It reminded me once again how quirky and complicated people's memories could be. With so many questions left unanswered in Poland's recent history it is almost as if people are embarrassed by the period even though it paved the way for Michnik's 'evolutionary revolution.' And with so many people dissatisfied with the outcome of that revolution it is not surprising that its heroes are not always revered as outsiders might expect them to be. Given the Polish tendency to pour scorn on authority, neither is it surprising that many have already rejected yesterday's heroes as a new 'nomenklatura'.

However, Zbigniew Bujak is unlikely to be attacked by Poland's disillusioned electorate or branded as a member of a new political elite, an elite that, it is alleged, rival the former regime's nepotistic tendencies. This self-educated worker-hero of the underground has not found easy the path from single-minded anti-communist resistance and dissidence to realistic, deal-making politics. In many respects Zbigniew Bujak epitomizes the problem post-communist countries face in building democratic and parliamentary procedures. Often the idealistic people whose roles were pivotal in securing freedom lack

the skills necessary to take part in the building of effective bureau-
cracies. It can be even harder for the former heroes to learn the often
cynical game of politics. The fact that after two and a half years of
democratic politics that the one-time alternative to Walesa was the lone
representative of his Social Democratic Movement in the Sejm said
reams both about the man himself and about the way the political map
was shaping up in Poland.

Zbigniew Bujak was born in November 1954, the youngest of a large
peasant family that farmed at Lopuszno near Kielce. When he was
three the family moved to Ursus near Warsaw, where he later got a job
at the mechanical engineering plant. Then it was famous for its trac-
tors. Later, as we have seen, the town's fame spread because of the
brutality of the suppression of the strikes there in 1976.

One of the first things Zbigniew mentions to journalists is that he
used the first instalment of a scholarship he received in his teens to buy
a three volume history of diplomacy. No doubt the impulse to know
more about the truth of Poland's past was a major factor in the politicization of this industrialized peasant's son. What's also more than
likely is that Jan Bujak's stories of anti-Nazi resistance nurtured a spirit
of opposition in the youngest of his sons and sewed the seeds of a
willingness to resist the status quo. Just twenty-two when the strikes
hit Radom and Ursus in 1976, Zbigniew was appalled by the treatment meted out to the workers: 'It is hard to make decisions and get
involved when one is alone. But the beginning of my political activity
was when I met Zbigniew Janas (now a deputy). We worked in the
same brigade at Ursus. Together we approached our local priest and
asked him for underground literature including *Robotnik*. After that we
got in contact with KOR and met the intellectuals; we started distributing some of the KOR press at Ursus. A lot of people from, or
close, to my family worked at Ursus, so from the beginning, we had
people we could trust in almost every department at the plant.
Originally fifteen people took the independent press from us but after a
while we were distributing between forty and sixty copies. By the spring
of 1980 up to one 180 people were reading *Robotnik*. It is hard to describe now, what we believed in and hoped for then, but we were
convinced that we'd win out in the end. I was very much under the
influence of KOR at that early stage. The clear aim was to do something at Ursus. We were fighting communism but at local level. Our
goal was long-term. When we started reading material by people like

Vaclav Havel we became convinced that we'd succeed but we certainly didn't anticipate how immediate the success would be. Initially we wanted to organize alternative trade union structures at our own company level, but in the spring of 1980 the whole thing started to accelerate. It was then that we started talking to people like Jacek Kuron and Jan Litynski about an all-Poland trade union. After a hunger strike in defence of a worker accused of stealing a printing machine, our contacts with the intellectuals became very close. If you ask me to define myself politically at that time, all I can say is that what dominated was an anti-communist attitude. We were also very critical of how the economy was being run. I can't say that I was not aware of concepts like social democracy, Christian democracy and liberalism, but I didn't even try to get into them or compare them with the Polish experience then.'

I first met Zbigniew Bujak in late July 1980. The meeting was secret and was held as I remember at the flat of mathematician Janusz Onyskiewicz, who would later become known to every Eastern European correspondent as Solidarity's press spokesman. Interestingly the aspect of the meeting that I remember most was his keen interest in hearing about Ireland. Krystyna Litynska told me that I would like Bujak. When I met him I thought straightaway what a great politician he would make. He was handsome, athletic looking and gave the impression of being interested in the opinions of those around him. He was a powerful presence in any room and radiated a rapport with those around him. He had a twinkle in his eyes and was highly amused to learn from me that one could neither buy an unprescribed condom or get a divorce in Ireland in 1980. I remember explaining that the sad plight of Irish women was not the same source of amusement for me as it was for him.

At that first meeting I did not really fully appreciate how important Bujak was to the process of worker politicization being engaged in by the intellectuals associated with KOR and *Robotnik*. But once the August strikes began and the Gdansk settlement was reached, Bujak was to leap to prominence gaining control as chairman of the whole Warsaw region of Solidarity. But it was his unofficial leadership of the underground's Temporary Coordinating Committee that made Bujak a national hero and household name.

Zbigniew Bujak was like many other Solidarity activists annoyed with himself in the first few days and weeks after General Jaruzelski introduced martial law because he thought that he should have anticipated it. He escaped arrest as did his friend, Zbigniew Janas. Both men had gone for a meal after the Solidarity Congress ended on the night of 12 December in Gdansk. They intended getting a train to Warsaw which was due to leave in the early hours of the morning. In the meantime the two men were killing the few spare hours with a couple of brandies. When they eventually headed off to the station they were approached by another delegate who told them that the police had been arriving in force at the hotels used by the thousands of delegates. Realizing that something was wrong, the two made for the hotel where most of their friends were staying. They found it locked and apparently quiet. From behind the hotel's front door a woman told them to get away quickly, warning them that everyone had been arrested and that a clean up operation was underway along the hotel corridors. Bujak and Janas belted down the streets outside and split up both heading for safe houses.

For the next four and a half years Zbigniew Bujak lived underground. He was the symbolic leader of Solidarity's resistance and living proof that Solidarity had survived.

In retrospect the purpose and impact of the underground period is easily recognizable but in those first few months of 1982 it was by no means clear what shape or purpose this new movement was to assume. In the first place those who had escaped were generally laying low and avoiding contact with each other. Secondly, apart from trying to avoid arrest most of the escapees had no clear cut plan of action: 'The introduction of martial law was very important for Solidarity. There was a feeling that maybe Solidarity had lost. That view was shared by some of the activists. There was a strong feeling of defeat right up to 1984. It was up to the activists who hadn't been arrested to decide if Solidarity was to exist at all. It turned out that among the leaders there was no doubt that the movement should survive. There were very different views however as to how it should be organized. The question was what would keep it alive? What should the symbol be? I was convinced that we had to hide, but that we needed a named underground leadership as a symbol of resistance.'

The debate about the shape and purpose of the underground centred on whether it should attempt to set up a centralized alternative state with clear lines of command, whether it should retain its non-violent commitment or whether it should establish a loose structure to help coordinate and encourage peaceful resistance. In the end, despite the fears of many of those who had been caught in the 13 December dragnet, the movement opted for a framework of activity that was very close to KOR's concept of the 'civil society'. No doubt the fact that Bujak had been so heavily influenced at the outset by KOR intellectuals was a factor in his decision to back the decentralized approach of non-violent conspiracy.

'Our main aim as underground leaders', he explained, 'was to delegate people to organize regional structures around the country. I think that the underground press was a major factor in keeping Solidarity alive. Another important group were the resistance units who painted propaganda on walls and passed on information and literature. On another level the secret supporters who kept up a presence at the factories played an important role.' In the background there were memories of wartime resistance and of the conspiracies of the nineteenth century but at the end of the day there was very little direct action a mixum gatherum of intellectuals and activists could take once the possibility of guerrilla or violent action had been dismissed. Neal Ascherson, who covered Poland for the *Observer* newspaper, noted in his book, *The Struggles For Poland*, that the opposition suffered from a clear lack of perspectives: 'Its activists could neither prepare insurrection nor expect foreign liberation. The best they could do was to preserve independent thought and discussion, publish as many facts and figures about the past and the present as they could, and wait patiently for something to change.'[1]

In the meantime Bujak and the rest hoped that by stimulating a wide range of activities that they were helping to prepare people for a time when they would really live in a 'civil society'. People were continuing the process of learning which began after August. They were learning to organize themselves, to print and distribute ideas and to think about what kind of society they wanted to emerge in Poland. At the heart of what happened during the underground years was the emergence of an opposition so broadly based and so peculiarly tolerated by the authorities that in the end its existence was tacitly recognised by the Party. The significance of that development cannot be overstated.

It is not at all a cliché to say that Zbigniew Bujak and all the others including Wiktor Kulerski, Bogdan Borusewicz, Bogdan Lis, Wladyslaw Frasyniuk and later Jan Litynski lived a cloak-and-dagger

existence. Bujak remembers that he 'never stayed longer than one
month, it was often shorter, in one flat. Each underground person was
designated a flat. We never lived in the same place. The flats were
generally near other flats used as meeting places. We never met each
other in the flat where we were living. Normally there were two flats
picked out in a district. One to sleep in and one to meet in.' Three
administrative bureaus ran the underground operation in Warsaw.
Zbigniew Bujak looked after all the contacts with the former Solidarity
branches which were than clandestine. Wiktor Kulerski was in charge of
the underground press and printing operations as well as the huge
amount of cultural activities while Ewa Kulik ran the office which provided the cars, organized the apartments and sorted out provisions.
They also arranged for doctors to visit when necessary and lined up
couriers and decoys.

Bujak explains that his 'main activity was writing and reading letters and reports. I used to meet the front people from the old union
branches and enterprises about twice a week. I was also heavily involved
in the maintenance of our security measures.' He took an active part in
running what was known as the Hygiene and Safety department, which
checked out flats, followed security leaks and generally tried to gather
relevant information.

It is very difficult to assess how fearful those in hiding were about
being caught and arrested. In general violent incidents initiated by the
police were rare enough to be notorious when they occurred. On the
other hand the mentality that allowed for the murder of Solidarity supporter, Father Jerzy Popieluszko, and indeed the other union activists
who lost their lives in suspicious circumstances, must have been in the
backs of the minds of underground members as they lived their life of
shadows. Bogdan Borusewicz, who ran the Gdansk underground, was
shot at twice during martial law, but he says that there were rules of
engagement: 'They were very serious about catching us and arresting
us. But there was an unwritten agreement. Generally they didn't shoot
us and we didn't shoot them. We didn't go over certain limits. In so far
as we were tolerated, they didn't keep us for too long in prison.'

Zbigniew Bujak says he was not depressed during the underground
years: 'The predominant feeling was of danger. In fact it was the
people around us, our friends, who were not hiding who felt it the
most. For them each time a knock came to the door there was the fear
that it was the police. Our families were being constantly harassed. I

knew that if the door bell rang it was probably a neighbour because the police didn't know where I was. I told myself that in my case the police would only come once. The greatest problem I experienced was what I would call the emotional burden of living with people one didn't know. Of course I knew I could trust these people, but I didn't know them. It was difficult. We all had to get to know so many new people all of the time. It's funny the things one learns. Even now when I go to a new apartment I always recognize straight away the place where the head of the family sits. It was so important not to be a burden on the family with whom one stayed, never to occupy the position of the head of the family, or to sit where he (or she) sat. Another problem was disposing of letters and reports so that there was no suspicion cast on the family. You obviously couldn't put the material in the garbage, so some tried to flush it down the toilet bowl. But if you did that and it didn't all go it was a dead give-away if outsiders visited the house. I used to try and burn the stuff in the toilet bowl and then flush it away. That worked, but I cracked a couple of toilet bowls in the process. It was a bigger problem than you'd think.'[2]

'Figures in the shadow of the big man' is the evocative phrase Krystyna Litynska uses to describe the situation of many Polish women. In particular she uses the phrase to describe the emotionally complex position of the wives and girlfriends of men who were underground. With some men gone from home for up to five years the women were left in a virtual limbo, where, on the one hand, they were to all intent and purposes alone, but on the other, they were meant to play the role of the noble and committed partner, frozen in time and awaiting the hero's return. Zbigniew Bujak is direct on the subject: 'Half of the history of the underground is the history of the political actions; the other half is the history of the human problems. The second part is the history of the divorces, the new loves, short relation-ships, of the babies that were born and of the abortions. The story is common to all conspiracies but this second part will never be written about because conspiracies are run by gentleman. So the story will never be told.' The latter remark was delivered by Bujak in what can only be described as the effusive and gushingly sexist fashion that Polish men favour when, metaphorically speaking, they are performing a peacock dance.

And then getting closer to the bone that many underground wives would probably prefer to forget, Bujak proffered, that the experience 'required from both people, great love and trust. For some time after I was out, if people asked me if I had any children, I would say that after four and a half years, I couldn't answer the question.' He then emphasized that the remark was meant as a joke: 'During the underground I met my wife once or twice a year. During the holidays we'd arrange a two-week visit together. The whole thing was very difficult. They were watching Wacia all of the time, so she'd have to organize a disguise. But as you can imagine, when we did meet it was a very hot meeting. We didn't worry about where we were or the food or anything.'

In trying to discuss the issue seriously with Krystyna Litynska I was very conscious of not crossing the barrier. She remembers private conversations with her friends whose partners went underground. She does not want to break confidences or be disloyal to those who have shared their hurt. Hesitantly, Krystyna admits that many underground wives are now 'a little bitter. But in life you learn to forgive. When a partner goes underground there has to be an agreement. It needs both sides. You expect their behaviour to be the same as one's own. It is a very hard lesson. There are shadows left.' I have never heard Krystyna speak in nostalgic terms about the past except when she compared the underground years with the atmosphere in 1980 from the woman's perspective: 'Then there was a great sense of men and women working together.' There was a definite sense of loss in her voice when she spoke about the collective experience of the women involved.

On a personal level, Janek going underground was an important experience for Krystyna: 'It was good for me. For the first time I was completely independent. Of course I couldn't get a job. If I did get one, it was badly paid. I couldn't be involved in a relationship. But I didn't want that anyway. Suddenly, nobody was looking for dinner. Nobody was coming home with six friends when I had one chicken leg in the flat. I didn't spend my time waiting. It's such a freedom. An excellent freedom.' But, as Zbigniew Bujak pointed out, conspiracies are run by 'gentlemen'. So the story, largely the story of the women's experience of the underground, will never be written. And for Krystyna there's another factor which makes it difficult for women to speak with ease now about their feelings: 'It is normal for wives to think in a manner which puts their husbands first. Perhaps it is the difference between Western and Eastern wives. What's good for him is good for the country. Everyone expects so much responsibility, one has to be a respectable wife. If your husband suffers you must be noble. You can't be seen to let him down.'

After many near misses, some of which have been embellished and mythologized, Bujak was finally caught and arrested on Gandhi Street in Warsaw on 30 May 1986. It is somehow ironic that Poland's great pacifist resistance leader should be caught on a street commemorating the most famous pacifist of them all. But Bujak was in luck: 'I served around a hundred days and was released after the general amnesty on 11 September. I went home to a new apartment – to my mother in-law. My wife had moved while I was gone. I wanted to go back to Ursus but I couldn't get a permit. No state owned company would employ me. I worked from time to time and I tried to establish my own business fixing and curing trees. I became the "famous tree-doctor, Zbigniew Bujak", but the idea didn't work. People didn't want to employ me because there was still the problem of my politics. But we survived because I received a human rights award from the Robert Kennedy Foundation while I was in prison. My wife worked in Ursus which helped. She'd managed to keep her job mainly because of the attitude of the manager there who stopped her being sacked.'

Bujak became politically active immediately after his release. And of course it was not long before there was a clash between the former underground leadership and the public wing over future strategy: 'The survival of the union as a political force was the big issue. I was in favour of open structures. I didn't think it should be secret anymore. I was convinced at that point that the communists were no longer strong enough to take us on. So I favoured an open leadership and set about creating one. The period of disagreement between the advocates of an open leadership and a secret one lasted about two months. There were a lot of rows over the abilities of certain individuals, fortunately it was short. My relationship with Lech Walesa was tense. It still is today. Lech always saw me as a rival but then in November the open and underground leadership came together to form a new National Executive Commission.'

Of all the politicians who now question Lech Walesa's judgement and who express dislike for the man, Zbigniew Bujak probably has the most cause. In 1987 he founded the Citizens' Committees. Starting in Warsaw, they developed nationwide. With the political

map in disarray, in early 1992, Bujak was saddened by what he saw
as the committees' lost potential: 'Now we can see how much such
institutions were needed. They were social-political organizations, not
just a trade union. I think that the situation was developing correctly
then. On the one hand there was the strong structures of the trade
union, while there was a parallel political organization developing.'
Obviously hurt, and politically crushed by the manner in which
Walesa sacrificed the committees, Bujak is hugely defensive of their
potential role in the immediate post-communist period: 'The Citizens'
Committees exerted a lot of pressure and influence. Without them we
wouldn't have been as strong at the Round Table. In retrospect I
now know that Lech was afraid of their political power. But in the
early days he accepted them because they helped him. After the
Round Table, the emotions and political ambition in the committees
grew; Lech didn't stop it and they finally broke down. What followed was the biggest political mistake of all, even from Walesa's
point of view. If he'd decided to keep them as a homogeneous body,
now we'd have an efficient strong political party with the support of
the Solidarity union.'

Bujak traces the political fragmentation and weakness of the union
back to Lech Walesa's role in the 'War at the Top': 'The only thing
that could have kept Solidarity together was Walesa. Had it remained
whole it would have had enough professionals to run the country.
Now the intellectual force is gone in different directions. You can
see what I mean by looking at all the different governments. When I
talk of the benefits, I mean it would be good for the whole country if
the split hadn't happened. And of course Solidarity would now be
strong. The whole thing is a tragedy. The union lost its authority,
power and influence. It has been bad for Polish politics. Now politicians cannot deal effectively with the problems here. The cost for
society is very big. It has even been bad for us abroad. What's happened is irreversible.'

Today Zbigniew Bujak describes himself as a social democrat. For
the first two and a half years of post-communist government, Bujak sat
alone in the Sejm. Many thought that the one-time hero was on a limb
forever. Given the fluidity of political thought within the many parties
on the Polish political scene, it is difficult to understand why Zbigniew
Bujak took so long to find a political base. His tempered commitment
to the market economy, his concern about the pace of economic reform

as well as his liberal views on women's and religious issues would make him welcome as a member of the liberal end of the Democratic Union, for instance. But like so many aspects of the political scene in Poland now, choice of party often seems to have more to do with personalities than philosophy. But perhaps Bujak was just waiting for the time to arrive when socialism would once again be respectable. Whatever his reasoning he is now one of the leaders of the socialist Labour Union (UP), which had 41 seats in the Sejm following the September 1993 election.

The central and most important issue which Poland faced in the early nineties was the transformation of the economy. Over three years after the first non-communist government was formed many key structural changes still remained to be carried out. The failure to complete the reform process quickly enough, initially jeopardized Poland's inter-national reputation and resulted in a dramatic slackening off in foreign investment after the first year of democratic government. There were and still are many complex factors militating against rapid economic reform and industrial development. Undoubtedly some of these factors are ideological but at the heart of what many regard as the slow pace of change has been the squabbling within the political elite and its failure, until the summer of 1992, to form a strong and stable government.

Zbigniew Bujak is highly critical of all of the post-communist governments. At the heart of his criticism is the view that the pace of reform has not been fast enough: 'The first Finance Minister, Leszek Balcerowicz, created a framework under which we could start our economy. His fiscal reforms could have been the basis of success if, at the right moment, the monetary changes were supported by a proper industrial policy. But that didn't happen. Instead, enterprises were told, "Now we have a free market; get out there and take care of yourselves." In the West, entrepreneurs have government agencies advising them, a go ahead banking system, expert consulting companies, a whole range of services at their disposal. Here in Poland, it's the same as leaving a small child in the middle of the city without any instructions about the red and green traffic lights – you can't do that.' Looking at the deterioration in industrial performance follow-ing the introduction of market reform, many who sympathise with Bujak's view, put the problems down to a higgledy-piggledy approach to structural change: 'Look, the rate of changes in various spheres are not compatible with each other. For example, the changes in the

banking system are too slow by comparison with the whole privatization process. There were all kinds of plans and theories. Theoretically
employees are meant to have a right to buy a twenty per cent share
of an enterprise that's being privatized. But in order for that to function properly, if at all, we need a viable credit system so that people
can get access to the money they need to buy the shares. The credit
doesn't even have to be direct cash, but the system here simply isn't
developed enough. We're not familiar with the methods or schemes of
modern financing and banking.'

As the euphoria and expectation diminished in the aftermath of 1989
the public grew critical of the social consequences of the transformation
process. That concern, emotional deflation and criticism crystallized in
September 1993 when the electorate told the post-Solidarity parties that
they'd had enough of the bad times. Bujak had long feared that the
public's *angst* about social security, wages and unemployment would
translate into a rejection of the whole transformation process: 'Now there
is very little public support for privatization. Fundamental things that
were necessary for the introduction of a market economy were neglected
by Mr Mazowiecki's Christian Democratic government and by Mr
Bielecki's Liberal-led government. These first two governments made
crucial mistakes. A really important factor here is the need to rebuild the
trust in private ownership. Remember, people here simply are not used
to owning anything. First of all the previous governments should have
invested in reprivatization and secondly money should have been spent
to try and sort out our system of transferring the ownership of property.
It's a mess. There's lots of work for lawyers there. But the budgets
didn't make enough money available. The whole policy of privatization
is badly constructed. As things stand many foreign companies wanting to
buy into Polish firms cannot even establish who the owner is. What's
really lacking here is the creation of new private enterprise. Instead we're
just transforming the old state firms into private ones. In fact because of
the complexity of the way it is done, it isn't really private enterprise at
all. The essence of privatization – risking one's own capital – isn't part of
the picture here yet at all.'

Apart from an obvious growing lack of public support for the
changes there's also an increasing sense of social vulnerability: 'The
whole process of transformation has caused a huge feeling of insecurity.
People cannot be sure of being able to earn a living, of finding somewhere to live, of getting an education and more and more they're afraid

that if they become sick, that there'll no longer be a health service to take care of them. As far as I'm concerned I think that people should at least feel secure about having somewhere to live. Land prices should be kept low so that construction companies would find it cheaper to develop land. In relation to these issues I'm in favour of a policy of protection for workers. Health service and medicine costs should be low.'

Prior to the left wing landslide in the '93 election the whole area of social security, unemployment benefit and labour law was still undergoing a fundamental overhaul. In a country moving from a notional position of total employment to increasing unemployment, there are many who would argue that the early reform of this area should have featured higher on the political agenda: 'From the beginning this is the area that should have had priority. Again, very concrete things need to be done. Given the enormous amount of companies which have gone bust as a result of the new conditions, a special bankruptcy office should have been established to look after the interests of both the employees and the State Treasury. It wasn't done. So, as you know, there have been very serious strikes. I could go on and on. Look at the government's social security department. Its legal status is unclear and there have been times when it hasn't had the money to pay old age pensioners.'

Essentially Zbigniew Bujak argues that it is simply unjust that the workers should pay the price of Poland's economic transformation: 'The focus should be on how the workers are affected. Their fate can't be left to the market. Job creation can't be left to the free market. The government and local authorities must be responsible. On the issue of reform and privatization we are no different from the right wing parties. Where we differ is on the consequences. Job creation and social security must be a priority. If these issues are not taken care of there will social unrest. There'll be occupations and strikes.'

While there's no doubt that Zbigniew Bujak was isolated politically after the break up of Solidarity and appeared to place himself on the political margins of Polish politics, there's equally no doubt that his reasons for doing so were sincere. It would, for instance, have been much easier for the son of a peasant, espousing strong Catholicism, to have taken a less prominent position on Church-State issues during a period of intense public debate on moral matters. But being the maverick he undoubtedly is means that he has discriminated between private devotion and the public role of the Church: 'As far as the Church engaging in the political life of the country is concerned, it's well known that I'm critical of it. I don't like this engagement in national politics. It diminishes the real role, the social role, that the Church should be playing.' And in a country which rivals Ireland in its obsession with moral issues he has not been afraid to state his opposition to the mainly Church-led campaign to criminalize abortion. He campaigned hard for a referendum on the abortion bill, arguing that the issue was too important not to be decided by the people.[3]

There's no doubt that it would have been easy for Bujak to have played a prominent role in the Democratic Union because of the good relations he has with many old comrades there. Instead he chose a far more difficult road. He chose social democracy at a time when it was being embraced by the vast bulk of the reformer wing of the old Communist Party. It was no easy task to establish the identity of a social democratic party emanating from Solidarity and therefore intrinsicially anti-communist but not anti-socialist in its social and economic policy on the human consequences of the transformation process.

Having had the courage to face down one power it is probably not surprising that Bujak is not now afraid to argue that the war is over. He is vehemently against anti-communist witch-hunting, regarding it as a means to an end for many populist politicians: 'I'm definitely opposed to what most supporters of decommunization mean by the phrase. For me decommunization is simply the changeover to a new mechanism. But many of these people are calling for decommunization for personal reasons and of course I'm against it.' Given the ugly allegations of communist collaboration which were made against many former dissidents following the release (by the Olszewski government, December 1991– June 1992) of an alleged list of collaborators from secret police files, it requires courage to refuse to join in ritual denunciation.

Zbigniew Bujak is a big, earthy and generous-faced man, without a hint of the paranoia that would be forgivable in a man who spent four and a half years conspiring underground. 'Many friends think that I should hate the secret police. I was willing to meet the man who finally discovered where I was hiding. I felt respect for that secret police agent because he was clever enough to find me. Even if I was underground, I never conducted this fight from a position of hatred.' In conversation with Bujak, one is profoundly struck by his political wisdom. At a time when many nationalist politicians were seeking to have General Wojciech Jaruzelski impeached for his involvement in martial law, Bujak went one step further than those who simply argue that the time of trials is over. Perhaps with a wider vision than most, he is prepared to give Jaruzelski credit for a move which literally reversed the domino theory in Eastern Europe: 'I think that when Jaruzelski decided to begin the series of talks which led to the Round Table, he became the main person in the decommunization process because the Round Table Talks was the event that began the end of communism.' Perhaps this refusal to view Poland's recent past in black and white terms is a threat to those who want easy answers to what are complex political and moral questions.

THE ROUND TABLE TALKS

THE 'CONTROLLED OPERATION' THAT WENT WRONG

There was but a faint glimmer of Mieczyslaw Rakowski's renowned chicanery in evidence when I met him in March 1992. A frightened man, Poland's last communist prime minister seemed more concerned with the contemplation of his own mortality than with the certified death of the system for which he'd long laboured. Out of misplaced politeness I didn't point out the irony of his impending trip to Berlin for a by-pass operation. On second thoughts, however, I remembered that the Party elite had never really hidden their enjoyment of privileges, not available to the masses, in the so-called classless socialist order. Was this a tacit admission that Big Brother's medical facilities weren't up to scratch in Poland?

Entering Rakowski's room at the office of the magazine *Dzis*, in Warsaw's Poznanska Street, I was forcibly struck by the palpable air of vulnerability. As always when a person is met by the opposite of what's anticipated I reacted with a combination of uncomfortable sympathy and anger. Here was the Party's one-time frontman, apologist, reformer, editor, bon viveur and of course survivor, shuffling around feeling sorry for himself in an invisible grey cardigan. I was angry with myself for feeling sorry for him. This was the former peasant's son made good, who'd called Zbigniew Bujak 'that little shit'.

Back in 1980 I was never quite sure whether the esteemed members of the international press corps actually liked Rakowski. His name often rolled off their lips. As editor of the official weekly newspaper *Polityka*, Rakowski met foreign journalists both as a skilled commentator on the Polish scene and as a mouthpiece for the reformist wing of the Party. Then he was the acceptable face of communism, the man with ideas who prompted observers to believe in the possibility of reform within the Party. Or was he simply an elegant spider who wove the web of illusory deceit?.

From the outside, his appointment as head of the newly established 'Permanent Committee' for government-union relations in February

1981, looked like a possible step forward from Solidarity's perspective. In retrospect much of his contact with the union over the next ten months looks at best like a cosmetic exercise designed to create the impression of dialogue while the Party worked out what it was going to do. Needless to say Rakowski denies this as well as any suggestion that he actively knew of the plans for martial law. There is a sense, however, in which his version of events can be regarded with credibility. But that credibility depends largely on semantics – in other words, on an understanding of what communists meant by words like negotiation, reform, power sharing and responsibility.

One could be forgiven for imagining that the Party must have temporarily lost its sanity when it agreed to Round Table talks with Solidarity at the beginning of 1989. It it is hard to see how any rational politician contemplating the process which was to pave the way for the first semi-free elections could believe that they would lead to anything other than the collapse of communist power. But in the end the Party was the victim of its own propaganda. It had forgotten that its power was but a semantic illusion once it failed to exercise it.

So given the fact that the Party had no sense that it was about to facilitate a handover of power, what was the communist apparatchiks' perception of the deal it made at the Round Table? 'In the eighties,' Rakowski says, 'I don't think that anyone from the party saw the possibility on the horizon of us losing power. My belief was that we could arrange a political, social and economic situation that would allow us to retain power. Nobody dreamed we'd lose power.' Essentially Rakowski seems to be arguing that the aim and thrust of the Round Table process was to produce a social democratic model for Poland's future based on a consensus approach by the government and opposition. Inherent in this argument is the claim that, following the massive Solidarity victory (at the first semi-free elections) and the installation of the first government, Solidarity broke the agreement by accelerating the process. 'Jaruzelski's staff thought that the end result would be a sharing of power. We thought we'd work out a new concept of economic policy based on the market system. Politically we thought we'd share power but the June 4th election result wiped out that concept. Society wanted change. But the economic concept was accepted by people. Remember nobody at the Round Table had thought that Poland's future should start with capitalism. The economic agreement was based on the mixed economy approach. It was clear to us and the opposition that we should revitalize the economy but step by step.'

As a reformer Rakowski argues that while he failed to anticipate the collapse of communism in the entire region he had long anticipated the need for change: 'I saw that the vision of socialism had no future. The main question was how to transform society from a vision of socialism which had lost any internal force. How to go forward and to find out how far and what were the possibilities. We hadn't a clear concept of how to move and of how to transform to democratic socialism such as exists in Spain, Sweden and Austria. The system here had historically lost. In the economic sphere it was clear that we couldn't compete with the West. Our system had condemned the market concept so for many people in the ranks of the Party it was clear that it was finished. For me it was also clear that in the visible future we would have to create a situation where the Party shared power with the opposition. But that in the end we knew that the opposition would end up on top. However, I thought that it would be a ten-to-fifteen-year process. And you must remember that they thought that it would take time as well. Walesa made a speech at the beginning of 1989 in Gdansk to a meeting of young people where he told them that he expected Solidarity to be sharing power at the end of the century.'

Timothy Garton Ash (in his book *The Polish Revolution*) describes the communist understanding of sharing power as 'consultative authoritarianism', while Professor Wnuk-Lipinski points out that the reformers 'were trying to restore the power of the Party by sharing responsibility but not power'. Lipinski argues that those who remained communists after the grotesque series of purges and the politically sterile response of martial law were simply determined not to let go: 'The reality of reformism and of the Rakowski element was that it was a way of clinging onto power.'

Rakowski strenuously denies any suggestion that the notion of power-sharing was merely a pragmatic foil to retain power: 'Every politician wants to retain power – but what kind of power? There was no future for any kind of dictatorship based on a one-party system and not only because of Solidarity; but because of the historical tendencies that were becoming evident. There was no time for postponing the inevitable.'

Whatever history will make of Rakowski's claims, there is no doubt, as Timothy Garton Ash points out, that the main motivating factor which prompted the Party to seek 'talks about talks' (to borrow a phrase from the Northern Ireland context) was the series of Solidarity strikes staged over the spring and summer of 1988. The Party was once again overtly in conflict with the very group on whom its legitimacy was based. With the economy in a state of virtual collapse and with no apparent way ahead in sight, and in the context of a different wind blowing in from Moscow, General Jaruzelski decided to act. Former Central Committee spokesman and adviser to Jaruzelski, Jan Bisztyga claims that the general moved on the basis of the answers to three questions: 'First, he asked if it would be possible to keep the economy stable. Secondly, was it going to be possible to retain power; and thirdly he asked if it would be possible to wipe out Solidarity. The answer to those three questions were negative.'

Professor Jerzy Wiatr, a political sociologist and former Communist Party member, argues that the communists had a totally unrealistic perception of what they were doing at the Round Table: 'There were clearly two different elements on the Party side. The dominant role was taken by fairly open-minded pragmatic representatives of the establishment. Behind this group was General Jaruzelski. A secondary role was played by the reformers who had been co-opted at the last moment. They didn't have enough authority to shape policy however. The fundamental mistake that Jaruzelski made was that he started the process of opening the talks with Solidarity before he did anything with the Party. In my opinion the 10th Party Congress in 1986 solidified the position not of the extreme hard-liners but of the moderately conservative elements who believed that the worst scenario from their point of view had already happened and had been corrected. In other words the bad dream of Solidarity was over. Two years later Jaruzelski authorized the opening of talks with Walesa. He had enough lead time. He should have reversed the order of things and should have dealt with the situation in the Party first. The consequence of that was that the government side was internally divided. Those running the government team perceived the Round Table as a controlled operation which would expand the political base of the regime. It was a bold initiative compared to the way other ruling communist parties behaved. At the same time their perception of what was going on was unrealistic.'

What is mind-boggling to the outside observer in retrospect is why the Communists failed to anticipate the possibility that given the chance the Polish electorate would reject the Party outright. Rakowski still seemed bemused by events almost three years later: 'In May after the end of the Round Table the opinion polls showed that fourteen per cent of the electorate would vote for us and the Peasants (nominally independent Communist coalition partner), while forty per cent said they'd vote for Solidarity. The rest had no opinion. Till now I don't know why we thought that the rest would vote for us. We were prisoners of our past, when the elections weren't free. It just didn't register that the don't knows wouldn't vote for us.' I then asked Mr Rakowski if the Party had believed in its own propaganda? He replied: 'Somehow yes.' And did he get an awful shock, I asked? 'Yes, indeed.' Rakowski then added that there were many reasons why the Party had failed to anticipate electoral defeat: 'It wasn't only the reason of being prisoners of the past, the tradition of unfree elections, and the fact that the end of the Round Table Talks looked good but there was also the fact that the opposition told us that they were not interested in power. So I think that there were many reasons why our behaviour was such as it was.'

Professor Wiatr explains what seems like an enormous gaffe in terms of a massive underestimation by the Communists of the calibre of the opposition representatives at the Round Table: 'They became victims of their own wishful thinking. They underestimated the other side; in particular they underestimated the people they were negotiating with in the political committees.' I served on the political committee. Solidarity played the game masterfully. This was particularly because of the Solidarity co-chairman Bronislaw Geremek. He never over-committed himself. He never said anything that could now be read back to show that he violated any commitment he made. But he allowed the communist side to be carried along by its wishful thinking. I remember that following a small caucus meeting there was a decision to allow completely free elections to the Senate. Rakowski called me early on a Sunday morning to tell me. My first reaction was that we'd lose. So Rakowski said he thought that I'd be pleased by the decision. I told him that I was in favour of fundamental change. But you see even open-minded people like Rakowski were prisoners of the self-definition of the situation. They didn't realize what was going on.'

Essentially Professor Wiatr is arguing that having thrown all caution to the wind the communist side left themselves exposed to a level of electoral defeat that they simply failed to anticipate. In the Solidarity landslide following the first round of voting on 4 June, union-backed candidates took 99 of the 100 seats in the newly created Senate as well as 160 of the 161 seats in the Sejm (lower house) set aside for opposition and independent candidates. Although the remaining 299 Sejm seats automatically went to the communists, only five of their candidates actually got the required fifty per cent share of the vote. Rakowski was one of the most prominent victims of the débacle.

Of the 35 well known Communist candidates who ran unopposed, 33 had their names scratched off the list by voters. The result was constitutional chaos and a genuine fear of a communist backlash.

At the time, Solidarity adviser Professor Bronislaw Geremek described the result and the communist role in it as a 'monstrous political and technical mistake.' He claimed it resulted from, not only a 'lack of imagination' but also from 'the sin of pride'. On one level victory on the scale Solidarity achieved was the last thing it wanted. Firstly, there had been no intention of actually taking part in government. The Round Table was a trade off as far as Solidarity was concerned. Constitutional and political freedom on a step by step basis in return for social peace and gradual economic development. But the communists did not fulfil their part of the bargain. That failure left Solidarity enormously exposed to the inflated aspirations of their victorious supporters who now thought the time was ripe to take power.

Immediately after the landslide, Solidarity MPs such as Jan Litynski were still voicing the official line that they would not be taking part in or forming government. The strategy was still seen in terms of a gradual process of reform from below and constitutional change from above by the enactment of new laws and the blocking of anti-reform legislation. Just how cautious the Solidarity side was in the immediate post-election period came home to me when I listened, once again, to an interview I had conducted with the former Solidarity press spokesman and then elected MP Janusz Onyskiewicz: 'That [the size of the electoral victory] gave people the feeling that we have power already. But power is not measured by simple mandates or election results here in Poland. That is the case in democratic countries. Here the power is where the instruments of power is. Power is with the army, the security service and the police. And that still means the Party. The election result starts a certain process. We will have the power in parliament to block certain legislation. After such a tremendous victory we can think seriously of dismantling the system of 'nomenklatura.' Up to now the Party nominated people to every managerial post not only in industry but in education, medicine and to every state agency. It controls everything in a country like Poland. Now we can begin dismantling the whole system. To put it in a nutshell we want to begin a process of regaining our country, our state which belonged to one party and was dominated by one ideology. And we simply want this country to belong to the people.'

Janusz Onyskiewicz would later become the first non-military Deputy Minister of Defence in the Warsaw Pact. In the immediate post-election period in 1989 he was enormously conscious of the dangers inherent in taking office: 'We can't for instance take certain portfolios in a situation where the Party is dominant. Defence and the the Interior are the two obvious ones. We would be seen to be puppets. Solidarity promised the people we'd stay in opposition. We can offer parliamentary cooperation to the communists on an issue by issue basis. But we cannot partake in a coalition or help form a government. First we must change the situation at the grassroots level. We are treading a very delicate path. We must not lose the confidence of the Warsaw Pact and we must make sure that the process of democratization is gradual. There can be no leaps. The orthodox elements within the Party shouldn't be frightened. We must leave space for the Party to change and leave time for them to turn into businessmen. We must avoid a backlash. The process should be smooth but fast.'

The conviction that the Party had to be given space to transform itself is at the centre of the argument over decommunization. Many of the critics who found the opposition's handling of the Round Table negotiations too soft see it as the fatal flaw which has resulted in old communist power structures and spheres of influence being left in place. In the aftermath of the September 1993 post-communist election victory many Round Table critics would argue that it was the most important factor which paved the way for a Lazarus like resurrection for the disbanded party.

The veteran anti-communist leader of the fiercely nationalist KPN (Confederation for an Independent Poland), Leszek Moczulski, would have preferred for Poland's freedom to have been won by other methods: 'The Round Table could have been avoided. There was a chance in 1988 when the massive strikes took place of overthrowing communism like it happened in Czechoslovakia. The strikes were stopped and the Round Table began. Had the talks not been organized and the strikes allowed run their course the end result would have been the same but without having to barter with the communists.' Moczulski is a leading proponent of harsh anti-communist measures and believes that the Round Table deal was a mechanism which left an escape route open for Party apparatchiks. It is also claimed by some including

Moczulski that there was too much fraternization between Solidarity and the Party sides during the talks process. That's a claim that, as we shall see later, germinated into a bitter row with allegations that well known dissidents were in fact communist agents.

Professor Wnuk-Lipinski looks at the process in a more dispassionate light: 'In human terms people did get closer. The question is who got closer to who? Did the communist reformers move closer to Solidarity or was it the other way round? Those who now look back and criticize the Round Table forget the historical moment at which it took place. It wasn't totally clear whether the Brezhnev Doctrine had been abandoned by Gorbachev.[2] The communists were still in control of the military and security aspects of the state. The surrounding countries were still communist regimes. There was no sign then of the incredible changes that were to come later in the year. So Solidarity was moving very cautiously. It must be remembered that the talks didn't just open the way for the transformation in Poland: it paved the way for the rest of the Eastern Bloc. So on the human side I believe in the conversion of St Paul. A certain part of the communist elite realized that change was inevitable and they were smart enough to change. From the political viewpoint it is not that important whether it is a real conversion or tactics for as long as it works. It allowed for bloodless change. You can argue that those communists who realized the inevitable moved out into the market and exchanged one privileged political position for another commercial one. From a social justice perspective it should be condemned but from the Machiavellian perspective it is probably fortunate. The main precondition necessary for the collapse of communism was a split. Having an alternative and being left a way out supported the chance for them to change.'

After the momentous changes that took place in Eastern Europe at the end of 1989 it is perhaps easy to become blasé about the significance of the Round Table itself. Those who criticize the negotiators for getting too close to the Party or for not making even greater demands perhaps forget what the reality was and how quickly that reality changed. Just after the election in 1989 Janusz Onyskiewicz was still almost overcome by the enormity of the process in which he had taken part. He remembered vividly his feelings on the day the talks actually began: 'It was a quite surrealistic experience. I remember the first moment when we [Solidarity side] entered Government Buildings. We were opening a small office and putting up our Solidarity banner to identify where we were. And, I thought, here we are, Solidarity is illegal and now we are inside the very building of government. Here we are talking freely when we could be in jail. People were almost amused at first by the incredible change. Then people began saying, "Remember who they are; not so close." But, remember, we were there to sign a sort of compromise it wasn't a situation where we could expect them to sign an unconditional surrender. We couldn't treat them as our enemies.'

For Onyskiewicz looking at the talks process from the perspective of just a few months its significance was clear. 'The fact that the Party has accepted pluralism is of enormous historical importance. The Communist Party here was never totalitarian in the sense that Poland never became a totalitarian state. The Church and the peasants always remained independent. But the Party never gave up its totalitarian aspirations. But at the Round Table the Party finally declared its acceptance of pluralism as a fact of political life. It was the end of their totalitarian dream.'

Even after the shock of the massive Solidarity victory Mieczyslaw Rakowski still thought that the transfer of power would be gradual: 'No doubt I thought that we'd go step by step together. I thought that the people from the opposition would learn what it meant to govern, because of course, they were not prepared. But the events in Czechoslovakia, in Hungary etc showed that it was the end of the system. I think that in July 1989, after an article by Adam Michnik[3] called 'Your President – Our Prime Minister', it was clear that the time of our governing was over, our power was in the past. But still in the next few months with Jaruzelski as President and four ministers from our Party in cabinet we thought that a total transfer of power would be postponed for the next months perhaps for a year or two. Now, looking back, it seems we were very naive. But it happens.'

Former communists now argue that Solidarity didn't keep its side of the bargain. It is claimed that the rapid implementation of measures to transform the economy on market lines was not part of the package and of course it is claimed that the acceleration of the democratization process was not agreed either. But then it could be said that nobody appears to have anticipated the obvious: given the opportunity Poles voted en masse to wipe out the Party. The electorate decided to ignore the rigged arrangement and vote like free men and women. It seems rather odd that having left the cookie jar open the communists were dumbfounded by the scale of the theft.

Professor Wiatr claims that the formation of the first post-communist government under Tadeusz Mazowiecki went beyond the spirit and philosophy of the Round Table agreement. The tendency of former communists to maintain this lack of faith on the part of the opposition seems conclusive evidence of the Party's failure to respond to the rapidly changing political situation in the weeks following the election. Given the scale of the communist defeat, Solidarity was forced to fill the political vacuum once it became clear that there was to be no military defence of the old order. Professor Wiatr claims that because Solidarity didn't expect to be taking part in government that they selected candidates who were 'excellent radical speakers for the opposition. People who would be good trouble-makers for the government. But then they became the government. The combination of radical parliamentarians and the collapse of the other Eastern European regimes made it very difficult for the moderate voices within Solidarity.'

As Timothy Garton Ash comments: 'once it became clear that communism was really finished all over Eastern Europe, once Czechoslovakia had Vaclav Havel as President and entirely free elections were being held in neighbouring countries, then Poland's rigged coalition – the product of the Round Table agreements – seemed increasingly a relic of the past rather than a model for the future.'[4]

Having tried to look at the Round Table from the Party's perspective it is clear that its biggest failure was its inability to grasp the fact that Solidarity was not a monolith and that therefore it could not be expected to respond in the manner that the Party itself would. In other words because the Party had in the past defined the rules it somehow still believed that it would continue to do so. The fact was that by the middle of the summer of 1989 the entire game had changed.

Poland's last communist prime minister still believes that the reforming wing of the Party lost its opportunity to save Poland: 'The tragedy of our Party was that the reformist wing was weaker than the one which was maybe not pro-Soviet but more dogmatic. To the end of the Party the dogmatic wing and their vision of power was stronger and the reformers lost. The question was, what possibilities were there for presenting reform in the sixties, seventies and eighties. We were limited until Gorbachev.'

Sitting opposite Mieczyslaw Rakowski in his grey, Spartan office, I wondered what it must feel like to experience not only the disintegration of one's own power but the disintegration of the power of an

entire ideology. Perhaps it was his impending operation but I kept
thinking that much of what Rakowski was saying was being voiced
stage left as if he was somehow looking at his own performance in
wonderment from the wings.

I asked him how he felt having devoted his entire life to a failed
ideology. 'I think', he replied, 'it wasn't easy to accept the situation.
But because I'm a historian I know that all systems have their begin-
nings and their ends. And in the last two hundred years there have
been many different parties and systems; a lot of losers. I have accepted
it from the historical perspective but it is not easy. Such is life.' In a
very detached way Rakowski argues that communist ideology has not
failed: 'Of course there have been a lot of errors. The most important
error was that the whole movement was not prepared intellectually and
politically to take into account the changes that were going on in the
world. So it lost its dynamic. I think that from the time in the twenties
when the concept of Leninism was replaced by Stalinism that the movement was in crisis from this time. But it did influence the development
of the world. It's just been ill for many years.'

Other writers have commented on how much Rakowski yearned to
be recognised as a liberal reformer. Now he feels that it is unlikely that
he will get a fair historical assessment in the foreseeable future: 'No
doubt because I played a rather important role not just in the last ten
years but as *Polityka*'s editor in chief for over twenty years I helped
educate a critical generation especially among the Polish intelligentsia.
You know it's difficult to get an objective opinion about people like me
because we are still under the pressure of the situation of on-going political battles. My government was criticized for creating huge inflation.
Mazowiecki criticized me and Bielecki [second prime minister] criticized
Mazowiecki and now Olszewski [third prime minister] criticized the lot.
It's difficult to get an objective opinion.'

Looking back at his own writings from the days when he was a
young Stalinist, Rakowski nowadays sees more and more evidence of his
early criticism of the Party. The instinctive ability to survive and to
change colour has been Rakowski's hallmark. As he sat staring into the
middle distance it struck me that the chameleon had changed colour
once too often: 'I would like to be remembered as someone who wanted
to change the system – to improve the system. As someone who prepared the way for the changes.' The emphasis in his otherwise bland
voice confirmed my impression that he didn't really expect history to
vindicate his claim.

Shuffling in and out of the offices of the magazine for which he now works, the former much-sought-after and acceptable face of the Party appeared relieved by his lack of responsibility and apprehensive about the pressure within Poland to punish those responsible for the past: 'No, I don't miss power. It's a very pleasant status not to be responsible for what's going on. Now I know what power is I don't think that power makes people happy. No I don't think so.'[5]

PLURALISM AT GUNPOINT

The concept of Lech Walesa as communist 'agent Bolek' would have been funny had it not been so tragically serious for Poland's burgeoning economy and political landscape. Through the spring and early summer of 1992 normal, or at least constructive, political activity was suspended as politicians grappled with revelations concerning attempted coups and claims that some of the most famous anti-communist warriors were in fact signed up agents of the former security apparatus. So, instead of attention being focussed on getting the budget through the Sejm or perhaps on the complex question of a new constitution, Poles were fed a diet of innuendo and intrigue which did little to improve the tarnished reputation of politics in a country where people yearn for the fruits of capitalism and are less and less enamoured by their recently won democracy. And though the formation of Hanna Suchocka's Democratic Union-led coalition government in mid-summer did much to enhance Poland's reputation abroad, it did little to quell the interminable cacophany of charge and counter-charge which appeared to consume the interest of the nation's politicians.

Abuse and vilification are regarded by some as the norm in the world of politics, but when the poisoned cup is passed from associates who were until very recently marching under the same anti-communist banner, the result is a phenomenal putrification of the political atmosphere. From the outside it is perhaps not difficult to regard the release of an alleged list of former communist agents (and the claims by Defence Minister Jan Parys that President Walesa's advisers had planned a coup) as simply part of the cut and thrust of politics in a country where the rules have yet to be written. However, the shattering of Solidarity's homogeneity following the 'War at the Top', the inability of the anti-communist political elites to make government work, not to mention the vitriolic immolation inherent in the secret security files and Parys' affairs, have been a sad and bitter experience for many of those who struggled for democracy in Poland. This apparent compulsive destructiveness is seen by many commentators as an essential part of the Polish national psychology, and though this interpretation is often regarded as clichéd it is nonetheless a major obstacle to the nation's political and economic development.

Priest and philosopher Father Josef Tischner was Solidarity's chaplain between 1980 and 1981. He now teaches at the Jagiellonian University at Cracow. A giant of a man in both body and mind, it is Father Tischner's humanism rather than his Catholicism that first strikes the visitor to his booklined 'cell'. behind St Mary's Church just off the beautiful square in Cracow. An outspoken commentator, he is not afraid to criticize the Church's role nor has he been afraid to attack the new political elites for their populist anti-communist slogans. 'The essential issue,' he maintains, 'is that for the first time in two hundred years we are trying to build an independent democratic country. We are rather specialists at destroying things and in this area we have special achievements. We know how to lie to the authorities and destroy communication. We know how to bribe. If there is a need for a general strike, we can do that too. We've also made uprisings against foreign invaders: we always failed, but we got better at it as we went on. Now it's a very bad situation because we have to build a country. The key question is: if the state is to be democratic – do we know what democracy is? The problem is that we don't have any democratic customs or habits.'

Seeing Poland's difficulties in establishing normal political life as uniquely the legacy of communism is dismissed by many including Professor Wnuk-Lipinski: 'Polish society is generally hard to govern. Poles are excellent at organizing protest but disastrous at trying to do something constructive. In short, Poles are giants with regard to national issues but dwarfs regarding social matters.' So, what were the factors that transformed an apparently mass movement of opposition into a self-destuctive and constantly fragmenting political elite? One must always be wary of the opinion of the opponent, but former Communist Party member Professor Jerzy Wiatr believes that the break-up of Solidarity follows a classic model: 'First of all, Solidarity identified all Poland's problems as based on the fact of communist power. There was an implication in their argument that the communists took over a perfectly happy society. In a sense there was a moral defeat for Solidarity in victory. When what is essentially an anti-system movement is transformed into a ruling block, there is inevitable frustration. Solidarity became a victim of its early rhetoric. It had promoted aspirations for Western-style development in a country without Western ways.

Solidarity was a common crusade against communism rather than a political or social movement with clearly defined objectives. Once the adversary was gone the movement inevitably split.'

As we have seen, Solidarity was not prepared for governing. But the disastrous performance of the communist side at the June 1989 election transformed the Round Table deal and created a power vacuum that Solidarity was eventually forced to fill. Following an intense period of negotiation, Lech Walesa's veteran adviser, leading Catholic intellectual journalist Tadeusz Mazowiecki, formed a grand coalition government in early September 1989, which included four Communist Party members who held key cabinet posts including Defence and the Interior. Of course, while the formation of Mazowiecki's government was an important historical moment, it was from the outset doomed, not least because it created an untenable situation in which everyone appeared to be playing for the same side. There is bitter disagreement among Walesa's friends and former friends about how he exploited this phenomenon, but there is no doubt about one thing: the 'War at the Top' signalled the end of Solidarity as a cohesive movement. With the exception of the row over the security files and the allegations of communist collaboration, the 'War at the Top' was the most bitter episode in post-communist Poland.

Democratic Union MP Jan Litynski was part of a grouping within Solidarity which supported Mazowiecki and his style of leadership and opposed Walesa's more populist approach: 'After the election,' he says, 'we realized that some political organization had to be established. Many of us thought that Solidarity as a social movement would be a good basis for a political movement. Zbigniew Bujak tried to develop the idea in the Warsaw area, for instance, but the local Citizens' Committee rejected his proposal. The activists there were afraid of central organization. Then after the Mazowiecki government was formed, it was obvious that a broad basis of support was needed for the reforms we wanted to bring in. That support did come from the Committees but Mazowiecki stayed outside the Committees. They were never properly organized. So, at the end of 1989 there were three groups: there were the Citizens' Committees, Solidarity itself, and the government. Within the Sejm, there was the Parliamentary Citizens' Club. It was like a multiple power. But Lech was on the outside; he was still the leader of the union. He was unhappy because he wasn't a statesman. It's hard to say when the "War at the Top" actually started, but as the standard of living deteriorated and as the impact of the fiscal reforms hit the country, a natural conflict developed between the government and the union. Walesa exploited that conflict. That was the beginning of the split, really. Obviously what I'm saying is an over-simplification, but there were basically two points of view about how we should proceed. We thought that the situation should remain the same. In other words we didn't want to push the pace of the transition where the communists were concerned. We wanted to allow the reforms to go ahead under the protection of some social peace. Then Walesa enters the ring with his slogan of a "War at the Top" and calls for "acceleration".'

'Acceleration' was the catchword of Lech Walesa's presidential campaign which began almost as soon as General Jaruzelski entered the Belweder Palace after his election as president by the National Assembly. Apart from demanding Jaruzelski's resignation, Walesa called for early presidential and parliamentary elections and the speeding up of the privatization process. 'Looking back now it was a mistake to oppose Walesa's election as president by the National Assembly. The two Kaczynski brothers' proposed it. But because it had been obvious during the Round Table that Jaruzelski was to be president because that was the communists' gurarantee of influence, we thought that his election was the optimum route to democracy. Then, when it first appeared that Jaruzelski wasn't going to get the votes at the Assembly, Bronislaw Geremek proposed that Walesa put his name forward. But we disagreed, [the group that would eventually form the Democratic Union] because we were afraid that the communists would have resisted the idea.'

It appears that politicians like Jan Litynski, overcome by the scale of the communist defeat, simply were not able to respond quickly enough to a rapidly changing political scenario. But then they could not have been expected to have had foreknowledge of a wide range of inter-connected events, both within Poland and Eastern Europe, which were to completely transform the basis on which decisions were made. Professor Jerzy Wiatr blames the 'intellectual leaders of Solidarity for what followed: 'Look: technically they treated Walesa correctly. He was the leader of a trade union. He wasn't elected. But he was more. The fact that Walesa played the "acceleration" card merely reflects his own exclusion from the decision making process during the Mazowiecki period. After all Walesa thought that Mazowiecki and Geremek were his men, they'd been his advisers for years. He didn't expect the new cabinet to turn its back on him. For the Round Table arrangement to have worked, they would have had to have given Walesa a proper role. By deviating from the Round Table, by stepping up the pace of the process, Mazowiecki's people left themselves vulnerable. They became prisoners of the radical elements such as the KPN [Confederation for an Independent Poland] and of course Walesa's group.'

The moment when the backroom stabbing became public could not have been more dramatic. Walesa turned up very late for a packed and televised meeting of the Citizens' Committee in Warsaw on 24 June 1990. All the Solidarity glitterati were there. Walesa's late arrival was seen by many as an indication of his attitude to both Prime Minister Mazowiecki, who was chairing the meeting, and to the rest of the assembled power-brokers present. Jerzy Wiatr looked at the ensuing mêlée on television. 'There were so many incredible moments like when Wladyslaw Frasyniuk [prominent underground leader and MP] got up and told Walesa that he hadn't served years in jail to now serve at the court of a despot. Then there was the moment when Walesa shouted at Jerzy Turowicz, the elderly and respected editor of the Catholic newspaper, *Tygodnik Powszechny*, to come to the podium as all of Poland awaited his criticisms. People winced as Walesa treated this venerable man in this condescending fashion. Walesa wasn't stupid. He knew that there was a price tag for that sort of behaviour. He did want to get rid of the barons and the elites, but there was the personal element as well. He wanted to get rid of those who, he thought, looked down on him. This was their Frankenstein. They had created him but they failed to fully appreciate the formidable Frankenstein they'd created. They underestimated him and those who did so eventually had to pay the price.'

That rancorous debate was the end of any pretence of unity. From then on the 'War at the Top' permeated the entire former opposition. At its simplest it would be perceived as a fight between the old intellectual dissident opposition, fighting under Mazowiecki's banner, and the new breed of populist Walesa supporters.

Though many would disagree with Wiatr's interpretation, his view that Walesa is dangerous when he's excluded from the main stage is an opinion voiced in many quarters, even by admirers. Wiatr doesn't hold the view that the 'War at the Top' was purely the product of Lech

Walesa's ambitions: 'He [Walesa] sensed that Solidarity wasn't cohesive and he exploited the divisions. Why was it so easily split? Why was it so bitter if it was just a case of rivalry between Walesa and Mazowiecki? There was a big force behind Walesa – what you might call the third echelon of power who were rebelling against the great power barons. It's a common historical phenomenon that there is a high degree of resentment against the main leaders taking all the cream of victory. That combined with a huge ideological diversity and the strong personality of the elders led to the split. Remember that Solidarity grew rapidly from a small group of seventies' dissidents into a mass movement in the eighties. That had its cost. The KOR and Free Trades Union people were just a few hundred people at most. Large numbers were recruited who were never part of the inner power broking nucleus. That set the scenario for future conflict. Martial law and the underground period suppressed that conflict but sooner or later it had to emerge.'

While the potential for fragmentation might have been obvious to those looking at Solidarity from the outside, there were many inside the movement who shared Jan Litynski's hopes of cohesion. 'We didn't expect that degree of fragmentation,' he says. 'We hoped to keep Solidarity together. Now I can see that we were naive. Our idea was that political activity would come out of the social movement. We didn't expect the depth of the split. Judging by what actually happened, you can see that the support for our vision of a liberal democratic system is much smaller than we anticipated. It's a minority political view. What we underestimated was the scale of the changes taken place. The problem was that Solidarity wasn't easily changeable. The people in positions of power within the union stopped progress. It wasn't just the "War at the Top". There were political splits everywhere all over the country. When there was a common aim of defeating communism things were simple. It was when we had to restructure the system that the problems arose. It wasn't long before there were big differences on how to build the new Poland. In reality those divisions were there all along. They were there in the Solidarity of 1981, and with different people involved, the divisions were there in the various movements in the seventies. And it wasn't just a left versus right thing either.'

Jacek Majiarski, a member of the Centrum Alliance, agrees that the divisions were there from the beginning: 'The divisions were there but were hidden. There were left-wing revisionists, Nationalists and

Catholics. It wasn't important. The divisions were secondary then. People now say that Solidarity has been defeated (in the September '93 election) because of the split. I think the opposite. Solidarity was splitting because it was defeated. Solidarity was unable to fulfil the job of the transformation. As a trade union it had to protect the interests of the workers but at the same time it was part of a government that had to fight workers. Solidarity had to fight communism and then find a place for former communists within the new regime. As a result Solidarity as a concept became very unclear for ordinary people. Political parties flourished and they all sought to find their legitimacy out of Solidarity. They were all sure that the ship was going down so they eagerly started getting their own boats ready.' Majiarski opposes the view that Lech Walesa destroyed Solidarity with the 'War at the Top': 'Walesa opposed the domination of the intellectuals. He opposed the power of Mazowiecki and Geremek. He wanted to allow other voices. He simply said what was happening. He didn't start the "War at the Top". He named it. It was then that he lost his big chance. It could have been very clear. One camp of intellectuals and liberals around Mazowiecki and another traditional, nationalist group around Walesa. But Walesa seemed to prefer some sort of Polish goulash so Solidarity ended up in pieces.'

Democratic Union leader and chairman of the Sejm Committee on Foreign Policy, Bronislaw Geremek deeply regrets the consequences of the split: 'The fragmentation of Solidarity was inevitable. I had thought that in the transition period to a market economy that we needed a force which could support such a painful process. I thought that the unity of Solidarity would ensure some measure of confidence and support. In '89 and '90 I felt that we should preserve unity so that we could build political pluralism around concrete programmes for the future rather than around groups that were the continuation of the old historical parties. But I wasn't successful and now it looks like the fragmentation was always inevitable.'

Professor Wnuk-Lipinski credits Lech Walesa with a deeper understanding of the dynamic of what would have happened had Solidarity remained at full strength after the communist collapse: 'From the very beginning, Solidarity was in a paradoxical situation. On the one hand, a new democratic order was its main goal and on the other hand it supported the introduction of a market economy. But had Solidarity not been manipulated by the politicians the transition to a market economy

would have been stopped or impeded because the union would have had
to support the workers who after all would be the first victims of the
fiscal changes. So Walesa decided not to restore Solidarity to its full
strength in the autumn of 1989 because it would have stopped the economic changes he was striving for. As regards the "War at the Top", I
think it is far too simple just to say that it was Walesa's lust for power.'

But not everyone is as dispassionate as Professor Lipinski. Jan
Litynski is adamant: 'Of course I blame Walesa. What's obvious to me
is that when he announced that there was a split, then a split took
place.' Solidarity's former press spokesman, Janusz Onyskiewicz, is also
critical of Walesa's role in the affair: 'I do blame him absolutely. My
view, which many others shared, was that we should have kept a degree
of cohesion to get through the complex political and economic changes,
to get through the most difficult period of the transition. I think that
splitting Solidarity was to Walesa's advantage to a certain degree. In a
fragmented situation one can seek the position of ultimate arbiter, the
moderator role. But with one unified political movement, a leader
can be a hostage to it. His announcement of the "War at the Top" was
a mixture of his own and the nation's interest. He wanted a pluralist
situation, but he wanted to speed it up too much. But Walesa played
the game too long. Now he has no solid base of his own, the political
scene is excessively fragmented. He has been left with no firm base of
support.'

Talking to Janusz Onyskiewicz one is reminded that the bitterness
of the split did not just damage political relationships. A whole web of
friendships were shattered during what should have been a year of
victory. Onyskiewicz says, 'I do regret what has happened. Everyone
who was in Solidarity regrets it now that it is gone. In fact I think
there is a tremendous nostalgia for times which were much happier in a
way. It is painful to learn to take beatings from people who you fought
alongside in the past. I always hoped that some things wouldn't be
questioned, like a person's good intention and commitment. I hoped
the debate would be hot but fair. I hoped our colleagues would treat us
as opponents in political debate but not as enemies. The trouble is very
often that if you look at the Polish political scene now the fight
between the former factions of Solidarity is hotter than the battle with
the former communists.' Janusz Onyskiewicz echoes Jerzy Wiatr's
comments when he acknowledges the narrow base of the political elite
which Solidarity spawned: 'The split was on personal lines, not on

matters of policy. The main problem, and this view was shared by the people I was close to, was that the political elites that emerged from Solidarity were far too narrow to run the country. It didn't incorporate all the people with political talent and ambition. In the first Mazowiecki government, after the division of positions in the parliament and the new political structures, we found that we hadn't enough people while others were left out. Then people that we considered outsiders began to question the leadership – and that wasn't well handled. They were seen as trying to destroy things and so that created the initial critical mass of bitterness.'

If Lech Walesa was trying to achieve a degree of pluralism, as he claims, the reality is that while there were dozens of political parties, up to thirty of them with seats in the Sejm prior to September '93, they were predominantly personality-based and often lacked a clearly defined political programme. Janusz Onyszkiewicz was obviously saddened, when I first talked to him just before the files scandal broke, about the state of the Polish political scene: 'It is true that there is a lack of philosophy in the parties. What divides us is not our views on the future but our views on the past. And not just our views on the past but our roles in the past. I don't want to go into the *anciens combattants* syndrome and talk about whether people joined the movement [anti-communist activity] at five minutes before midnight or five minutes after. But many of those people are dangerous because they are trying to undermine a certain ethos. Those who came late to the anti-communist side are trying to diminish the role of those who came earlier. They are saying all sorts of things. They are making hilarious accusations such as accusing people of collaboration. We might even have a Stasi phenomenon. It's horrifying. It's so unpleasant.'

Professor Lipinski argues that the 'mud-slinging' has been worsened by the fact that all four post-communist governments emanated from the same root: 'Normal politics will only start when real politics starts. When they stop sitting on the same branch and when a politician's credentials cease to be based on his or her underground activity. Then one government condemning the actions of the previous one will be normal. It won't be so personal. It's part of the communist legacy. Politicians don't come and go in Poland, they're denounced – just like in Communist times'.

Having admitted that he was perhaps naïve to have hoped that Solidarity would not split following the communist collapse, Bronislaw

Geremek was concerned about the detrimental effect that the perceived poor performance of the new democratic institutions could have on the Polish electorate. In the spring of 1992 he argued that people needed to be shown not only a clear image of pluralism but an understanding that 'the system of political parties is the very condition of the existence of the democratic order. The question is – what kind of parties we should try to build? They must be orientated towards the future. If not, the young generation will turn its back on politics and parties. The high level of abstention was a very important and dangerous sign at the last election. Now, in parliament, there are many small groups, but six basic parties. Of course they can try and build alliances or they can continue to fight. The real question is what kind of system will they build? We have a choice between the Anglo-Saxon tradition of pragmatic parties or the Continental model which is ideologically based. Right now we don't know what Poland will choose.' A little over a year later Geremek's concern that the young would turn away and that people would tire of seemingly endless political struggles was proven to be justified as the Polish electorate voted somewhat nostalgically for security and the promise of better times.

Analysing the political scene prior to the post-communist election victory, Geremek argues that there were really only two basic lines of division, even though there were dozens of parties: 'Firstly there were the fundamentalists who displayed an ideological aggression on issues like abortion and religious education. The second tendency was the populist one who used social demagogy against the forces who favoured a pragmatic reform oriented progamme. During one of the debates on the budget in early 1992, I remember that one could see that four groups were working together. The ex-communists, the trade union Solidarity, the nationalistic KPN and the Peasants Party. Such a coalition was directed against the reform process and was based on populist slogans. Looking at the situation in parliament in that period it sometimes seemed that short term-political alliances were more important than the most important issue of all – the economy.'

This tendency towards short-term alliances and campaigns based on personal emotions and the settling of old scores has dominated the political scene since 1989. Many observers would resist commenting on the phenomenon, fearing that they might be accused of reducing the political scene to some stereotype version of Polish life in which Poles are often portrayed as romantics, incapable of efficient and systematic political activity. But of course there are perfectly logical reasons why Poland's new political elites had enormous difficulties exercising power after the fall. Firstly there is the obvious problem of transforming conspirators into legislators. The fact that the present political class emerged out of the counter-elite of communist times has meant that they evolved not to govern but to fight, undermine and weaken the status quo. Even in conditions of freedom the basic instict of these *ancien combattants* is to function in a semi-conspiratorial way. Jeffrey Sachs, the guru of Eastern European economists, once commented that Poles had so much energy and that most of it was spent on destruction. The effect of the underground, the years of conspiratorial meetings and political activity, which was based on the antithesis of consensus, has meant that few politicians emerging from this class have any knowledge of political behaviour, language or norms. It is therefore understandable that the tendency to adhere to the rhetoric of the freedom fighter leaves these politicians in a time-warp where they talk about the ideals of the family, morality, religion and the nation, when the country is crying out for dynamic economic and political models.

It goes without saying that the communist period did not favour the development of a class of statesmen, leaders or efficent bureaucrats. However, many intellectuals, artists and writers who remained aloof from the commuist regime were key players in the anti-communist activity. Many of those who stepped forward to fill the poltical vacuum had also emerged from this group. Again it is obvious that academics, like conspirators, are not necessarily the stuff of the cut and thrust of politics. In short then, as Bronislaw Geremek remarked, the time of the *anciens combattants* is over. The question is whether they know it and whether they will step aside or learn to operate within a democracy.

Jaroslaw Kaczynski leads the Centrum Alliance, the onetime mouth-piece for Walesa's 'acceleration' campaign and the vehicle of his successful bid for the presidency. Kaczynski was well rewarded for his loyalty and was given the job of heading Walesa's chancellery. He and his brother Lech were two of the new President's closest confidantes. They had played Walesa's hand during the 'War at the Top'. When the brothers fell out with the President, the Centrum Alliance did an about-face and metamorphosed as a virulently anti-Walesa party. Jaroslaw Kaczynski appeared to spend much of 1992 and early 1993 writing and talking about the alleged KGB status of Mieczyslaw

Wachowski, Walesa's former driver, who now heads Walesa's chancellery. Looking at the vehemence of Kaczynski's rhetoric and the sheer hatred of his attacks many observers wondered what it all had to do with governing Poland. This view was apparently shared by the public who when given the opportunity at the September '93 election failed to give the party the five per cent it required in order to get into the Sejm.

Kaczynski's rhetoric was firmly based in the politics of the counter-elite. A key player in the calls for greater decommunization, most of his speeches and interviews are peppered with references to the 'Reds': 'We have to destroy the old structures. The "Reds" are getting rich while in some places sixty per cent of the villages are unemployed. Social unrest is possible, even unavoidable.' He accused Lech Walesa, the KPN and the ZChN of utilizing social unrest for their own ends. The man who led the anti-Walesa march on the Belweder in January '93 denies, that he or his party would engage in whipping up public emotions': 'Walesa would like to use social dissatisfaction in order to remove certain elites from power. He wants to concentrate power in his own hands. It's more difficult for him now because he's not as popular. But he's good at getting support when he sees a chance. That's why I see his behaviour as something dangerous.' Kaczynski is typical of the breed of post-communist politician's whose sights are firmly fixed in past controversies and battles. Like so many others it is very easy to discover what Kaczynski is against but very difficult to ascertain what political philosophy, economic strategy or plan of action he supports.

It is perhaps significant that one of the first groups to organize themselves following the legalization of political activity after the Round Table was the Christian National Union (ZChN). Having played a pivotal role in opposing totalitarianism, the Catholic Church was unlikely to miss the opportunity to put its stamp on the new order. With 61 deputies in the Sejm, ZChN was the third largest caucus following the October 1991 election. Party leader Wieslaw Chrzanowski became Speaker of the Sejm while another leading light Antoni Maciarewicz became Interior Minister. Maciarewicz was responsible for the decision to reveal the names of alleged communist collaborators. Those who formed the ZChN were very much opposed to the liberal and secular end of Solidarity. 'We were opposed', Wieslaw Chrizanowski recalls, 'to the leftist thinking of those who said that the period of parties was over. They wanted a great social movement', and the right-wing faction disagreed with that approach. He claims that 'it was necessary to create new structures but it wouldn't have been rational to re-establish the former historical parties. After forty-five years we thought it wouldn't work to continue the old divisions. We wanted to rely on tradition, but only some of them. We wanted the traditions that were characteristic of Poland. We looked to the national democratic, Christian democratic and Christian trends in the peasants' movements and then we looked at some national trends such as Pilsudski.'

Conversation with Chrzanowski is peppered with references to Christian culture: 'The fulfilment of humanity is not possible without culture. Our culture has this very strong Christian element. One cannot forget that we are Christian for over a thousand years. I underline it because our nationalism is different from pagan nationalism. That kind of nationalism becomes fascism. Our concept of nationalism is based on the social teachings of the Church as developed by our former Primate, Cardinal Wyszynski and by Pope John Paul II. For us the nation is the nation of families.' ZChN favoured proposals to have the concept of the separation of Church and state removed in any future constitution: 'The Polish republic, as a social and political community of the Catholic Polish nation, should be described in the Constitution as a Christian state which accepts God as the master of creation, participates in acts of worshipping God, and respects the citizens' Catholic conscience.'[2]

Wieslaw Chrzanowski is very pronounced in both his politeness and speech. His missives are delivered in the studied fashion reserved by clerics anxious to emphasise solemnity and elaborate seriousness. A tall thin man, he often wears clerical grey. His movements are slow and deliberate. Chrzanowski did not bear the burden of his high office lightly. It was rumoured that at one time his greatest concern was the fact that, as the leader of Poland's Catholic party, he had not been granted a private audience with the Pope. What concerns Chrzanowski and the ZChN more than anything else is the moral fibre of the country. They are perceived as being involved in a crusade against liberal or left-wing influences which they see as alien to Poland's Christian national character. ZChN has been to the forefront in making sure that, what it calls 'Christian values' dominate Polish life. The party put the criminalization of abortion and the reintroduction of religious education in schools at the top of the political agenda. Unfortunately for Mr Chrzanowski, astute political observers in the Catholic Church anticipated the left-wing landslide in September '93 and moved to distance itself from the ZChN. That, combined with public disquiet at the level of state invasion into the area of private morality, were two of the factors which ensured that the ZChN and its coalition partner, the Conservative Party, did not reach the magic threshold for seats in the Sejm.

While the voices of parties espousing populist, xenophobic, national-ist and Catholic policies have on occasion appeared to dominate Polish politics in recent years, it must also be remembered that the second post-communist government was led by the Liberal, Jan Krzysztof Bielecki.[3] Bielecki is very much the European; his manner is cool, analytical and somewhat detached. He describes Poland's huge trans-formation process as a 'live experiment'. Though pragmatism is a very important word in Bielecki's vocabulary, he also failed the five per cent threshold test because he could not convince his party to coalesce with the Democratic Union in the run-up to the election. Looking at the other political parties, Bielecki was only concerned about whether he could do business with them; whether or not cooperating with them would further the democratic and economic transformation process: 'We're a pragmatic, market-orientated party with a good sense of the interests of private property. For us, freedom and responsibility are important values. We're not interested in playing around with the Church in re-shaping Poland. We believe in the separation of Church and state. Of course, the Church has a role but not in the arena of politics.'

Bielecki regarded much of the political activity, including the long campaign before the first fully free parliamentary elections at the end of 1991 as having delayed more important business: 'We have to be pragmatic. The essence of good political activity at the moment is to be able to respond quickly to the changing economic situation. We have to be able to improve the programme of economic reform and withdraw from plans if they are seen to have been a mistake. It's impossible to predict two years ahead in an environment of constant change. And of course the people are afraid. They are afraid of the future. There are many psychological problems with so many structures having to be changed. People want the easy option. It's normal for people to want to believe in miracles. All the research shows that Poles are short-term orientated. Opinion polls show that there is a negative attitude to foreign investment. It's not rational. People want to travel; they want

Western style and standards but they're afraid of Western companies and investors. But these attitudes are more connected with the threats that people are being told about than with anything else. This xenophobia and nationalism is connected with poverty. People like Moczulski [leader of the nationalist KPN] talk of printing money to solve Poland's problems. The KPN want power, so they tell people that it's simple – just print money. But it's not only dishonest: it's stupid because it only works in the short term. And the people will hate you afterwards for such policies. One of the biggest problems Poland faces is how to get a proper balance between the accountability of parliament and a strong executive. So much time has been wasted. Some Poles think that our new democracy is good but weak. There's more crime and more corruption now. People say it was easier to fight under communism. That's true because if someone was suspected, he was arrested. You looked for the evidence afterwards. People dream of an authoritarian solution. And because we don't have a strong executive, there's the temptation of the strong-man idea. That's why Walesa says that we need strong decisive leaders. But one guy cannot manage forty million Poles.'

Bielecki is not a man without passion, but he refuses to see issues such as decommunization in anything but rational terms. He is highly critical of those politicians, who from his perspective, exploit xenophobic instincts and whip up moral hysteria for their own political ends: 'Decommunization is a delicate problem. But it is not a question of trials but a question of telling the truth about the past. It is sufficient for me to say how it was. It's necessary for Moczulski to talk of impeachment [of Jaruzelski] in order to get power.'

When issues such as decommunization and what might be termed the moral and social agenda are out of the way, the omens look good for the rationalization of Poland's political parties. But as things stand, with the majority of politicians emanating from the one root, sharing old hatreds and vendettas, the development of issue and programme based parties depends largely on whether Solidarity's *anciens combattants* will be prepared to hang up their holsters and let the new generation try its hand.

1 Lech Walesa and the author, Jacqueline Hayden, at Solidarity's headquarters in Gdansk. The photograph was taken in April 1981.

2 Jan Litynski campaigning during the June 1989 election in his constituency in Walbrzych.

3　Janusz Onyszkiewicz, Solidarity's former press spokesman. While Lech Walesa was the face of Solidarity, Onyszkiewicz was its voice. He was the first civilian Minister of Defence in the Warsaw Pact.

4 Bogdan Lis was once close to Lech Walesa in the early days of Solidarity but he
   refused a position in Walesa's chancellery because of the calibre of the President's
   advisers.

5 Alina Pienkowska stopped Walesa prematurely ending the Gdansk Shipyard strike
   in August 1980. In the September 1993 election, Alina did not run for the Senate,
   where she had held a seat since 1989. She feels that there are better and more
   productive ways to use her talents.

6   The Gdansk Shipyard strike initially focused on the sacking of Anna
Walentynowicz from her job. Now she believes that her former friend Lech Walesa
was a spy and agent for the Polish secret police. She is convinced that the 'Party'
has not relinquished power in Poland.

7 Andrzej and Joanna Gwiazda were members of the Gdansk strike committee. Andrzej became a prominent member of the Independent Trade Union and was vocal in his opposition to Lech Walesa's leadership in the early eighties. Both are now disillusioned with Solidarity and believe that Poland is ruled by a KGB–CIA conspiracy.

8 Jan and Krystyna Litynska were regularly jailed because of Jan's participation in the dissident opposition. Their flat was a well-known haven for foreign journalists on the look-out for information and analysis. Both were arrested on the night that martial law was introduced in December 1981. He subsequently went underground. Jan is now an M.P. and member of the liberal Democratic Union. Krystyna works as a psychologist.

9 Krystyna Litynska has no nostalgia for the heady days of dissident opposition. She wants to get on with living a 'normal' life in the 'new Poland'.

10 Regina Litynska was once an ardent Communist. Eventually the conflict between the ideal and reality became too much for her. In 1980 she helped her son, the dissident Jan Litynski, type the underground newspaper that he edited. Now she says she is confused by the poverty and problems Poland has faced since the beginning of the democratic transformation.

MORE CIRCUS THAN BREAD

Paranoia is an inevitable by-product of totalitarianism. It leaves scars of deep and profound suspicion in the minds of those whose only concept of political activity is conspiratorial. In Poland the problem was compounded by the fact that totalitiarianism was negotiated out of existence. There was no big *putsch*, no bloodshed and no violence. There was no day of victory or day of reckoning. As a result many people believe that nothing has really changed. Some like Anna Walentynvowicz and Andrzej and Joanna Gwiazda believed that even under Solidarity governments communism had simply changed its face: the monolith remained. Now, with former communists once again in power, they believe that Poland is the victim of the ultimate conspiracy. Others argue that the very process of negotiation was in itself a contamination of the anti-communist political elite and that the Round Table deal left the social and economic system in communist control. Then there are those who, while accepting the validity of the Round Table process, argue that rigorous decommunization is necessary in order to wrest institutional and financial power out of communist hands.

Decommunization is a complex issue involving questions of justice, punishment, financial and political redress, as well as the emotional and symbolic needs of post-communist society. It has become the benchmark of difference between liberal, middle-class and secular orientated parties and those espousing more populist, nationalist and traditional politics. For the liberals, legitimate decommunization has been contaminated by those who they perceive as using it as a diversion to hide political redundancy in the face of the huge task of the political and structural transformation of Poland. The populist and more traditional parties, on the other hand, charge their opponents with, at best being tainted by contact with the communists at the Round Table, and at worst, with having been communist agents in the past.

It is certainly arguable that while the post-Solidarity political parties have been tearing themselves asunder, knee deep in security files, alleging that even Lech Walesa had been a communist agent, that the new post-communist business elites are getting on with the job of feathering their nests.

The first two governments formed after the 1989 elections steadfastly refused to have anything to do with the opening up of the old regime's security files. Krzysztof Kozlowski, a member of the Mazowiecki cabinet and the first civilian Interior Minister since the War, argued that the SB (communist secret police) files had more than likely been doctored by the communists after they lost power: as a result the archives probably contained only those files which were designed to compromise the party's opponents, and that many were false and simply represented an unreliable account of who was or was not an agent or collaborator. This view was supported by Henryk Majewski, Kozlowski's successor as Interior Minister in Jan Krzysztof Bielecki's Liberal government. This consensus was shattered with the formation of the third post-communist government of Jan Olszewski. Formed largely with the support of the populist Centrum Alliance and the Christian National Union, this government from the outset made it clear that it would initiate a purge in all branches of the public service. Gone was the conciliatory and pragmatic compromise approach of Mazowiecki and Bielecki and in were the politics of vandetta and retribution.

In early 1992 Poland's new Interior Minister, Antoni Macierewicz, told a press conference that the new government intended to vet the past of public officials. He initially suggested that the vetting would include the last fifteen years of communist rule: 'All politicians, parliamentarians, and high-level state and justice officials who once worked with the former security service, the SB, should be allowed to withdraw from public life. However, if they do not do so of their own free will, they must realize that any information compromising them will be presented to the public.'[1] Macierewicz also called for the establishment of a special institution to vet all candidates for high level state jobs. The new minister set about his task eagerly. As spring drew to a close he had already presented two anti-communist bills to the Sejm, while some seventeen recruits were labouring away at the new Studies Bureau examining its files and formulating lists of possible SB agents. The first bill provided for a special committee, attached to the prime minister's office, which would investigate the pasts of candidates for positions with access to state secrets. A second bill dealt with high executive, judicial and legislative positions. It gave anyone formerly connected with the secret police between three to six months to resign from their post. Any individual failing to resign would have his past revealed by the

Ministry of Internal Affairs. Another ministry bill proposed that all officials and collaborators of the old regime be temporarily barred from virtually all public offices. Potential candidates for such positions would have to submit an honesty certificate, issued by the Internal Affairs ministry declaring that they had never been a party secretary, employee or collaborator.

While in principle it was clear to most politicians that some legislation was necessary, it was also abundantly clear that such vetting procedures could be used against political opponents. The people who were most obviously vulnerable were the generation of dissidents who had moved from an early involvement with communism to participation in anti-communist activities in the late sixties and early seventies. Jan Litynski knew that there were huge dangers involved for many politicians, simply on the basis of the old maxim that there is no smoke without fire. He argued that those accused of collaboration would be discredited no matter how hard they fought off the accusations. He feared that Macierewicz's move would spark a nationwide response, similar to those in the former East Germany and Czechoslovakia.

Macierewicz had no such fears: 'There is no chance of a successful forgery which would show that someone never involved with the SB was a collaborator. We can uncover and verify every attempt at doctoring dossiers – and there were such cases. Because the system is so complex, and because it has been internally verified by simultaneous and overlapping checking, mistakes in this area can be ruled out.'[2] Many politicians, including Prime Minister Mazowiecki's Internal Affairs Minister, Kryzsztof Kozlowski, simply rejected Macierewicz's assertion. Kozlowski claimed that he was sure that up to eighty per cent of the information contained in the files had been fabricated. It was suggested by others that at best Macierewicz was embarrassingly naive.

No doubt the whole affair would have trundled on for much longer, impeding the execution of more important matters both in and out of the Sejm, had it not been for the intervention of Janusz Korwin-Mikke, a deputy from the small right-wing party, Union for Realpolitik. On 28 May 1992 a nearly empty Sejm chamber passed a motion, proposed by Korwin-Mikke, obliging the Minister for Internal Affairs to present the Sejm with 'full information' including the names of former secret service agents. The resolution also demanded that a list of collaborating deputies, Senators and civil servants be presented before 6 June. As Jan Litynski pointed out rather tersely at the time, 'It's difficult to ignore the fact that the resolution is passed at a time when the future of the Olszewski government is in doubt. Democratic Union circles were not penetrated as deeply by the secret service. So if Macierewicz's lists contain the names of many of our politicians, it will be proof that the Ministry of Internal Affairs has been dabbling in a little forgery.'

Almost immediately there were suspicions that the 28 May resolution was not unconnected with moves to save the beleaguered Olszewski government which had failed to pass a budget and was facing a no-confidence motion tabled for 5 June.

Following the resolution in the Sejm, Macierewicz acted swiftly. By 3 June his list of alleged collaborators was drawn up and brought by guarded convoy to the chairman of parliamentary caucuses and to the Speakers of the Sejm and the Senate. The sealed lists contained 64 names, dates of birth, pseudonyms and in some cases the signatures of those who were named. An introductory letter explained that the document was not a list of agents but extracts from Ministry of Internal Affairs documents concerning the files. A second list shown only to the Speakers, the former Prime Minister and the President – four people – was rumoured to indirectly accuse Lech Walesa himself, albeit without naming him.

The manoeuvre created instant chaos. Rumour was followed by counter rumour as to who had been named. President Walesa issued a statement saying that the screening operation was being conducted on the basis of a number of forged documents: 'The procedure being followed is illegal. It permits political blackmail and completely destabilizes state structures and the political parties.'[3] Within hours Walesa sent a note to the Sejm calling for the immediate dismissal of Prime Minister Olszewski. In the early hours of the following morning, Walesa watched from his seat in parliament as his wish was carried out.

The fact that the names were not published probably made things worse. Some deputies who did have access to the lists were stunned to see that individuals who had merely been approached to collaborate were mentioned in the documents alongside people who it was alleged were actual collaborators. Veteran dissident and Democratic Union MP Jacek Kuron reacted angrily: 'This is simply a pack of lies. The list contains names which I simply do not believe, and I have lots of evidence in support of these people. Macierewicz has decided to ruin the country, because apparently he is sick.'[4]

As the day wore on and pro-government politicians attempted to postpone the vote on the dismissal of the Olszewski government, deputies were further excited by the news that the prime minister was to address the nation. In his speech, which went out on radio and television, Olszewski said: 'The people should know that it is no accident that now that we can finally break free from the bonds of communism, a surprise motion to dismiss the government has been put forward.'

Rumours then began circulating both in and outside the Sejm that Macierewicz had put the Vistula military units (which were under his direct control) on combat alert. Many believed that an unconstitutional attempt was about to be made to prevent the dissolution of the cabinet. In that context of heightened tension, the Sejm decided by a decisive majority to continue the debate and vote on the dismissal of the government that night. Within minutes of the commencement of the debate, the Sejm was to hear the first of what were to be many allegations of illegal and unconstitutional behaviour by Antoni Macierewicz. Adam Slomka, speaking for the Confederation for an Independent Poland (KPN) rose quickly to tell the Sejm that, during negotiations on KPN's possible participation in the coalition, Macierewicz had attempted to blackmail the party by saying that he had evidence that party leader, Leszek Moczulski, had been involved with the communist security service. That was but the opening shot of what was to very quickly become a morass of allegation, innuendo and political opportunism. Most independent observers quickly concluded that the security files issue, which should have been afforded serious consideration and debate, was in fact being used by elements of the Olszewski government to discredit and destabilize the opposition.

This proposition gained credibility when it became clear that Lech Walesa himself was becoming the focus of a sustained campaign of leaked information concerning an agent named 'Bolek'. In a special announcement a few days after the Macierewicz's lists were circulated, President Walesa stated that he had 'signed three or four documents' in December 1970 (during the strikes and unrest in Gdansk) during his interrogation by the SB: 'I would probably have signed anything except my consent to betray God and my fatherland, just to get out and continue the fight. They never broke me and I never betrayed my beliefs and friends.'[5] There was nothing new in what Walesa had to say at that point. He was merely reiterating what he had often said publicly and had written in his autobiography.[6]

And so in an atmosphere of both menace and farce, of refutation and counter charge, the Sejm voted to appoint a special commission to investigate how the 28 May resolution allowing for the revelation of names had been implemented. As the commission set about its inquiries Walesa's name was being openly associated with that of agent 'Bolek'. *Nowy Swiat*, a newspaper which was at that time associated with politicians connected to the Olszewski government, published details from the 'Bolek' file, and while not directly naming Walesa, gave an unmistakable hint as to 'Bolek's' identity.

The relevant documents stamped: 'Secret – Of Special Importance' were kept by Piotr Naimski, the former head of the State Protection Office (OUP), in his personal safe. Naimski went on Polish television in mid-June and further fuelled speculation that 'Bolek' was in fact Walesa. He claimed that the documents contained in his safe were of unprecedented importance to the work of the Sejm commission investigating the affair and said that the safe 'contains unique archive documents of immense importance concerning the President of the Republic of Poland'. He indicated that the material was from both the OUP central archive and the local archive in Gdansk. With no firm details coming from the investigating commission the media had to base its specualtion on leaks which were very thick on the ground. Various leaks suggested that the documents included summaries of Walesa's interrogation in the period between 1970 and 1973 while others were said to relate to information from informers as well as reports from the security service officers responsible for handling Walesa. Then the man behind all the allegations told the investigating commission that he had been blackmailed while he was preparing for the release of the files. Initially Macierewicz did not openly name Walesa, saying that he needed first to consult with his former prime minister. A few days later, however, Macierewicz unequivocally pointed the finger at Walesa, at last removing the veil and placing the allegations firmly in the public domain. Macierewicz also used the opportunity to name Walesa's controversial chief of staff, Mieczyslaw Wachowski, as one of the alleged blackmailers. Rarely out of camera shot when Walesa was in the frame, Wachowski had been Walesa's driver for many years before his unusual promotion. It was common gossip both in and out of political circles that Wachowski was everything from a KGB agent to a CIA minder. His reputation was not enhanced by articles in *Gazetta Wyborcza* and in magazines such as *Nie* (edited by Jerzy Urban,

the former Communist Party press spokesman) which claimed that
Wachowski extorted money from individuals with the promise that the
President would be well disposed toward them in return.

At a news conference following Macierewicz's statement Walesa was
still trying to laugh the whole thing off. But it was not long before the
laughing stopped. Facing the fourth Congress of the Solidarity trade
union Walesa felt obliged to provide delegates with proof that he was
no traitor. Delegates were given four documents which Walesa claimed
proved his innocence. One, a statement by an anonymous employee of
the Interior Ministry's chief inspectorate alleged that the 'Walesa Files'
had been faked. According to this source, material designed to incrim-
inate Walesa had been collected by a Solidarity regional chapter
chairman, Eligiusz Naszkowski. It was further alleged that Naszkowski
was a SB agent. The rest of Walesa's proof largely relied on previously
published denials including fragments of his book – *Droga nadzei* (Path
of Hope) – and his repeated statement that he had never signed any
document that betrayed either his country, cause or friends. The Solidarity Congress was not a good experience for Walesa, who appeared
rattled and out of sorts. Many delegates were critical of Walesa for
harping so much on the 'files' issue. However, that reservation didn't
prevent the Congress indulging in its own 'vetting fever' with lists of
alleged union collaborators being circulated amongst delegates.

On 14 June, Walesa hit back. The Polish public were given the code-
name of yet another alleged agent. The President's office announced
that it would disclose the identity of agent Zapalniczka (Lighter).
According to the Belweder, Zapalniczka was responsible for the compilation of materials designed to discredit former Solidarity leaders.
Meanwhile, the coup scenario was gaining further credibility as leaks
multiplied out of the Ciemniewski Commission which was examining
the affair.[7] On 19 June Walesa went on Radio Zet claiming that a plan
had been hatched to blackmail the President as well as the Sejm and
Senate Speakers: 'With such a situation in hand, it would have become
necessary to elect a new temporary President throught the Sejm and
the Senate. The best situation would have been to have Olszewski as
President. Macierewicz would have made the best Defence Minister,
Wlodarczyk the best Sejm Speaker, and Najder the best Foreign
Minister.'[8] There were of course lots of other scenarios and even
more interpretations of the incredible behaviour of some elements of
the Olszewski goverment during the 'files' affair. Leaks from the

commission showed that dossiers 'doctored' by the communists to discredit members of the opposition were among those included in the documents released by Macierewicz. Even the names of men such as Wieslaw Chrzanowski, the Christian National Union leader and Sejm Speaker, had been included without any attempt to check whether the charges could be proven. This, it would later turn out, had been the way Macierewicz had conducted his screening.

On the same day that Walesa went on television to publicly acknowledge the existence of the coup scenario, Poland's Constitutional Tribunal decided that the Sejm's 28 May resolution which initiated the screening process had been illegal, unconstitutional and contrary to Sejm procedures. It also obligated the Sejm to repeal the resolution. Unfortunately for those who had been wrongly named, the decision was too late. During the celebration of Corpus Christi in Warsaw, the Polish Primate, Cardinal Josef Glemp, recalled the words of St. Paul in his letter to the Galatians: 'A sentence is hanging over him who sows discord among you, whoever he might be . . . And if you bite and devour one another, mind that you don't eat each other.' The Primate warned that justice and love had been violated in the furore over the files and offered those who had been slandered and wrongly accused a Christian apology. President Walesa was one of the participants in the ceremony who heard the Cardinal assure the faithful: 'We will come out from the turmoil cleansed.'

The 'Bolek' and security files affair highlighted, as if it needed highlighting, the distrust and fragmentation of Poland's post-communist political elites. The Ciemniewski Commission, established to examine how Macierewicz implemented the 28 May resolution was very quickly the centre of intrigue. It was even suggested that its members included former security agents. There were disagreements about how the 'Bolek' dossier should be handled and who should have access to it. The controversy was made even more muddled by the leaking of conflicting testimonies from officials and witnesses. Individuals who might have been expected to support the screening process initiated by the Ministry of Internal Affairs failed to do so. Piotr Wojciechowski was, as director of the newly established Studies Office, directly responsible to Macierewicz. He acknowledged that the 'Bolek' file had been forged. Earlier Krzysztof Koslowski, a former Interior Minister and supporter of Tadeusz Mazowiecki during the presidential race, suggested that the material had been planted in order to discredit Walesa during the presidential campaign. He claimed that the 'Bolek' files had been forged at a time when Walesa's role in the democratic opposition was growing, especially after his election as Solidarity chairman.

The Ciemniewski Commission took over a month to reach a conclusion. It was not unanimous. By the time the report was published the Sejm had finally formed a new coalition government headed by the Democratic Union's Hanna Suchocka, the country was facing a serious round of strikes and another divisive issue, abortion, was about to hit the headlines. Olszewski and Macierewicz were disgraced in the eyes of many. Macierewicz had been expelled from his party, the Christian National Union, just before the Constitutional Tribunal found the 28 May resolution illegal, while Olszewski had established a new party, the Movement for the Republic. The Commission placed full responsibility for the whole affair on the shoulders of Macierewicz and Olszewski. It concluded that those responsible for the vetting initiative had planned to hold onto power illegally: 'After making public the dishoneslty drawn up lists, the idea was to disgrace the state's supreme authorities, paralyze them, and subsequently have the architects of the lists take over the centres of power.'[9]

An important point well worth remembering is that both Macierewicz and Olszewski had honourable pasts as Solidarity loyalists. Jan Olszewski had been the lawyer who defended many of those activists facing charges after the Radom and Ursus strikes in 1976 and he was a man long associated with the defence of the anti-communist opposition. Macierewicz had been a founder member of KOR, a former adviser to Walesa, and was interned after martial law. But, like Anna Walentynowicz and the Gwiazdas, he too succumbed to the belief that the battle had not been won. For Macierewicz, the Solidarity take-over was in fact 'a controlled handing over of the facade, so as to retain real power over the country.'[10] If Macierewicz really believes that, then his behaviour probably makes sense!

Perhaps the most disastrous side-effect of the files affair was the fact that the issue of legitimate vetting became compromised. The defensible notion of protecting society from people whose former allegiances might compromise their support for post-communist Poland has been destroyed in a web of false accusation where informer and innocent were deliberately bungled up together. Decommunization is at the best of times a complex issue for any post-communist society. But, by using the security files issue in an attempt to prevent the dissolution of a government, those behind the Macierewicz move destroyed any hope there was that decommunization would not be used as a means of discrediting political opponents. The fall-out from the affair ensured that decommunization would remain a fragmenting and divisive issue; an issue which in the context of the return of former communists to government leaves many question marks over the efficacy of the Mazowiecki government's policy on decommunization.

Wiktor Osiatynski, a co-director at the Centre for the Study of Constitutionalism in Eastern Europe, argues that, 'The Polish drama is that at the time when society wanted and needed at least a symbolic sign breaking with the past, the elite which took over power could not really provide it, nor did it even feel the need to do so. It must also be remembered that at the time the police and the army were still controlled by the communists and the situation in neighbouring countries was fluid.' Osiatynski argues that the elite who negotiated the Round Table accord failed to grasp the social mood because 'the elite physically sat at the round table, made the contract and felt bound by it. Also in the course of the discussions, the opposition's resentment toward the opposite side lessened because it was given satisfaction. But the rest of society did not sit at the table and its resentment remained.' However, Professor Wnuk-Lipinski maintains that 'the rest of society' has had very little to do with calls for decommunization or demands that security files be revealed. He argues that only about ten to fifteen per cent of the population are concerned about it, though of course, that figure increases as passions are inflamed by populist political rhetoric. Speaking just before the formation of Hanna Suchocka's government in mid-1992, Professor Lipinski argued that 'The historical time for decommunization has passed, though it's not too late to throw the issue out to public opinion. The need for a scapegoat is growing. Real decommunization should have been initiated after the party collapsed. But it was not possible, because it would have consolidated the communist opposition, who it must be remembered still held contol of the military and police.' In fact the resentment that Osiatynski talks of has festered, not so much in the hearts of the people, but in the hearts of elements of the political elite who used the issue as a battering ram against political opponents.

One-time kingmaker, Jaroslaw Kaczynski, was a close confidante of Lech Walesa and head of his chancellery until they fell out. A classic *éminence grise*, Kaczynski epitomizes the populist politician. He is the leader of the Centrum Alliance, a party initially established to provide a political platform for Lech Walesa in his battle against the liberal and intellectual dominated Mazowiecki wing of Solidarity. Now utterly opposed to Walesa whom he accuses of being a communist agent, Kaczynski plays the anti-communist card as if nothing has changed in Poland since 1989. 'The media,' he says, 'paint a picture of me as a man holding a gun: the real issue of decommunization is not explained at all. We don't see it as looking for revenge or witchhunting. Look the witches were innocent. Here we're not talking about innocent people. Here the issue is not revenge but restructuring – so that we can create a just society. If we don't, we'll be like Argentina. If a lot of people continue to feel that the old structures have remained, that nothing has changed, then they will not try and change their habits or try to develop the economy. The restructuring is necessary to bring a feeling of social justice. If the old system remains, the new economics cannot develop. Look at the situation in the banking system. It's still dominated by the old structures. If you don't have contact or friends from the old system, then you won't get credit. Secondly there is the moral issue of prosecution or punishment. If you punish people for robbing a store, then why not punish for greater crimes? If, in the past fascists were punished, why not punish the communists now? If the old communists are not punished there will be a feeling of social injustice because society will know that criminals have not been prosecuted.'

Kaczynski took his crusade to the streets of Warsaw in late January 1993. Burning an effigy of Walesa decked out in Bolshevik symbols, the 5,000-strong demonstrators chanted: 'We want a president, not an agent.' Ostensibly the march on the President's headquarters was organized by the newly founded Social Protest Committee – mainly former activists of the Independent Students' Union. But the real force behind the anti-Walesa movement was an *ad hoc* rainbow group led by Kaczynski and men such as Antoni Macierewicz, former Defence Minister Jan Parys, and Jan Olszewski, the former Prime Minister. Perhaps the only issue on which this diverse group agreed was their hatred of Walesa and their obsession with outing agents. One journalist, commentating on the event, observed that the politicians were 'all marching arm in arm, as if time had stopped. It almost looked as if they were expecting a charge by the riot police about to pick them off one by one and pack them into police cars, the communist way.'[11]

Jaroslaw Kaczynski is not now prepared to accept the verdict of the people and appears to question the validity of the electoral process. He describes the SLD–PSL election victory as a counter-revolution.

For Solidarity's former press spokesman Janusz Onyszkiewicz, the decommunization bandwagon was merely a diversion from the more important issues facing Poland. As a Democratic Union MP and Minister of Defence, he saw it as endangering the progress of more important processes: 'There is a cynical tendency among some politicians to use what I'd call socio-technical tricks on the people. If you can't give them bread, give them circuses. The circus in this case is decommunization and abortion.' In simple terms, people such as Onyszkiewicz believe that time has marched on and that the settling of old scores should not be the dominant theme of post-communist political life. He opposed the vetting measures passed by the Senate in August 1992. Under the terms of that bill former communists would have been, in effect, excluded from public office for ten years. Onyszkiewicz reacted to the passing of the bill angrily: 'If vetting is introduced, I'll be left with three generals in the army – one of them a bishop. I don't intend to contribute to the liquidation of the Polish Army.' Poland's first non-communist Defence Minister was adamant that he would resign were the measures introduced.[12]

KPN leader Leszek Moczulski took an entirely different view. He regards men such as Onyszkiewicz who negotiated the Round Table deal as having made a huge blunder. While he is certainly careful in public not to imply that the anti-communist opposition who sat down at the table were collaborators, he insinuates that their opposition was not as noble or as complete as his own: 'Before 1980 there was two kinds of anti-communist opposition. One part of it thought that internal reform was possible, that communism could be made more human. The other part, the part that I belonged to, wanted to destroy the communism in this country and the Soviet bloc. The reformers found themselves in the unforeseen situation where there was no more communism to reform. Now they are lost. My side of the old opposition movement isn't happy either. They got more than they bargained for. We got much less. The changes brought about by the Round Table are not as big as we wanted. This is definitely not a fully democratic country, because we don't have enough democratic institutions as yet. The general structures of the state are the same as in the communist times. We still don't know who makes the most important decisions.

The communists still hold up positions in banking, in the state apparatus and in the press.' Moczulski sees the whole Round Table process
and the subsequent political decisions as anti-democratic and compares
it to the activities and intrigues of a royal court. He claims that Poland
is run by a mafia. His approach to decommunization is therefore hard-
line: 'Jaruzelski should definitely be.impeached. He was responsible for
many crimes. His biggest was the promulgation of Article 123, the *coup
d'état* against the Polish people. The approach of my party is that those
who acted illegally must be punished no matter what their political
convictions were. It's not good enough for the communists to argue
that they must not be punished because of their ideology at the time.
They are not to be punished because they are communists, but because
they committed crimes. This issue should be treated according to the
law and not according to ideological consideration. Certain professions
have to be cleaned up because of what society expects from them in
moral terms. Judges who made decisions not according to the law but
on the basis of instructions are not fit to be judges. Teachers who spied
and reported students to the secret police should not be allowed teach.
People who used their political power to create wealth must be punished. Mechanisms must be introduced, so that at least part of the
stolen wealth is returned. We should consider a tax on those who made
money in abnormal times. Look: some people think that we should
move away from communism in a humanitarian way. It's like cutting a
dog's tail. To cut the dog's tail all at once is not humanitarian: it's
thought better to cut it, bit by bit, like salami. But with time the dog
won't be able to bear this humanitarian approach any more.'

Father Josef Tischner feels that the exploitation of decommunization
as a political football by populist politicians is unwise: 'I'm against
decommunization. But I'm not against explaining how communism
happened. I would like future generations to understand how the
totalitarian system enters the body of a country and society. The
majority of the people didn't want it and yet communists came here
anyway. Remember it was not all done by force. The communists came
here by little compromises. And a man hardly knew it and he was in
the middle of the system. This fact has to be shown. But not in order
to accuse anybody, but just to show how it happened. Poland is in a
good situation compared to Russia where each generation has some
murders on its hands. Those who organized the revolution murdered in
the thirties; and those who murdered in the thirties were themselves

murdered in the forties. That didn't happen in Poland. Those who did murder are dead or very old. Communism ended in Poland in 1968. After that there were people with power but it had very little to do with communism. You can accuse them of financial crimes but not of communist ones.'

Father Tischner sees the Round Table accord as a continuation of the process of compromise, of positive decommunization that had been happening in Poland since the Gierek era: 'I think that demands for decommunization are immoral because many people were compromised by the arrival of communism and that in turn many communists took part in the first efforts to begin the decommunization process that led to the Round Table.'

Jan Litynski is vociferously against decommunization and rejects passionately any suggestion that the Round Table process in some way robbed Poles of their great moment of anti-communist catharsis: 'Look at Moscow and at what Boris Yeltsin is doing. Look at the bloodshed in the Russian White House. That's what happens without a Round Table. Of course it is a problem that it was not a big social movement, a big moment when the old system was abolished. But I don't believe in catharsis. They had their moment of catharsis in Czechoslovakia and it didn't help them maintain one state. It didn't help with the decommunization problem. We would never have been able to make real decommunization. You can't clean the past. You can't point the finger and say you were bad and you were okay. Who can make trials? Who prosecutes? Prosecutors from the old regime. We did try to clean the prosecutors' office but we failed. It is impossible to achieve real justice.'

GENERAL WOJCIECH JARUZELSKI

POLISH PATRIOT OR TRAITOR?

'I have been frequently asked if I regret my decision to declare martial law [on 13 December 1981]. I have made many mistakes in my life, but I do not consider this particular decision to be a mistake. I have not changed this assessment in hindsight. I would even say that the reverse is true: I am gaining more and more evidence and confirmation, including the opinions of various statesmen in both the West and East, that this move was unavoidable. What I do regret is the situation, and the process, which led to my decision' Wojciech Jaruzelski's in the introduction to his book *Stan wojenny. Dlaczego ...* (Martial Law: Why ...)[1]

'Then they [Solidarity] called the general strike for 17 December. Undoubtedly, this would have meant the confrontation they exposed in Radom. The bloodshed. The civil war. At this moment, the only alternative to martial law was to raise our arms and let ourselves, the state itself, be destroyed'[2] Mieczyslaw Rakowski.

Over a decade after its introduction the apologists of martial law still maintain that its immediate trigger was the alleged call to arms by Solidarity delegates at an emergency debate held in Radom on 3 December 1981. Three days after the meeting, secretly recorded and edited extracts of the proceedings were broadcast on Warsaw Radio. The tapes allegedly exposed the true nature of Solidarity's plans to overthrow the state. In simple terms this was the basis for the claim that martial law was justified in order to deal with the 'internal' threat to Poland's security. The other threat was of course the anticipated offer of 'fraternal assistance' from the Soviet Union or members of the Warsaw Pact, concerned that the Polish disease might spread.

The assertion by Party spokesman, both at the time and since, that the decision to introduce martial law was an unplanned direct response to the 'Radom tapes' has been proven fallacious most effectively by Timothy Garton Ash. Even Mieczyslaw Rakowski now concedes that 'the concept of martial law was prepared many months before [13 December] but that's normal.' Before Boris Yeltsin's release of the secret

Suslov Commission documents, which contradict General Jaruzelski's claim that he introduced martial law in order to prevent a Soviet intervention, opinion polls showed that the majority of Poles believed that the decision was legitimate and that the general had acted to prevent Soviet intervention. Very few, only sixteen per cent, accepted the Party's main claim at the time that it was introduced to prevent the disintegration of the state at the hands of Solidarity. However, despite the apparent acceptance of the legitimacy of the operation, a high percentage of those polled believe that the behaviour of the authorities at the time was excessively brutal.[3]

Martial law is still the focus for much debate within Poland because the claims and counterclaims relating to any attempted assessment of the legitimacy, motivation and perceived purpose of its introduction is at the heart of the wider debate about Poland's historically complicated relationship with its eastern neighbour. Central to that debate is the chasm between the 'Insurrectionists' and the 'Conciliators' – between Poles who absolutely opposed Russian invasion and domination and those who sought to achieve tolerable freedom through appeasement. Any objective critical analysis is additionally hampered because the row over how far decommunization should go is far from being settled. In a sense then the progress of the historical debate has been stymied by the demonizing of both the issue and those held responsible, most especially General Wojciech Jaruzelski.

The question as to whether General Jaruzelski is patriot or traitor puts at issue the definition of patriotism itself and highlights the complexity of the concept of loyalty as well as the huge difficulties involved in sifting through the individual's perception of his or her motivation in an historical event.

General Wojciech Jaruzelski is one of those figures whom most people recognize at a glance. A caricaturist's delight with his iron-rod back, bald head and dark glasses, he was, in the early eighties, the antithesis of the flabby octogenarians of the Soviet politburo. Always in uniform and apparently austere, there was literally an aura about Jaruzelski, no doubt partly encouraged by the fact that nobody ever saw his eyes.

When I met him in the late spring of 1992 he was working on the final draft of his book. Replacing the general's uniform was a heavy brown tweed suit, worn buttoned over a black poloneck sweater. I was not quite sure whether the glasses were different or whether it was just that, at close range, they did not look as impenetrable. I was struck immediately on entering his office at his publishing house by the fact that he was presenting an image very unlike the one I had known previously. It was very clear that he fully appreciated the fact that the rules had changed. He wanted to be liked, not just understood. His book and his willingness to be interviewed, albeit with the questions submitted in advance, was his bid to influence how history treated him.

'To be a good journalist,' he told me, 'one must be hot. To be a good politician one must be cold. But to be a good historian one must be ice cold. The issue of the introduction of martial law is not cold yet. It needs a bigger distance of time to talk about the issues without emotion. It's still too recent and is therefore a tool in current political controversies. Nevertheless I came to the conclusion that I had to write my book. I want to help society to look at this period in a proper way. I'm trying not to be prejudiced and to be objective. I'm trying to see the reasons the other side [Solidarity] had. This is not easy – and in this sense I'd like the book to serve the national understanding; to show that at the same time we were all right and all wrong. I want people to understand that it was a certain historical period; and it must be looked at in a rational and balanced way so that we can find a level on which we can meet. I'd like the book to serve the current situation and help in the future. I'm sure that there is still a lot more for historians to do.'

Martial law's apologists have always argued that it was the lesser of two evils. Jaruzelski emphasizes that time has made him even more convinced that he was right: 'I'm often asked if the decision was right at the time. I invariably reply that the decision was right and that I don't regret it. What I do regret is that such a decision was necessary at all and that certain processes were going on that required it. I also regret that during the implementation of this decision we made a lot of mistakes – that a lot of people were harmed – that, I really regret. And when I'm saying that it was the lesser of two evils this is what I have in mind.'

Jaruzelski rejects out of hand any suggestion that he mounted a *coup d'état* against his own people and country: 'In the West the introduction of martial law here has been compared to a *coup d'état*. In a *coup d'état* a legally based government is overthrown. In Poland martial law was introduced by the legal authorities – with the constitutional power of the Council of State. The decision was on my initiative as a legal prime minister. Of course I was at the same time the Minister of

Defence and a general – which of course gave me the support of the army. But it was legal. So the decision had legal authority and was supported by numerous resolutions and the agreement of different political and social organizations who put forward the initiative. I am taking responsibility because it's my moral duty to do so but formally the decision was taken by the Council of State.'

Jaruzelski argues that it is impossible to deal with the threat of Soviet or Warsaw Pact intervention in isolation from what he perceived as the threat of escalating conflict and chaos in the months before December 1981. From his historical vantage point the rest of the Soviet bloc had a legitimate interest in the internal affairs of Poland: 'The external and internal threats were interrelated. But we must always begin with what's inside the country. I think Poles tend to look outside to place blame for our failures. Look at our history. At the end of the eighteenth century Poland lost its independence at the hands of our powerful neighbours who divided us into three parts [Prussian, Austrian and Russian annexations]. But before that we were one of the biggest powers in Europe. Poland made itself weak and we became easy prey for the aggressors. I look at the events of 1981 in the same way. It's easy to say that there was Brezhnev, the Warsaw Pact and the Soviet Union: we are innocent. We had started jumping at our own throats before that. I, the authorities and Solidarity created such an inflammatory situation – such an explosive situation that it led to the introduction of martial law. Poland is not an island. Then Poland was part of a divided world and according to elementary logic we had to think that what was going on in Poland concerned the rest of the system that we were part of. Because of its size and its geo-strategic location Poland is the essential component of the Warsaw Pact. Had we not solved the situation ourselves, intervention would have occurred sooner or later. It was the logic of the time – the logic of Yalta. I have said many times that if I had been a Soviet general and if I had looked at the map with their eyes I would have thought in the same way that they did. The evidence is there now, many publications and memoirs show that they would have intervened. East Germany was ready, although they would have hesitated for longer because intervention by Germany would have been seen as a big provocation for historical reasons.'

In his book Jaruzelski argues that in the eighties 'Poland was seen by its allies as a heavily contaminated zone. In the changes taking place in our country, they saw – not without reason – a danger for the whole [Soviet] bloc, a threat of weakening its stability and unity. Hence the active penetration, including what can be called persuasive – indoctrination activities. One of the recurring tunes was the attempt to underrate ([former Polish communist party leader Stanislaw] Kania and myself. In some of our circles, these voices would fall on eager ears, and even bigger contributions were made. I was said to be a secret advocate of the Finlandization of Poland, and that I wanted a strong government supported by the army and a weak party without influence on state politics.'[4]

Jaruzelski cites Polish Army intelligence to support his claim of Soviet infiltration into Poland: '[They] reported increased activities of Soviet civilian and military intelligence, that is, KGB and GRU, and also of the [former East German] Stasi and the Czechoslovak SB. My informants quoted specific names and verifiable facts. Some of this information was confirmed via military channels. Several periods of especially vigorous infiltration were recorded. The first period was in August and September 1980, and the second was in November and early December 1980, the third was in March and early April of 1981, and finally the fourth period in November and December of 1981.' Jaruzelski also claims to have been provided with proof of Soviet penetration of Solidarity's organizational structures.

The Internal Service and National Defence Minister, General Czeslaw Kiszczak, agreed to investigate the Warsaw Pact's intentions towards Poland during the summer of 1980: 'He did this very cautiously, using for this purpose trustworthy officers and his personal connections among top-ranking employees of Warsaw Pact intelligence and counterintelligence . . . These officials said that the leaders of the Warsaw Pact countries were so seriously alarmed over the development of the situation in Poland, that they were afraid of the possibility of the [Polish] 'plague' being transferred to neighbouring countries . . . They told Kiszczak more or less openly that a decision was maturing to grant Poland "assistance" modelled after the invasion of Czechoslovakia in 1968.'

Former communists like Professor Jerzy Wiatr see the issue in cut and dried terms: 'I think he was right. He was doing everything possible to gain time, to delay Soviet intervention and to allow Solidarity time to work out a compromise. But when it failed he took control himself by

using the Polish military rather than watch the Soviet Army march in.'
Professor Wiatr became emotional when he described a secret meeting
between Jaruzelski and members of the Soviet politburo including
Brezhnev in April 1981: 'Kania and Jaruzelski made a trip to the
border for a meeting which was held on a train. It resulted in the
Soviets deciding to wait and not come in, but the circumstances were
very dramatic. Before he left for the border, Jaruzelski asked the head
of his office to promise him that he would take care of his wife and
daughter. He swore his adjutant to secrecy and asked him if consider-
ing the circumstances he would accompany him. When the man said
yes, Jaruzelski embraced him and wished him good luck. They had an
absolute realization that they might not return alive.'

Unfortunately for General Jaruzelski his version of events is completely shattered by the contents of the documents from the Suslov
Commission handed over to President Walesa by President Yeltsin
during the summer of 1993. The Suslov Commission was made up
of the Communist Party chief ideologist Mikhail Suslov, Minister of
Defence Dmitri Ustinov, KGB Chief Yuri Andropov, Minister of
Foreign Affairs Andrei Gromyko, and Konstantin Chernenko. The
Commission monitored and analysed the situation in Poland during
1980 and 1981 and was responsible for policy towards its neighbour.
The secret documents which were taken from the Kremlin archives
appear to show that the Soviet authorities ruled out armed intervention
against Poland in 1981. The documents handed over include a verbatim
account of the Soviet Communist Party's politburo on 10 December,
the text of Leonid Brezhnev's letter to Jaruzelski in mid-November and
records of conversations both between Jaruzelski and Brezhnev and
other Polish leaders.

The mythology of important historical events is often as important as
the facts when it comes to understanding how those events are subsequently interpreted. Jaruzelski has always chosen to accept the burden of
the decision to introduce martial law alone. That position is no doubt
convenient for men such as Mieczyslaw Rakowski who have always
sought to distance themselves from any preparation or knowledge of the
planning of martial law. Rakowski rejects any suggestion that Jaruzelski
was put under pressure to move against Solidarity by the Polish Army
Command.

'I think,' he told me, 'that Jaruzelski's colleagues, the generals, the
people with whom he had everyday contact approved of the step. But

the decision was made by himself. I think that he has always said that "I'm responsible" and no doubt it's true.' Jan Bisztyga, a one-time spokesman and adviser to Jaruzelski, disagrees. He maintains that he was put under enormous pressure from a number of senior Polish generals who had close contacts with their Soviet counterparts: 'They threatened him with martial law-himself if he didn't act. He's a noble-man, with the mentality of an aristocrat. Work, dignity, friendship have a different value for him. His father was from the old Polish nobil-ity. He will never admit that he was put under pressure by the generals – but they were the ones that were close to the Russians.'

There is no dispute about the fact that Poland was descending into economic chaos as 1981 drew to a close. The only issue is to what extent that chaos had been fostered by the authorities in order to pro-vide grounds for radical intervention. Publicly the Party, in the guise of Rakowski, continued to negotiate with Solidarity, while a much heralded meeting was held between Cardinal Glemp, Lech Walesa and General Jaruzelski in early November. Both Jaruzelski and Rakowski still main-tain that the negotiations between the government and Solidarity were real and that the party was genuinely seeking a national agreement. Both claim that, on the basis of their information then, that Solid-arity was planning a major strike, that would involve armed resistance, for 17 December. Inherent in this argument is the rejection of the sug-gestion that the collapse of the system within Poland was being used to isolate Solidarity and therefore justify any action that would return the country to some degree of normalcy.

Rakowski still claims that it was the discredited Radom tapes that made Jaruzelski change his mind and agree 'at the last minute' to introduce martial law. He brushes aside the suggestion that the tapes were doctored: 'I know [Adam] Michnik and many others have said that no confrontation was planned at the meeting. But for Jaruzelski the facts played a part. There was strike after strike, the demonstration planned for the 17th, winter was upon us and living conditions were getting worse. These facts pushed Jaruzelski and the generals towards martial law. It will be the subject of discussion for twenty or forty years. It's my opinion that if we hadn't acted the physical future was grim. It's clear from books by people such as Edward Shevardnadze that there is no doubt that the Soviets would have invaded. But maybe before all of that – the atmosphere was such at the time – that there

might have been civil war; people forget that such a danger existed.
For Jaruzelski the main task was to avoid such a development: we saw
the possibility of barricades in the streets. For us it was a dramatic
step: nobody in the leadership was happy. In my opinion there was no
other way.'

Employing the oldest weapon of them all, the Party continually
claimed in the pre-martial-law period that agreement could not be
reached because of the radical elements within Solidarity and that the
movement had been hijacked by the Jewish intellectuals. In a less than
subtle reworking of that argument Rakowski seems to be shifting the
responsibility for 13 December on to those, within both the party and
Solidarity, who lacked the vision to compromise. With hindsight he
now appears to argue that martial law was an historical inevitability. In
this scenario Rakowski imagines reformers such as himself as lone
beacons of light being enveloped by the dark clouds of unreason: 'I
think that at the time the two sides were not prepared psychologically
or politically to find a compromise. It's a tragedy, but it happens. On
our side there was no will to share power; on the other side there was
no will to find a way to people who were [Party] reformers and therefore willing to look for a solution. Therefore practically there was no
possibility of an agreement.'

Another key argument used to justify martial law is the claim that it
was the will of the people. General Jaruzelski says that 'people begged
us to stop what was going on. People couldn't stand any more. The
situation threatened everyday life. There were many meetings, and
many letters begging me to re-establish order. The impression was later
created among foreigners that martial law was imposed on the majority
of society; that was because opinions were taken from sophisticated
people, from intellectuals, from some of the workers and from people
in the big cities. But Poland is not only Gdansk, Cracow and Warsaw:
it's not only the university, hall and cafe. It's hundreds and thousands
of villages and small towns. They all demanded in some way the
introduction of order by disciplinary means. They said, "Mr General, I
have to feed the horse and the cow, but in the cities people go on
strike and because of strikes I cannot buy fertilizer."' Jaruzelski claims
that opinion polls taken in the autumn of 1981 support his view that
martial law was a remedy acceptable to many Poles. Unfortunately from
the general's point of view, his claim is dismissed by Ms Lena Kolarska-
Bobinska, the head of Poland's independent opinion poll service,

CBOS. She points out that research carried out during communist times is not regarded as reliable.

Leaving aside the vexed debate about the level of communist connivance in the economic collapse and the questionable sincerity of the Party's commitment to its negotiations with Solidarity, the question remains as to what perception of principle, set of values or notion of the state justified the use of government forces against the people. 'I was protecting three values,' the general says. 'First, I acted to stop civil war; to stop brother killing brother. There's nothing more terrible than that. I survived elements of such a war in the first years after the First World War. Secondly, I wanted to prevent economic disaster – we were at the edge of winter, we were threatened by hunger and cold. The economy was in ruins. Thirdly, I wanted to protect Poland's sovereignty – limited as it was – from outside intervention.' In an interview in the *Warsaw Voice* Jaruzelski was asked if he had acted to defend the system? 'I defended the state,' he claimed. 'A state which obviously had a defined system. I acted on behalf of its stability. Even if it was an imperfect state, functioning with a limited sovereignty, it was still the Polish state. I regarded the need to ensure its security – its territorial integrity and permanent borders – as the supreme value. The system of international security in those days, created as a result of Yalta, was ailing but did exist. The system in Poland constituted one part of it. In this sense, I also defended the system, as I was defending the stability and security of the state.'

General Jaruzelski baulked at the prospect of discussing his own sense of patriotism. But when I asked what was the essential difference between his sense of what it meant to be a Polish patriot and the view of those who regarded him as a traitor and collaborator, he replied: 'I think it is very uncomfortable for someone to have to defend whether he or she is a patriot. I think patriotism is a moral issue and shouldn't be talked about. I remember in the period when Poland was overwhelmed by growing strikes that our national flag was used and our national anthem was sung. It looked like patriotism but it wasn't patriotism at all. Patriotism should be considered in two dimensions. Firstly, there is the question of how a man perceives himself and secondly what are the objective effects of that. I grew up in a climate of deep and eager patriotism, I inherited family traditions going back hundreds of years. I was brought up in a spirit of great hatred for the

Russians. My grandfather took part in the uprising and then he spent eight years in Siberia – my second grandfather almost got hanged by the Bolsheviks – at the last moment he escaped. My father was a volunteer in the war against the Bolsheviks in 1920. Later on I suffered as many people did in those times. We were deported to Siberia: I was there, with my father when he died. You may ask why I don't hate the Russians? It is because I understand that it is not possible to identify the pathology of the system with the nation – because the Russians are also victims of this system. And you must remember that Russia is a great nation.'

And yet despite his personal experience of the horrors of Siberia, which included the irreparable damage done to his eyes by the glare from the snow, Jaruzelski like many other Polish communists differentiated between the ideal and the reality. As a young man he attended a training school for Soviet officers and joined the Soviet-inspired Polish First Army and took part in the liberation of Poland. Jaruzelski was one of the many Poles who came back to Poland to take part in what became the very brutal crushing of anti-communist resistance. Later he became a member of the Polish Workers Party in 1947. By the time of his appointment as prime minister in February 1981 he had been one of the most powerful and trusted communist leaders in Poland for a decade. 'I'm not a unique case here,' he explained. 'I think that a man should stay above his personal experiences – in the interest of his country. I know people who spent years in prison, Stalinist prisons or Polish prisons after the war and they still remained faithful to their communist ideology. I can think of three communist leaders – and I don't want you to think that what I say is my personal estimation of them – but Husak, Kadar and Gomulka went through a lot of things and they still remained faithful to the ideology. So I think that if a man finds an ideology that he likes and wants to follow, he must be able to divide his personal tragedy from his sense of what is good for the country.'

From the post-communist vantage point of Professor Jerzy Wiatr, Jaruzelski is 'a genuine Polish patriot. Firstly he is a man of the left but a man shaped by his nation's experience of war. He learned the hard way that a weak nation must watch its step. He learned that the leaders of such nations have a moral responsibility not to do what Poland's leaders did during the Second World War – for which Poland paid an enormous price.' Jaruzelski's former spokesman Jan Bisztyga argues that his loyalty is to 'the Polish nation – not the romantic Polish Nation. For Jaruzelski, Romanticism is the most dangerous phenomenon for his country.'

Professor Edmund Wnuk-Lipinski places Jaruzelski firmly in the anti-romantic tradition of Polish leaders: 'Political and historical legitimacy is very important to former communists. But to understand Jaruzelski you must understand the historical context. In the nineteenth century there was no Polish state on the map of Europe. There were two basic attitudes to that situation. There was the Romantic and what is called the positivist approach. The positivists believed in a step-by-step route to the recreation of an independent Polish state. With the Romantics it was all or nothing. Jaruzelski is in the anti-romantic tradition of Count Alexander Wielopolski (1803–77) who collaborated both with the Russians and with the officers who organized the January Uprising in 1863.'

Norman Davies argues in *God's Playground* that 'The politics of Polish Nationalism were conditioned from the start by the uncompromising nature of of the established order. At no time did the authorities of the partitioning powers look with favour on the re-creation of a sovereign and fully independent Polish state . . . As a result, the politically conscious Pole was faced with a very limited choice of action. If he loyally acquiesced in the policies of his government, he was tempted to surrender his Polish nationality in favour of the official nationalisms of the imperial regime. By pursuing a career in the Tsarist, Prussian, or Royal and Imperial service, the chances are that he would adopt the culture and the outlook of the ruling elite, and would come to think of himself not as a Pole but as a Russian, a German, or an Austrian . . . If, however, he were to give priority to Polish aims, he was immediately confronted with a fundamental dilemma. He had either to work with the authorities, or against them. In the context of autocratic, authoritarian, or absolutist regimes, where pluralist political aims were not permitted, there was no middle way: there was no concept of a loyal opposition.'[5]

This was precisely the same dilemma that Jaruzelski and others like him faced when they considered what it meant to be a patriot. For him there was never the remotest possibility that he would go down the Romantic and insurrectionist road. And, as Wnuk-Lipinski points out, 'When he defends his version of the good of the nation, the line between collaborating with the oppressor and defending the national interest becomes blurred. Jaruzelski wants to be an ambiguous figure in our history. There will be endless discussions for future historians about his role. His personality can be examined in terms of three rhetorical models. Firstly, he can be viewed as an opportunist; secondly, as a Young Turk – as a man who was taken to the Soviet Union, educated and then returned as an obedient and loyal communist; thirdly, there is the Konrad Wallenrod model. I think Jaruzelski will try and present himself as a new Wallenrod. I feel that his own perception of himself is closest to this clichéd figure in Adam Mickiewicz's epic in which a young Lithuanian is taken away by the Teutonic knights as a baby. He is promoted and later becomes the leader of the Order but in the final battle he changes sides.'

The historian Bronislaw Geremek, now the leader of the Democratic Union, rejects the notion that in introducing martial law Jaruzelski was acting in the national interest: 'Until 1989 I had never met him. I knew him only as the leader of the Communist Party and the general who had introduced martial law against the Polish people. After the election I had some personal contacts with him and I learned to respect him as a person. However, I cannot accept that martial law was done in the interest of the Polish people. The decision was taken in order to pre-serve the communist regime. It was also part of an internal struggle within the communist leadership. One can defend Jaruzelski's decision on the basis that if he didn't do it, someone else in the politburo would have done it. But one cannot explain the decision by saying that it was in the interest of the people, that it was the lesser of two evils, that it was that, or Soviet intervention. I don't think so: the Soviet plan was to force the Poles to deal with the political situation themselves and by doing so preserve the Soviet interest.'

In an earlier chapter I have already discussed aspects of the motivation behind communist participation in the Round Table process. Jaruzelski now argues that once it became clear to him that it was impossible to reform the economy without 'social support' and that 'social support' was only viable in the context of parliamentary democracy, it was a 'very short step to the Round Table. [It was] perceived as a particular philosophy of sharing power; not until then, handing it over, but sharing it. However, A leads to B. If you agree to elections – limited by a certain contract – which are not fully democratic, then it's clear that one day you'll have to accept totally free elections.'[6] Professor Jerzy Wiatr does not accept that the complete collapse of communist power was an inevitable result of the Round Table process – an interpretation which is implicit in Jaruzelski's argument. 'Ultimately,' he says, 'the responsibility [for losing power] goes to the man at the top. History will remember Jaruzelski for what he has done to save Poland from the fate of Hungary and Czechoslovakia. He did not use political and military power to solidify a sort of Pinochet regime. He used power to prepare Poland for democratic transformation. But he made mistakes. For too long he dealt with mediocre careerists – people with no vision at all. If you look at the people around him, almost until the last moment, they were people who were opposed to democratic change. In the end he got rid of the most stubborn of them, but with one exception – Rakowski; he replaced them with people who were not much better. The big problem with Jaruzelski right up until the end was that he surrounded himself with old Party hands who were good for any scenario: they weren't even hardliners.' Wiatr concludes that this mistake 'cost the Communist Party dearly'. If the Party had been put in order – prior to or simultaneous with the Round Table – it could have presented a better image of itself: 'When the election came the Party was full of discredited types because the choice of who would run was in the hands of the old guard. The arithmetic might have ended up the same, but the personnel would have been better and subsequent relationships better.'

Jaruzelski very obviously wants to be remembered as someone who saw the need for and promoted the idea of change and reform of the system: 'One thing is certain: the ideology was beautiful. But in the end it turned out to be Utopian and because it was introduced in under-developed countries, it turned out a failure. But, as I understood it, in serving this idea and this country, I wanted to reform the practical implementation of the idea so that the distance between the idea and reality was as small as possible. This turned out to be impossible. But I still believe in the concept of socialism, if it is freed from the fact of being Utopian and implemented in democratic conditions. However everything that happened to socialism after Stalin was a distortion of this idea.'

Implicit in all that Jaruzelski says is a total rejection of any suggestion that he sensed the winds of change moving across Europe and that he therefore played an opportunist's role. 'The process of change', he says, 'which took place in Poland happened much earlier than in other parts of Eastern Europe. I am convinced that, were it not for our changes and for the introduction of martial law, the Gorbachev phenomenon would not have occurred. Poland was a great warning to other countries in the bloc. They saw that without change an explosion would happen. We were a sort of laboratory where our reforms could be looked at and examined. I spent many hours talking to Gorbachev and I shared our experience with him. Our reforms were then reflected in *perestroika*. Of course I don't want to diminish Gorbachev's role in the process that took place in Poland. We could not have started the change without Gorbachev. He played a very big role. I must say that I respect him and I like him.'

Crucial to an historical assessment of Wojciech Jaruzelski is the issue of his sense of loyalty and his commitment to the socialist ideal. It is interesting that old foes such as Bronislaw Geremek do not doubt the bona fides of his beliefs nor the fact that he did genuinely change his political philosophy: 'Mr Jaruzelski is a dramatic person in Polish history. In his personal biography one can see the dramatic destiny of many Polish people and elites. Jaruzelski, a representative of the gentry and intelligentsia, becomes a communist because he thinks that it was the great hope for the world. Having served the interests of communism and the Soviet Union, he then sees it collapse in the eighties. And what is left? His national feelings and patriotic sentiments. Now I believe that Mr Jaruzelski is a different person – and this different person I have learned to respect.'

Catholic theologian Father Josef Tischner, once the moral voice of Solidarity, is totally opposed to calls for Jaruzelski's impeachment: 'He should be left alone. The blame and responsibility for martial law is not clear. One shouldn't punish when the facts are not clear. I think that the threat of intervention before martial law was very great. It is interesting that after the Napoleonic wars many Polish generals fought in the Russian army. That experience convinced many of them that the Russians were invincible. They became convinced that the army that had defeated Napoleon was the strongest army in the world. I think that, maybe, Jaruzelski had the same perception of Russian might after World War Two, that it was not possible to oppose it. I must say that I have a big understanding and even some liking for this man. I respect people who are able to change their opinion. He did change his views.

I used to read all his speeches. I think he was honest in them. Maybe he didn't always say everything about a situation – because maybe he couldn't – but he didn't lie. It was clear from his early speeches that he was a true communist but later, when it was apparent that communism was no good, he backed off as far as he could. He's like a doctor who sees that the medicine is not working; he changes the medicine and then finally gets somebody else to deal with the case. I think it's possible that, for him, the last argument was the economic collapse that followed the period after martial law. He recognized that military measures could no longer be used to resolve such problems. I think that realization opened the door to the Round Table.'

Father Tischner's assessment is *ad idem* with those who place Jaruzelski in the anti-Romantic and conciliationist tradition of Polish leaders – a tradition heavily burdened by the realities of geography and the historical fragility of Polish independence. Perhaps, then, it is possible to conclude, as Father Tischner does, that Jaruzelski's enormous sense of the reality of the world and the times in which he lived played the major part in determining his decisions: 'We Poles have big problems with reality. We are so free – we don't know the real world and what it looks like. I think that if Jaruzelski was sinful, it was because he had too big a sense of reality. I think that this feeling of reality is what differentiates him from the rest of us.'

9

JANUSZ ONYSZKIEWICZ

POACHER TURNED GAMEKEEPER

Janusz Onyszkiewicz suppresses an almost giggly smile as he contemplates the fact that he was the first civilian Deputy Minister of Defence in the Warsaw Pact. The nervous laugh highlights both a residual sense of disbelief and his awareness of the historical and political importance of the appointment. In a sense Janusz Onyszkiewicz is the epitome of the Polish revolution; he is the poacher turned gamekeeper. As Solidarity's national press spokesman he was known to all those who covered the Polish story. A small, neat, mustachioed man with impeccable Oxford-sounding English, his controlled and disciplined behaviour stood out from the cacophany of sound and beaverish activity at Solidarity's regional headquarters in pre-martial law Warsaw. He had a very 'English' way of expressing Solidarity's demands. It all sounded so reasonable until one pinched oneself and remembered that this was a country behind the 'Iron Curtain' where Moscow's will prevailed. The sort of reasonableness which characterized Onyszkiewicz's behaviour was of course the quintessential factor in Solidarity's initial survival. A mathematician by profession, Onyszkiewicz, unlike some of his fellow activists, appeared to stand back from the emotions and momentum in the post-August months. Always careful in his choice of words there was never an iota of bravado in his statements to the media, no element of provocation. Amid all of the chaos in those heady days Onysziewicz radiated an air of the controlled, expedient and calculated strategist. One never sensed any emotional response within him to either the people or the system that he and Solidarity were fighting. He had the measure of the enemy and like General Jaruzelski his response was based on generations of historical perception about Poland's possibilities and geo-political realities. Unlike Jaruzelski, however, Onyszkiewicz did not ultimately believe that the conciliatory, step-by-step approach necessitated outright collaboration.

I remember being struck on the first few occasions that I met Onyszkiewicz by the enigmatic aspect of his personality. Outwardly somewhat reserved and purposeful, his eyes shrouded a different story. A keen and enthusiastic mountaineer and caver, his first two wives died as a result of climbing accidents. Perhaps it was this personal tragedy that gave him the air of a man who could not be hurt or compromised.

Onyszkiewicz is not a man to linger on the past. Meeting him during the election period in the summer of 1989 his interest was completely focused on the present. He anticipated the potential danger in the size of Solidarity's election results, knowing that without a coherent opposition the trade union could easily run aground on the rock of the enormous diversity of its support. He was very conscious of controlling the public feeling that the war had been won and that power was now in Solidarity's hands. At that stage he knew that power could not gauged by electoral success alone. The Round Table and the first elections had started a process, but real power was still in the hands of the communists who had retained control of the army and the police. With the bloodletting of Tiananmen Square still dominating world headlines, he warned that no move should be made that would undermine Poland's position in the Warsaw Pact and that the democratization process should be gradual and cautious. Onyszkiewicz was pragmatic about how the Party would be absorbed in Poland's new order: 'We must always leave space for them. We must give them the time and the chance to change into businessmen. Otherwise there'll be a backlash.' Time, however, was not on the side of the communists in Eastern Europe, though in June and July of 1989 there were few who could have anticipated the scale or speed of the communist collapse that was to follow within months. For Janusz Onyszkiewicz the whole process of democratic change in Poland depended on playing the game by the new rules: 'The external situation is now different. Before we argued that Poland was different from the other countries in the bloc and that was why we needed reforms. It was a very shaky argument. Now Gorbachev says that the system needs reform and change – and that's what we are doing.' But as long as the party was still intact and the relationship with Moscow and the rest of the Pact a reality, Onyszkiewicz knew that Solidarity must accept its exclusion from certain portfolios of government. From this perspective, in the early summer of 1989, the army and the police were still the preserve of the party. Within a matter of just a few months however the party was gone having voted itself out of existence on 28 January 1990. And with the reforms process moving at a much faster rate than anyone had

anticipated, Prime Minister Tadeusz Mazowiecki decided that the time
had come to grapple with the heart of the old power. Onyszkiewicz
says that he was initially very worried by Mazowiecki's request that he
become Deputy Minister of Defence in what he calls this impregnable
area of the military: 'When Mazowiecki first approached me in the
spring of 1990 I didn't know what to do. My first reaction was not to
accept. I thought about my experience and interests. I was interested in
military matters but I didn't think that I could make a valuable contribution. After all the Minister was still a communist. I thought that
I'd stay with foreign policy and political issues. But after some time I
went back to Mazowiecki, who hadn't accepted my no in any case. I
told him I'd take the job provided I was given responsibility for all
international affairs and especially the Warsaw Pact. My idea at the
time was to try and work out how to dismantle the Pact. Mazowiecki
was in a panicky mood there was so much happening in Eastern Europe
and in Poland. Eventually after Mazowiecki returned from a visit to the
United States, he rang me and said yes to my provisos. So that's how I
got the defence policy.'

Onyszkiewicz emphasizes what an alien environment the army was for
someone from Solidarity: 'We knew nothing about it. For us it was a
big black box. There were two basic principles in Solidarity: stay clear
of the police and stay clear of the army. After the elections we were trying to avoid any suggestion that we were conspiring against the state,
and of course we wanted to reassure the Russians that they had the ultimate instruments of power in their hands. The army was an enigma for
us – we really knew nothing about it.' And with a grin Onyszkiewicz
adds that the 'police didn't leave Solidarity alone – so we acquired
rather a lot of information about how they were run. But can you imagine I was the first civilian Deputy Minister of Defence in the entire
Warsaw Pact? You can imagine the first time that I met with Yazov[1]
and the rest of the top brass at the Soviet Ministry of Defence. I must
have been like a giraffe to them. Something that should not exist. I
don't think they trusted me at the beginning but after time Yazov and
the generals became friendly. I don't think that it was a disguise because
they saw it as a trend that they couldn't stop. The generals said that
they accepted the changes that had taken place in Poland. They talked
about our common Slavonic background. At first I had found it very
difficult to organize a meeting with them following my appointment. It

eventually happened during a trip with President Jaruzelski to see Gorbachev in May 1990. When I got to Moscow I still wasn't sure if they'd see me or not. It was only after we buttonholed Gorbachev and he told Yazov to see us that the meeting took place. My impression was that Gorbachev was well briefed. He is quite obviously an interesting person with a capacity to win confidence very quickly. It was very strange for me. I was the only representative of Solidarity – of the new political establishment – to accompany Jaruzelski to Moscow. So when we met Gorbachev I was the only person from the new order – the odd man out. I got the impression that when Gorbachev was saying certain things that he was saying them to me. Actually he was looking at me all of the time. But of course it could have been accidental. I think he handled the encounter very well. Poland was very important to him and he had to accommodate the new situation.'

It was during this visit that the Soviet authorities admitted responsibility for the infamous Katyn forest massacre when thousands of Polish army officers being held as POW's were slaughtered. The admission was of enormous emotional and historical importance in Poland. It had been common knowledge that the Soviet NKVD (People's Internal Affairs Commissariat) had carried out the executions in the spring of 1940; however, in the official historiography of the Soviet Union and in Polish studies written in communist times the murders were attributed to the Nazis. 'When we got to Moscow,' Onyszkiewicz recalls, 'the Soviets announced their admission of the Katyn massacre. We asked them straightaway if we could go there. There was a problem because we wanted a Polish army unit to accompany us with a band. We wanted to have a proper ceremony. Gorbachev settled everything. We went and we had the first official ceremony there. We had a priest. The whole thing was very moving.' Whatever about Gorbachev's outward cooperation with Onyszkiewicz in arranging the ceremonies after the historical admission of Soviet responsibility, it was to be another two years before the full culpability of the Soviet authorities would be revealed. On 14 October 1992, the head of the Russian Federation's State Archive Committee, Rudolf Pikhoya, presented President Lech Walesa with a copy of the politburo's decision to kill more than 21,000 Poles interned in the Soviet Union after the Red Army seized Western Ukraine and Western Belarus in September 1939.

The document handed over by Pikhoya shows that on 5 March 1940 the politburo decided to kill the Polish POWs. The document, which was signed by Josef Stalin, Foreign Minister Vyacheslav Molotov, Defence Minister Kliment Voroshylov, and Supreme Soviet Presidium chairman Anastas Mikoyan, instructs the NKVD to handle the execution. The list of those officers to be shot was drawn up by the NKVD's head, Lavryenty Beria. Russian Federation President Boris Yeltsin claims that Mikhail Gorbachev knew about the Katyn documents which were held in the personal safe of successive Soviet leaders. Gorbachev claims that he never opened the file and only became aware of the existence of the documents when he was handing over power to Yeltsin at the end of 1991.

Onyszkiewicz also used his first visit to the Soviet Ministry of Defence to raise the sensitive issue of the withdrawal of thousands of Soviet troops stationed in Poland: 'We didn't raise it publicly at that stage because we didn't want to cause Gorbachev any problems. Also we thought it was a bad idea to raise hopes back home in Poland. When we raised the matter, the Soviet side indicated that its troops would be withdrawn if we demanded it. The problem with the Soviet troops in Poland was that they had nowhere to go home to. They simply came and stayed after the War. In Czechoslovakia, in 1968, the Soviet troops arrived from certain bases. They, at least, had a symbolic place to return to. Poland was the strategic backyard of the central front in Germany. The second echelon of troops coming from the Ukraine would be supplied by the bases in Poland. So we were left with huge stocks of arms, fuels, food, everything you need to supply an army. Now what can we do with these barracks? The Russians say they're leaving the housing stock and the barracks. We say that we don't want them. They were often built against our wishes. What can we do with them in the middle of nowhere. The ecological damage is huge. Farmers near one air base were able to drill holes and draw petrol or kerosene. These areas are often called "Little Kuwait" and the farmers there say they should be known as the "Polish Sheikhs". There is, of course, a huge human dimension to all of this. I have suggested during the course of the negotiations over the withdrawal that the soldier's families could remain in Poland while they await accommodation in the old Soviet Union.'

Negotiations about the withdrawal began in 1990 and an agreement was finally initialled a year later with the Soviets promising to have all combat troops out by November 1992. When Poland recognized the Commonwealth of Independent States in December 1991, the negotiations were taken over by the Russians who found themselves in the difficult position of being committed to the repatriation of thousands of troops and their families, but without the resources to deal with the problem. 'The Russians have a huge housing problem', Onyszkiewicz points out. 'The main Soviet barracks complexes are in the Ukraine and in Belarus. They've literally nowhere to house these people.'

The Katyn forest massacre and the withdrawal issue were two of the most serious impediments to the development of good Polish-Russian relations. During the withdrawal treaty negotiations Onyszkiewicz felt that it was impossible for the two armies to maintain and augment the kind of relations that would be appropriate in the post-Soviet era: 'We signalled that we wanted to maintain contact. But it was difficult during the negotiations. We were afraid that it would show weakness. We didn't want to dig a ditch on the border.' Tension surrounding the withdrawal issue eased after President Lech Walesa's visit to Moscow in May 1992. Apart from a Treaty of Friendship and Cooperation, the two sides also signed the final document agreeing the terms of the withdrawal. Within a couple of weeks General Viktor Dubynin, who had been commander of the Soviet troops in Poland, issued for the first time a schedule indicating a timescale for the withdrawal as well as a timescale for the Polish takeover of buildings vacated by the withdrawing army. Under the 'zero option', suggested by the Poles, hotly disputed property issues were settled. Under the terms of the agreement everything built by the Soviets within their garrisons was returned to Poland while the Russians retained the right to sell anything that moved. The right to sell everything from surplus fuels, scrap metal and household goods turned the garrison areas into virtual bazaars. The agreement provided a veneer of legality for a trade that was already well underway in bases across Poland, where all sorts of army equipment, including weapons, were being sold by soldiers and their families facing an unknown future in places some could barely locate on a map.

However, despite the odd hiccup, the 20th Special Communications Brigade, the last big Russian unit, left Poland in August 1993.

When Janusz Onyszkiewicz was appointed Deputy Minister of Defence he applied his well-tested stratagem of beating the opposition with their own rules: 'My immediate goal was to find out how the army functioned. I wanted to know what the power structures were, what the decision making procedure was. My aim was to change the nature of the Warsaw Pact. At that time – spring 1990 – dismantling this pact, even raising the issue, was very premature. But I persisted. I was reassured by an early visit I made to Czechoslovakia when I spoke to the then Minister of Defence. He nearly fainted when I mentioned that we must do something about the Warsaw Pact. My idea was to exploit to the full the potential for equality that existed within the charter. If you look at the charter it's fairly democratic, giving each country equal rights. But of course those equal rights were never applied. So I suggested straightaway that we could promote the idea of rotating the highest positions of command within the pact between the various countries. It was essentially a plan to beat the Soviets with their own rules by treating the charter seriously. I said that we should establish a liaison group of Warsaw Pact officers to liase with the Soviet Army. The funny thing was that each army did have a liaison group but it was made up of Soviet officers only – though it was not meant to. The next step was to establish a separate liason group within the Soviet army. The second problem was that the strategic planning structure of the pact was such that only the Soviets had an overview. The representatives of national armies within the pact were only handling the strategic plans which related to their own country. So my demand was for the entire pact to become involved in the central strategy planning process. I did get support for my ideas. But, you know, looking back, people think that the dismantling of the Warsaw Pact was somehow all inevitable. But when I took over at Defence the situation was changing each month. The whole process snowballed. The entire military structures of the pact were dismantled within a year, by the spring of 1991.'

With or without the collapse of the Warsaw Pact, Onyszkiewicz felt that the restoration of the integrity of the Polish Army was a major priority: 'I don't want to sound pompous but I wanted to restore the Polish Army as the Polish Army with a Polish command, Polish traditions, and without any shade of control from outside. And I had also to open our army to contact with the Western armies which I think I did. Now we have a vast array of contacts with Western armies and virtually no contact with the Russian army, which is deplorable. The only trouble is that we have nothing to talk about. I mean we made several offers to them and they didn't respond. To give you an example. The Polish side wanted to keep a mutual exchange of officers studying at our military academies. The Russians said, Fair enough, if you want to send your officers we'll charge you an exorbitant amount of money in dollars, but we won't send our officers to Poland. So that was the end of that. Another idea I had was that it seemed ridiculous that the Soviets and the Poles would only talk about defence policy and European security structures when we met in the West. I suggested that we do something about that but they never took it up. So I thought it would be a good idea to find a topic that would start the ball rolling. I suggested that we hold a seminar for our military and defence people on the conclusions that could be drawn from the Gulf War. They agreed and we organized a seminar at our Military Academy of National Defence and quite a big group of Soviets said that they would come. But the day before the seminar they cancelled. Perhaps it was because they were in such disarray. It was during the autumn of 1991. But anyhow they were unwilling to get involved.'

An early priority of Polish post-communist foreign policy was the establishment of formal links with the old Czechoslovakia and Hungary. Onyszkiewicz saw the importance of exploiting the military relationships that could be developed within the Visegrad Triangle, which had been set up in 1990 to promote common political objectives and trade activity: 'After the collapse of the Warsaw Pact I thought it would be a very positive idea to establish close military relationships between Poland, Czechoslovakia and Hungary. I thought that it would be good to get an agreement on cooperation. I didn't have manoeuvres in mind, but I thought that we could share training facilities, maybe even eventually agree a procurement policy for our military needs. The whole area of armaments could be looked at together with a view to making our equipment compatible. We would have a lot to share on many issues, like how for instance to educate our soldiers to be citizens in uniforms. There is also the question of closer military cooperation with the West.'

For Janusz Onyszkiewicz, the nurturing of military links within the Visegrad group is an essential part of Poland's wider foreign policy objective of convincing Western Europe that Poland and its two neighbours represent a stable and democratic zone in a region torn by ethnic strife. However, the disintegration of Czechoslovakia has not been helpful to those seeking to promote the stability of the Visegrad Triangle. At the heart of the debate about the future of Polish foreign policy is the old argument about whether Poland is a Western-orientated country on the Eastern fringe of Europe, an Eastern-looking country situated on the fringe of Western Europe or simply a country which sits bang in the middle, dividing East from West. Back in the autumn of 1989 the slogan of Solidarity's intellectual wing was 'a return to Europe'. For the political elites who formed the 'Democratic Union' there was no doubt about where Poland's heart lay. Historian and dissident Adam Michnic had been writing about the issue for years. For men such as Bronislaw Geremek and Tadeusz Mazowiecki the first plank of post-communist Polish foreign policy is a pro-European stance. Simply stated, this view of Poland's foreign policy interests depends on three interlocking policies. Firstly, an efficacious pro-European policy which would secure Poland a place in the process of European integration as well as eventual membership of the European Union. Aside from political and economic partnership this policy actively seeks full membership of NATO as well as the other Western security structures. A second dimension is the development of diplomatic, political and trading relations with the new Eastern republics. Traditionally Polish policy in this area has been to support local aspirations for independence while maintaining good relations with Russia. The existence of Polish minorities in Lithuania and the Ukraine in particular places barriers in the path of easy relations. The third objective is the maintenance of cooperation within the Visegrad group currently threatened by the fall-out from the break-up of Czechoslovakia and the problems generated for Hungary by the presence of a sizeable Hungarian minority in the new Slovakia. Apart from promoting the view that this group of countries is stable and democratic, Polish pro-European enthusiasts want it to approach its application for membership of the European Union on a quadrilateral as well as bilateral basis.

Janusz Onyszkiewicz summarizes this view of Polish foreign policy objectives in a sentence: 'We want to pull the Eastern countries westward.' Given Poland's history of annexation and obliteration from the map of Europe, it is natural that the issue of security looms large in the minds of those formulating a post-Yalta response to the nation's geo-strategical situation. 'Security,' he says, 'is a very important issue for us. We do not live with the level of threat to our security that existed in 1939, but we are not absolutely safe. The situation is not at all clear on our Eastern border. Anything could happen. The threats that are there are of a small military nature but they are there. Our relations with the Ukraine and other countries in this region are very important to us. Some of these relationships, for instance with Lithuania, are difficult for historical reasons, but it is very important that we work with these countries. In Lithuania we have a moral problem because we have an obligation to defend the interest of the Polish minority there. We must see that they are allowed to retain their Polishness. I think the chances of Polish-Ukrainian reconciliation are good. Ukraine has been the focus of much of our Eastern policy. Look at the level of the visits and the constant diplomatic dialogue. We are trying to restore the economic ties with the Ukraine. Potentially, on many levels, the Ukraine is an important partner for us. I don't think that that fact should make us move eastward in our thinking: we must pursue our policy in relation to the EU, but we cannot ignore the new potential of the territories in the East. And in any case we have responsibilities there. Many Ukrainians see Poland as their route westward, as their bridge to Europe; that's something we must build on. We can become a cultural, economic and geographic bridge between Russia and the West. The West can use us as a business bridge to the new independent states. If you look at the Russian, Ukrainian and Belarussian markets, they are potentially very important markets for the United States and the West in general. We have extensive knowledge of these areas, so there is a potential role there for Poland. But on the broader issue of security the biggest matter is the avoidance of another division of Europe. We must build very good ties and develop regional cooperation. That's why we are in the Hexagonal Group and the Visegrad Triangle, and why we favour Baltic cooperation. We think that the region can be stabilized through all of these contacts. Security can be best served by developing interlocking human, commercial, economic and political ties so that conflict becomes as unthinkable in this region as it is in the West.'

Onyszkiewicz regards the western response to the development of democracy in the CIS as vital, not only to the interests of the new federation, but to the interests of the entire region: 'It's quite obviously an historical moment. The Russian empire expanded from the fifteenth century onwards. Now we have seen the collapse, if not of the last empire, then at least, of the last colonial power. Our previous experience of the splitting up of so large a country has not been good. The British Raj left much blood and permanent conflict behind it in India. So it is important that something is done to help stabilize the region.

Unfortunately the collapse of the Soviet Union came during a con-
siderable recession in the West. Whatever happens, Poland lies between
two huge political entities. I don't know how long the CIS will last, but
Russia will certainly always be a very big nuclear power and probably a
big military power. And, more than likely, eventually a big economic
power. So Poland is in a delicate and strategic position. The recreation
of a division between the East and the West would be detrimental. So
in Poland we must help in the process which binds the East with the
rest of Europe. In Russia there are two basic tendencies, one looking
towards Europe, the other inward looking and messianic. If we turn
our back on those within Russia who want to anchor her in the West
then we may lessen their chances of success and we may condemn
them to going the other way. We mustn't do that. We must keep
Russia in Europe and by that of course I don't mean in the EU but,
philosophically speaking, Eurocentric.'

The difficulties of Poland's transition to a market economy have not
helped those promoting a pro–Western and and pro–European view of
foreign policy. As a result latent xenophobic tendencies have been given
new life by the post–Solidarity generation disillusioned by Poland's
failure to attain a Western standard of living in the immediate aftermath of the collapse of communism. 'Many parties here,' Onyszkiewicz
says, 'are drawing on people's xenophobic instincts. And no doubt it
will be exploited. Partly it's the legacy of communist policy which
exploited the fact that before the war much of Poland's industry was
foreign owned. The whole line of communist propaganda was close to
the National Democracy Movement before the war. It was pro–Russian,
anti–German and anti–West. Part of what's going on now is a hangover
from that propaganda. Two obvious examples are the ZChN and the
KPN. The ZChN is a very inward looking party; where we are orientated towards European values, structures and social behaviour, they
are wary of them. Unfortunately they have a lingering feeling that in
the process of reaching material prosperity Western Europe lost certain
spiritual values. They think that we – in Poland – can teach the West
something. I think this idea of a Polish messianic role is very dangerous. It's a repetition of the Solzhenitsyn, Slavophile concept which
is well rooted in Russian tradition. It's a struggle that we face in Poland
as well. I see it as the struggle between the outlook of Solzhenitsyn and
Sakharov. The KPN attitude is somewhat different. When they talk
about fears of Western domination they are really referring to

Germany. They both use right-wing phraseology but left and right mean nothing here any more. In essence they speak a left-wing rhetoric which, at heart, is populist.'

By the autumn of 1993 those Poles who had hoped that NATO would respond quickly to the changing face of Eastern Europe were beginning to wonder if in reality the spirit of Yalta was once again hovering over the region. Mieczyslaw Rakowski laughed out loud at President Clinton's response to Boris Yeltsin's handling of the sit-in in the Russian parliament: 'The idea of Boris Yeltsin as the guarantor of Russian democracy is laughable. We were condemned for martial law. Compared to what he's done and what he might do, it's a joke. If you are strong and you have an atomic bomb, then you get applause even if you do what Yeltsin has done. But if you are Poland you must accept the will of the stronger. There is no possibility that NATO will influence what happens on the Polish–Russian border, because the West sees the danger of the power of the Russian military. Anyone who knows Russia knows that the marshals are the winners in Yeltsin's battles. So the West won't offend the Russian military by inviting Poland to join NATO. Until Moscow fell, the world had two policemen. The West was much happier not to do this job alone. Now Yeltsin is offering to be the second policeman. It's quite simple: the West was more comfortable with its old spheres of influence.'

That cynical and pessimistic view is shared by Liberal leader Jan Krzysztof Bielecki: 'Now with the post-communists in power in Poland I think it's more comfortable for the West. From their point of view everything was stable before 1989. Europe was divided in two. The EC was developing integration policies, security was guaranteed by NATO and life was simple. The other half of Europe was integrated in a different way under the Soviet umbrella. That arrangement had been blessed in Yalta in 1945. Then there were four years of chaos and problems for Western Europe. All of these new countries were emerging and demanding market access and more assistance. They were looking for EC membership and security guarantees. Now Russia, where the hopes for democracy and the market are so limited, is talking about its sphere of influence again. A kind of iron curtain could easily be built up again while Western Europe gets on with integration.'

Journalist and former MP Jacek Majiarski believes that Poland's security will be guaranteed simply because it is in the West's interest to do so: 'As a poet I might like the West to think differently about Poland. But as a politician I must see my country as the West sees us. They don't want Kazakstan in the European Community and from London or Brussels that's how Poland is viewed. But on the other hand it is in NATO's interest to make sure that our region is secure; otherwise it's back to the days of Yalta. I think NATO appreciates that it is better that its border is further East than Berlin. Unfortunately it still looking at Eastern Europe through the eyes of Moscow.'

Two days after the 19 September election in Poland Boris Yeltsin dissolved the Russian Parliament. In the days that followed, the victorious Democratic Left Alliance leadership in Warsaw released a series of statements that made it clear that its position on the issue of NATO membership had changed. The question mark was gone, and SLD leader Aleksander Kwasniewski was emphasizing that membership was a top priority for his government. Professor Jerzy Wiatr argues that, as always, what is happening in Moscow is a key determinant of Polish foreign policy: 'We were never against NATO but now a pan-European security system is essential in the light of the *coup d'état* in Moscow. We are more vulnerable. The big winner in Russia is the military. They are looking for payment for supporting Boris Yeltsin. That will mean a more affirmative military policy from Russia. That's why we must declare ourselves in favour of as strong integration with the West as we can achieve. It's up to the West now. We have a different perspective from a year ago. Then we advocated a policy that would include Russia, but now, with the military riding high there, Poland's security depends on the active involvement of the United States and Western Europe, who must protect Central Europe.'

As Minister of Defence in the Suchocka government from the middle of 1992 until October 1993 Janusz Onyszkiewicz had a huge opportunity to assess the West's response to the process of change in Eastern Europe: 'I think that the latest election will cause some concern, but because we are not joining NATO immediately I think that the election will be viewed in a certain historical perspective as something that happened but which doesn't indicate a change in Polish policy. This election brought to power former communists, but the next election could bring together a totally different constellation of political parties. Politicians from NATO must look at developments here from a wider perspective. I do hope that our NATO membership could be achieved by osmosis so that our formal membership would basically formalize a cetain reality that would already exist.'

With the support of the post-communists, Democratic Union leader Bronislaw Geremek was once again returned to the chairmanship of the Sejm's Foreign Affairs Committee. Like Czech President Vaclav Havel, who has voiced fears that Democratic Europe will let its Eastern neighbours down as it did twice this century in the face of threats from Hitler and then Stalin, Geremek is disappointed by the West's inability to change its thinking: 'What is so important for us is that we need a feeling of security, a feeling that we are in the Western community. You know in practical terms this security means nothing because if the Red Army invades Poland it would be a world conflict and not a local one, regardless of our membership of NATO. What concerns us is that the priority in political thinking in international affairs is still caught in superpower terms. It's still Cold War thinking. There has been no response to the new situation. The West somehow lacks leaders with a vision of the future. They are without the intellectual courage to set aside this old analysis of world affairs.'

10

AND HE SHALL REIGN FOR EVER
AND EVER

The Catholic Primate of Poland, Archbishop Josef Glemp, admits that life was easier for the Church under communism. Then the enemy was obvious. Now Glemp finds himself at odds with many of the people who fought alongside a pro-dissident clergy in the battle for democracy in Poland. With the enemy vanquished, the real battle has begun to determine what kind of society Poland will become. There is, however, another battle and not necessarily one that the hierarchy wishes to acknowledge. That's the internal struggle between those who want the Catholic Church's definition of society to dominate Polish life and those who want the Church to play a guiding, spiritual role in a society based on pluralist principles. The battleground is strewn with argument over the traditionally polarizing issues of abortion, contraception, sex education and the conflict between freedom of expression and 'Christian values'.

The two faces of Polish Catholicism are most dramatically highlighted in the very different styles of two of its most famous churchmen, Primate Josef Glemp and moral theologian and former Solidarity chaplain Father Josef Tischner. Josef Glemp succeeded Cardinal Stefan Wyszynski as Primate in the summer before martial law. At fifty-two he was a young man for the job but it was rumoured that his appointment had been the deathbed wish of the internationally known and respected Primate.[1] Glemp's elevation could not have come at a more difficult or tense time. Within a short few months of his appointment, he faced the dilemma of eunciating the Church's response to the imposition of martial law. There are many Polish Catholics who will not forgive Glemp for the sermon he delivered on Sunday, 13 December. During that sermon, which was broadcast on radio and television, Glemp told his flock that the government's action was 'the choice of a lesser rather than a greater evil. Assuming the correctness of such reasoning the man in the street will submit himself to the new situation . . . Do not start a fight of Pole against Pole.'[2]

Cardinal Glemp is an austere figure. Short and squat, his jug ears are a cartoonist's gift. One detects no sense of personal conflict within

Glemp. He believes and proclaims traditional Catholic moral values as if there were no others. For him the Polish Church is the high ground of Catholic teaching, the moral base for the re-evangelizing of the godless Eastern hoards and the hedonistic West. A priest's priest, Glemp is not a man of the people; there is no laughter in his eyes. But perhaps that's because he witnessed so much terror when as a very young boy he was picked out for 'heavy labour' by the Nazi invaders. Another factor which must have influenced Glemp's behaviour and his perception of his role was the discomfort that he must have felt stepping into the shoes of the internationally renowned and respected Wyszynski at a time when Polish pride was at its height in celebration of its most famous son, Karol Wojtyla, Pope John Paul II.

It is impossible to follow the seemingly endless nature of the political debate over moral matters in post-communist Poland without first examining the moral and political vantage point of the Polish episcopate. Central to that view is the assumption on the part of the hierarchy that it cannot be considered as just one voice among many diverse voices struggling to be heard when moral questions are discussed. Cardinal Glemp refused to begin our interview, which was to focus on the role of the Church in post-communist Poland, until he had made it clear that he rejected outright what he claimed was the inference in my supplied questions that the Church was just another political group seeking to promote its version of social norms: 'I can only answer your questions on the understanding that you accept the terms in which the Church sees itself. The Church opposed Napoleon, Nazism, capitalism and socialism, and it is in opposition right now to everybody who sees man in a different way than the Church does. The Church is opposed to everything that negates respect for man. That's why we opposed Communism and why now we will oppose all the new ideologies which will question our basic truth. If an ideology of hedonism and secularism appears in society we will oppose that too.' Again, on the question of the kind of society that legislators should seek to enshrine in any new constitution Glemp appears at first to accept the notion of a pluralist state but then seems to imply a Catholic monoply on morality: 'We do understand that there are differences, differences in truth. And we do recognize those differences and we will approach everybody with love but provided they know the truth. No, our idea is not a Catholic, confessional state. Everybody is entitled to his religion. We are ecumenists. But we think that morality should be enshrined in the Constitution. Not Catholic morality, but Christian morality. It is after all the same morality for Catholics, Orthodox and Lutheran followers. And we think these values should be enshrined in our legislation.' It is this apparent insistence that there is only one brand of morality and that there are no differences between the churches on moral questions that leads many liberals to the view that, in effect, the Catholic Church is seeking the establishment of a confessional state.

After its 1991 conference the Polish episcopate issued a special statement restating its call for the abolition of the clause within the 1952 Constitution, which separates Church and state. The bishops claimed that the clause 'raised negative associations with the totalitarian system' under which it was used as a tool of domination of the state over the Church. The bishops also claimed that 'the public awareness is still dominated by a mistaken simplification that only the lay character of a state guarantees freedom and equality for its citizens.'[3] Cardinal Glemp is adamant that the Church is not interested in politics and that in fact the Church is above politics: 'The Church has a strong constitution – the Gospel. This is a negation of everything that sees life in political terms. The Church is the guardian of the Gospel. Therefore it is the Gospel that we want to see carried out in the world.' Glemp shrugs off the suggestion that the Church can appear to remain above the political chaos and fall-out from the abortion controversy because it could rely on the pro-Catholic line taken by the ZChN (Christian National Union). 'Yes, there are political groups who want to implement the rules of the Church. We respect them but it's their responsibility.' While Glemp publicly at least distanced himself from association with ZChN, the party itself never ceased to quote Church teaching and always explains its moral and social philosophy in terms of the teaching of John Paul II and the late Cardinal Wyszynski. Up until the 1993 election, when the party failed as a result of bad electoral tactics to get into parliament, it was regarded by political commentators as being a mouthpiece for at least a part of the Church.

Whatever about Glemp's equivocation now, there was little Church reticence in evidence during the presidential election in 1990. Many Polish clergy distributed leaflets and posters reminding the people that they faced an historical moment in which the 'fate of our homeland, Catholic Poland, was being weighed'. The Church unequivocally supported Lech Walesa's candidacy for President as a 'Pole and a Catholic'. Walesa's opponent, the then prime minister Tadeusz Mazowiecki, was also a Catholic but from the intellectual and liberal wing of Solidarity. During the election period his supporters claimed that he was the victim of a whispering campaign which alleged that he was of Jewish background.

The trend towards instructing Poles on how to exercise their newly won democracy continued in the first fully free parliamentary election at the end of 1991. In a letter from the bishops, voters were told that 'A Christian cannot choose a system which, in principle, denies God a place in public life. For this reason one must carefully examine the programme of individual parties and assess them in one's conscience, in keeping with the objective rules of Christian ethics.'⁴ If the public comments of certain bishops are anything to go by, it seems clear that the Church holds that it has a moral obligation to guide voters, and that that view is based on the opinion that people in post-communist society are not fully able to make decisions for themselves. Bishop Adam Lepa, chairman of the Polish Episcopate's Commission for Mass Media, when asked for his opinion on public dissatisfaction with the Church's high profile role, claimed that opinion polls expressing such views meant nothing in post-communist society: 'In my opinion, various opinion polls attempting to sound out the public's views fail to reflect the real situation. Many mistakes have been made in predictions based on such polls. I doubt if polls conducted in a post-totalitarian society are reliable at all. I suspect that they can mainly show the direction and efficiency of the current propaganda in some media.' Bishop Lepa went on to say that the issue of religious education in schools was an example of media bombardment: 'I am referring to this because the problem of the Church's presence in public life is reflected differently in statements made by political elites from that of the awareness and actions of media people, and still differently in the convictions and conversations of lay Catholics. Generally speaking, the latter group shows no dissatisfaction but on the contrary is clearly satisfied with any form of Church presence in public life. If there are any signs of disapproval in this area, they are a secondary phenomenon. I think this is a natural response to the well organized propaganda which has long been trying to tell society that it is threatened by the imminent clericalization of public life. This is undoubtedly yet another ersatz topic designed to divert society's attention from matters which are the most important for the nation. There are other such ersatz topics, for example, the alleged anti-Semitism of the Poles, the purported emergence of Church censorship, etc.' The people, it seems, are not to be trusted because they are not capable of making decisions. In an earlier part of Bishop Lepa's interview he offered the following assesment of the Polish public's ability to form an opinion: 'Actually, I doubt if this communism-saturated society is able, in its widest circles, to formulate the right diagnosis in the face of the current complicated situation. Church people are among those who display a fairly good orientation in this matter. After all, they are experts on human souls.'[5]

Theologian and moral philosopher Father Josef Tischner, though a close friend of Pope John Paul II, espouses a tolerant and liberal Catholicism. A big, burly man, his eyes full of laughter and pain; his surroundings, those of a monk. Unlike Cardinal Glemp he doesn't think that life was easier for the Church in communist times: 'I wouldn't say that the Church finds it difficult now. Difficult is the wrong word. Here, everything is easy now and because the situation is easy it is difficult to know what the Church should do. The political parties try and involve the Church in the political process and try to treat it as a political instrument. And unfortunately the Church is not impervious to religious rhetoric; sometimes it is seduced by this rhetoric. Religious rhetoric and real religious attitudes are two different things. I think that the support the Church gave to certain parties during the 1991 parliamentary election was as a result of the rhetoric. I'm going to be forthright here – and maybe I'll be criticized for it. But I would say that the size of the post-communist left-wing vote was increased by the Church's criticism of the Democratic Union's liberal and pluralist stance. The Church position was harmful to the Democratic Union, but this approach wasn't helpful to Catholics either. I think that the Church sees now that something went wrong.' Tischner is concerned that the Church, like many other groups in the new Poland, will not know how to build democratic structures because 'we don't have any democratic habits or customs.' He sees the danger that the Church can fall into the trap of allowing itself to fill the position of power broker vacated by the communists: 'Some time ago, a hospital director in this area was dismissed by the new Solidarity authorities. This man came to me and asked if I would intervene to help him. He asked me to intervene in the same way that, before, people went to the local Secretary of the Communist Party. There are many cases like this all over.'

Father Tischner argues that the traditional conflict between Church and State is no longer positive: 'The best way and the most positive

way to fight communism used to be to go to church. The basis of the
St Stanislaw celebrations here in Cracow are a good example. St
Stanislaw was the bishop of Cracow murdered by the king in the twelf-
th century. That was the historical basis of the conflict between Church
and state. During the celebrations each year in Cracow Cardinal
Wyszynski used the opportunity to give a sermon. It was interesting
that in 1991 Cardinal Glemp used the opportunity to attack the new
state. The outcome of all this opposition to the state is that the ordinary
man, the taxpayer, will cheat the state because he feels it is not his.'

For Father Tischner the burning issue is what role the Church will
play in constructing post-communist Poland: 'There are now big differences between this new, young democracy and the Church over
issues such as abortion and religious education in schools. The question
is whether the Church will support a state which is not built according
to its own ethic. The problem for the emerging democracy is whether
it will be enough to legitimize the democratic state or do we also need
religious legitimization. If we follow the first course, then we limit the
voice of the Church and of course the country will be more lay-
dominated. If, on the other hand, we go the second way, the Church
will have to accept a state that will not be built according to its own
ideology. Here I think that the Church should do a very heroic thing
and start accepting the state, even if it is not exactly as the Church
would like it to be – even if the state is not a saint.'

Father Tischner rejects the view that the Church is attempting to
construct a confessional state: 'I think it is true, especially in the lower
ranks of the clergy, that there is pressure to build a state based on
Catholic ethics. It's not that priests want power, but they believe that
the state is in a bad moral situation after communism. I think that this
is true. The ethical level of society is much lower than in the West.
For example, alcoholism is a big problem here. When the state owned
the stores, the authorities decided who could sell alcohol and when.
Now they are private and there are no controls. Also, the communists
destroyed people's ability to organize themselves. People didn't have to
make decisions. The main problem for priests is to teach people to
organize themselves again. If I was going to criticize my Holy Mother
Church it would be for not arranging enough help to teach people
to organize themselves. Wojtyla was very good at getting the laity
organized.' Father Tischner acknowledges that there are many within
the Church who oppose his view of Poland's future: 'My concept is of

a liberal democracy – so I represent Christian liberalism. The majority
are against my view. I think it is the view of the future, but right now
there are great anti-liberal tendencies in Poland – at least they are great
in terms of the language and the rhetoric they use. I don't think that
the Church needs state support to be strong. I think that the moral
strength of the Church is big enough. My God is the God of a free
people.'

Unlike many prominent churchmen and active Catholics, Tischner is
not convinced of the need for a Catholic or Christian constitution,
though he appreciates the view of those who argue that legislation, by
example, has an educational role: 'Up to now the state and its legislature was, by its very nature, immoral. But now I think it is not
important what is in the constitution. We should write down our
experience from the past – not, therefore, Christian or non-Christian
values. We should write in our constitution that during Solidarity times
we solved our problems without force. Our constitution should be
rooted in our history and our nation's experience.' From Father
Tischner's perspective the issue is not whether or not the constitution
is Catholic in its moral orientation. For him the real issue now is the
development of a society in which people identify with the state and
therefore owe it allegiance and respect its institutions. That is not an
easy task in a country where, for decades, institutions of state, such as
the police, had been seen as corrupt and regarded as agents of a foreign
master. 'Building a legal state,' he points out, 'in such a country is a
very hard task. There will be tension for a long time but I think that
in the end a liberal state will emerge, something on the lines of the
Austrian or German model.'

While the jury is still out on Father Tischner's optimistic and long-
term hope that Poland will become a liberal society, many observers see
the first four years of Solidarity government as a triumph for traditional
Catholic moral values. The Sejm took three years to debate how it
would change Communist Poland's 'on demand' abortion law which
had created a situation where abortion was just another form of contraception in a country where reliable contraceptive devices were difficult
to come by. While many liberals acknowledged the de-humanizing
effect of abortion as a primary means of contraception, they feared the
total ban sought by the Church-backed groups as the imposition of
sectarian values. Though opinion polls showed that seventy per cent of
the population favoured a referendum to decide the issue, liberal forces

within the Polish parliament and senate fudged the matter, fearing it would be the rock on which the delicate Suchocka coalition government would fall. In its original form the anti-abortion bill proposed by deputies from the ZChN would have banned abortion in almost every case except where the mother's life was at risk, as well as imposing jail sentences on both the woman and the doctor responsible for carrying out an abortion.

The chairwoman of the Parliamentary Women's Group, Democratic Union deputy Barbara Labuda, was a prime mover behind the referendum idea. The referendum, she proposed, would have asked whether Poles agreed with the criminalization of abortion and also their opinions on the legality of abortion when a pregnancy results from rape or incest, when it threatens the mother's life or health, when the foetus is seriously handicapped or when the mother is living in difficult circumstances. The referendum committee was headed by the former Solidarity underground leader Zbigniew Bujak, now a leader of the left wing Labour Union. Over a million signatures were collected backing the proposal while 120 Sejm deputies signed the referendum petition. Given President Lech Walesa's often stated opposition to abortion, it was not surprising that he also opposed the idea of holding a referendum. Cardinal Glemp on behalf of the bishops issued a carefully worded declaration in which he and they encouraged Catholics to pray to God 'so that he supports and blesses with his grace, efforts aimed at protecting each conceived human being.'[6] No doubt right-wing opposition to the referendum proposal was strengthened by opinion polls which showed that almost seventy per cent of Poles favoured allowing abortion when the foetus is severely damaged and where the mother's life is at risk, while fifty per cent would allow abortion where the pregnant woman was in financial difficulties.[7]

At the heart of the rancorous and often vitriolic abortion debate is the much wider issue of the conflict between secular and religious ethics and values. Zbigniew Bujak argues that the 'main division on the Polish political scene must sooner or later be drawn between fundamentalists and supporters of liberalism in its broad sense'. Rejecting the referendum idea, ZChN deputy Jan Lopuszanski highlights the enormous chasm that exists between the two sides: 'A referendum shows what people think about specific subjects. But in this case we are dealing with a moral issue. In such matters, you don't go around asking people's opinions. Good is good and evil is evil regardless of what the

majority or the minority think.' Fearful of the anti-democratic sentiments implicit in Lopuszanski's point of view, Zbigniew Bujak, and
liberals who share his opinion, feared the creation of a theocracy in
Poland: 'The tussle over anti-abortion legislation is a power game, a
battle for souls. Who has the right to determine what is moral and
what is not, what is compatible with Christian values and what is not?
The winners of this dispute would later want to dictate state policy.
That's why the dispute is so fierce and the bill so radical . . . The
argument that moral issues cannot be put to a vote has another side: in
reality, those who promote this view want to usurp the right to decide
what is moral and what is not. This shows their arrogance. Even the
Conference of Irish Bishops turned out to be more modest. As dedi-
cated as they are, they left the abortion decision up to their flocks.
Polish Sejm deputies, the President and the Prime Minister are trying
to impose their interpretation on the population.'[8]

Long before the Sejm and Senate passed the new abortion bill,
Poland's Supreme Doctors' Chamber introduced new ethical guidelines
for doctors which prohibited abortion for genetic or social reasons.
Under the terms of a new code of ethics introduced on 1 May 1992
doctors who performed an abortion in prohibited circumstances would
lose their right to practise medicine. Abortions in hospitals virtually
ceased after the introduction of the code, even though laws guarantee-
ing the right to an abortion, not only on the grounds of the protection
of the health of the mother but also where the mother was in difficult
circumstances, were still in force under the 1952 Constitution.

The law finally passed by the Sejm and the Senate allows abortion
in only three circumstances – where the foetus is seriously deformed,
where conception results from rape or incest and where there is a risk
to the life or health of the mother. A doctor who performs an abortion
in prohibited circumstances faces two years' imprisonment, though
under the revised bill the mother is not to be prosecuted. The bill also
guarantees access to contraception. In the pre-amended version,
favoured by the ZChN and the Church, abortion was allowed in only
one circumstances – where there was a risk to the mother's life. The
Sejm rejected liberal amendments that would have allowed a termination where the birth of a child would have added to the social or
economic difficulties of the pregnant woman. In the end the ZChN,
surprisingly, supported the bill in the Sejm, when it was finally voted

on in early January 1993. They regarded it as a bird in the hand which might well turn into two in the bush were it to be modified by pro-life Senators in the upper chamber. Those who opposed the criminalization of abortion voted against the milder bill, arguing that it was still too draconian. When the bill reached the Senate, those who favoured liberalizing it came just one vote short of pushing through an amendment which would have allowed a termination for social reasons. At the end of the day neither side was happy. Those in favour of a total ban know that the legislation is bound to be tested in the courts where it is possible that the clause relating to the risk to a woman's life could get a wider and more liberal interpretation. In the immediate aftermath pro-choice activists feared that the blanket protection provided to the foetus would be interpreted in such a way as to limit the availability of certain kinds of contraceptives. Some ZChN deputies openly said that they supported the idea of eliminating contraceptives from the Polish market altogether.

As the abortion row ground on, sex education was removed from the school curriculum in 1991 as part of a whole series of curriculum reform measures. With nearly half of all Polish marriages occurring after an unplanned pregnancy, this move was regarded as particularly retrograde by liberals conscious that the decision could only worsen social problems in a country where opinion polls show that very little is known about contraception. As work continued on the programme for schools, it was left up to teachers to decide whether or not to provide sex education courses to pupils. While some form of organized sexual instruction is normal in the big cities, many small towns and village teachers succumb to pressure from local Catholic clergy who tend to disapprove of instruction and promote only natural forms of contraception.

According to former Education Minister Andrzej Stelmachowski, 'there is no such thing as separation of the state from religion, because no human being is one hundred per cent a-religious.'⁹ A staunch Catholic, Stelmachowski has publicly stated that he saw no need for sex education in schools though he does regard religious education as an important element of the school curriculum. In April 1992 he signed an order introducing a new subject, ethics, into Polish public schools as an alternative to optional religious classes, which he increased from one to two periods each week. Though the order stated that the ethics/ religion class is not mandatory, those opting not to attend either class have a dash placed on their report card instead of a grade. The grade appears in the second position on the card beneath the mark for conduct. Following a demonstration organized by about a thousand students and teachers, opposed to the introduction of religion and ethics clases, Henryk Brunka, head of the Secretariat of the Polish episcopate, told the *Zycie Warszawy* daily that the demonstration was 'a protest by the sons and daughters of Russian officers'. Liberals, afraid of intolerance towards those· pupils who chose not to attend classes, argue that the new order branded a student for life, because their decision to opt out of religion or ethics would appear on their report card, thus creating the potential for the student to be discriminated against. Minister Stelmachowski's order also introduced the recitation of a prayer both before and after classes. Opponents of the order argued that the move is yet another example of the Polish educational system moving away from religious neutrality.

The ZChN's campaign in defence of 'Christian values' received yet another fillip at the beginning of 1993 with the passing of the radio and television law. The Sejm sanctioned amendments made by the Senate designed to compel the media to air programmes which would 'respect the Christian system of values as a basis, while accepting universal ethical principles'. In the final version of the bill programmes must 'particularly respect the Christian value system'. Because of the lengthy wrangling over the 'values' that were to be respected under the terms of the law, many of those deputies, originally opposed to the specific Catholic connotations, voted in favour of the final draft in order to allow for the introduction of private radio and TV stations.

Given the vagueness of the term 'Christian values', the introduction of the new law left many media professionals unsure about what it means in terms of programme content. However, there was no vagueness in the mind of Deputy Stefan Niesiolowski, one of the chief supporters of the bill in the Sejm. According to Niesiolowski, then the head of the ZChN's parliamentary party caucus, the new law bans satirical comments about the Church as well as prohibiting soft porn films and information about condoms. Again with only thirty per cent of the population supporting the measure and sixty per cent regarding the initiative as the first step on the road to censorship, it appeared that the public was having the ZChN's 'Christian values' imposed, whether it wanted them or not.[10] Though Niesiolowski had claimed that he was completely against the introduction of censorship, he has indicated that only journalists trained by the Catholic episcopate should be given the task of deciding what contravenes 'Christian values'. He apparently doesn't regard accepting the moral yardstick of just one church as conflicting in any way with freedom of speech.

Given the relative volatility of Polish politics, the make-up of the new National Radio and Television Council was yet another cause of concern to programme makers who wish to ply their trade without the interference of politicians and churchmen. The new council consists of four people appointed by the Sejm, two by the Senate and three by the President. The President will also appoint the chairman of the council. The fact that the composition of the council is to change by a third every two years could become a flashpoint, given the danger that its decisions will simply reflect the prevailing political balance of power. Opponents argue that it could simply become a super censor reflecting the ideological preference of the prevailing political elite.

The ZChN has not restricted its moral crusade to parliamentary activity. It stepped up its campaign in late 1992 by taking two separate public decency cases to the prosecutor's office. One case involved the infamous Benetton series of ads. The ZChN's objected to a poster which depicted a nun and priest kissing each other, claiming it was offensive on religious grounds. The party also pressed charges against the rock group Piersi (Breasts), whose song 'ZChN's Coming' became an instant hit following the party's complaint. The song, which is sung to the tune of a well known hymn, often used for children's Holy Communion ceremonies, tells the story of a priest who gets drunk during a visit to his parishioners. After the visit he speeds off in his car and crashes into a fence. Police smile and parishioners lament that once again they'll have to put more money into the collection plate. A radio producer bold enough to play the disc was sacked and was reinstated only after the intervention of Democratic Union deputies. ZChN deputies have also applied themselves to the consideration of what movies late night Polish viewers are allowed see. Having managed to twice stave off the screening of *Emmanuelle*, the movie was eventually scheduled for an 11 p.m. screening in October 1992. In the end, following yet more protests from the ZChN, the film was shown after midnight.

Commentators like Professor Wnuk-Lipinski acknowledge that the Church has been used by politicians anxious to give themselves a readymade impimatur. However, he argues that the Church in Poland will settle down and find a legitimate role for itself: 'After martial law the Church became a huge unconditional umbrella for the underground and for the entire opposition movement. It was no longer just a community of believers – its role was far bigger. But the Church must learn to live in a free society, just as others have had to. After the collapse of communism, the Church was like a balloon with no limits. It was expanding everywhere. Like Solidarity, which had to manage a self-limiting revolution, the Church will have to learn to manage a self-limiting expansion of its role. Part of the Hierarchy know that there is a price to pay for a big role in public life. The Church can only maintain its role as an independent arbiter in conflicts, if it is not directly involved itself. There's no doubt that in some respects the Church was more comfortable under communism. The main issue now for the Church is to find a new identity and role for itself as a public institution in a free Poland. I think that the Church knows society better than the communists did and knows that a confessional state would produce an atheistic state in the long-term. The Church doesn't want this. They'll learn to temporize.'

Former Liberal prime minister Jan Krzystof Bielecki (Minister in charge of EC Integration under Suchocka) warns that the Church in Poland should look to its more long-term interest: 'It cannot be involved in the creation of the new Polish political scene. During the election in late 1991, the Church was directly involved in the campaign – particularly in the countryside. Sometimes the priests even indicated who parishioners should vote for. But if Poland is meant to be ninety five per cent Catholic and the priests tell people how to vote and they still only manage to get ten per cent of the vote for the Catholic party, then something has gone wrong. What it shows is that the Church's influence is limited. This is evident when you look at opinion polls. Take abortion: the public is clearly against the criminalization of abortion. The short-term attitude of the Church is dangerous. Maybe dangerous is the wrong word, but it certainly complicates the political scene here.'

A combination of a massive tactical error and public disquiet at the level of Church influence on private morality resulted in the annihilation of the ZChN in the September '93 elections. The tactical error was the announcement of a coalition with the Conservative Party late in the election campaign. Under the new electoral law coalition groups had to break the seven per cent threshold in order to translate votes into seats in parliament. This the combined pair failed to do. ZChN chairman Wieslaw Chrzanowski admits that it is a disaster for his party but refuses to acknowledge that the electorate had rejected his party's message. Instead he blames television and radio for being pro-communist and anti-Church. He says the President should never have called the election in the first place and that Bujak's Labour Union was responsible for all the hullabaloo over abortion. Interestingly, Chrzanowski acknowledges that the Church moved to distance itself from the ZChN during the course of the election campaign. There is no doubt that this is the case, as even the slightest analysis of Church statements and interviews highlights. It is likely that two important developments affected the Church's attitude in the pre-election summer period. Firstly Poland and the Vatican concluded a concordat, which some liberals regard as giving the Polish Church too many concessions, and secondly Bishop Tadeusz Pieronek was elected secretary general of the episcopal conference. Pieronek is by Polish Catholic standards a liberal and would be regarded as closer in thinking to men like Father Josef Tischner than to the traditional and conservative wing of the Church. While many bishops might disagree with him, Pieronek made it clear before the election that the Church should not directly back individual parties. This was undoubtedly an easier pill to ask his fellow churchmen to swallow given the fact that the concordat enshrined the Church's position in a framework which claimed to establish the principle of the separation of Church and state.

This new caution was by no means to the liking of Wieslaw Chrzanowski, who regards it as a factor which confused the electorate and decimated his vote: 'Firstly it was put to us by people very high up in the Church that it was better that there be only one Catholic list of candidates. There is no doubt that the opinion of certain influential bishops had changed. So we announced a coalition with the Conservative Party in the last weeks of the campaign. The new secretary general of the episcopal conference, Bishop Pieronek, had a very different attitude to the previous man, Archbishop Dombrowski. It was clear that the bishops were worried about their relationship with the future government. They anticipated the fact that the left would do well in the election. They remembered that under Gierek and Jaruzelski that the Church was able to negotiate. They concluded that, if the SLD won, open support for the ZChN would complicate relations between the Church and the government. It was around the middle to the end of

August that the Church's attitude towards us changed.' Chrzanowski regards the change as a bitter blow and is very obviously not impressed by its exhibition of *realpolitik*.

Janusz Onyszkiewicz feels that the Church learned its lesson long before ZChN's painful experience in the September '93 election: 'They had their fingers burned. At parish level the priests were very involved in earlier campaigns. Certain parties were solidly supported by the parish priests. But it was a factor in the loss of popularity for the Church. It's the reason why the Church is no longer the most trusted institution in Poland. According to opinion polls the Army now is the most trusted group. They drew the lesson and kept a low profile this time around. I think that the hierarchy accepts the Pope's view that the Church should not mix with politics and should identify with issues and not with institutions and certainly not with political parties. The Church must now find its place in a democratic society. For over forty years they developed a tactic to ignore the law and challenge the authorities. That places them on a collision course with both the government and the legal system. Now the situation is changed, and it has taken the Hierarchy a while to realize this. They don't have to kick the door down anymore because it is already open. Now it looks as if the Church is well on its way to finding its place in society and their attitude is becoming more subtle.'

Former Centrum Alliance MP Jacek Majiarski agrees that the Church paid a very high price for its high profile during the abortion debate: 'They realized it and decided to take a back seat this time. I'm sure that they'll be much more cautious in future. It saw that it was placed in a difficult position by such open asssociation with the ZChN. Often much of the impulse for the social reforms like abortion came from extreme lay elements and politicans. But the Church couldn't say that they didn't support them.'

Mieczyslaw Rakowski says that the hierarchy gave the ZChN 'the shoulder during the campaign. They want to have influence now with the new government. And perhaps looking back they know that the best period for them was in the eighties because Jaruzelski saw them as a partner. A better partner than the revolting workers. But people are much more educated now and they reacted to this extremism from the Church. Polish people hate extremes. They are moderates.'

The former underground leader and Gdansk MP Bogdan Borusewicz agrees that the electorate reacted badly to the whole issue of Church influence on private morality. But he says the ZChN will be back: 'They got six per cent of the vote, so they do have a base. The result was a tactical error. The Church doesn't want the ZChN to set the agenda because within the party there are elements that are more extreme on moral issues than the Church itself. Our bishop here in Gdansk commented that some politicians from the ZChN act as if they were born without original sin.'

Democratic Union leader Bronislaw Geremek argues that the public was simply astonished by the level of direct involvement by the Church in politics: 'Poland is a Catholic country, but Poles don't accept such a heavy Church presence in politics. I think that they had a tri-umphalistic attitude and went too far in demands over issues such as their rights concerning former property. They went over the top on the issue of their role in society and the teaching of religion and sexual matters in schools. Their direct involvement in public affairs and in political affairs had a negative effect on their popularity. One of the reasons why the SLD and the PSL were so successful in this election is because of the attitude of the Church. Women were afraid of the abortion situation. Now there is a terrorism in Polish hospitals with women going to the Ukraine and such places for an abortion. It is non-sense. In fact I believe it is a good law. Now it is a question of how it is interpreted, but that depends on the climate in local hospitals and whether the priest can exert pressure and influence, whether the priest has the real power.' Geremek rejects any suggestion that the govern-ment exposed itself on the abortion issue: 'I believe that we averted a religious war in Poland which would have been disastrous with its ideological divisions. Perhaps the concordat was a mistake. It was intro-duced during the election campaign. I don't understand why. But the public didn't see it as an agreement between the Vatican and Poland but simply as a decision concerning divorce and marriage and Church finances. But this misunderstanding over the concordat was a factor in the election result and it was our mistake.'

Jan Litynski goes further than Geremek and recognizes that as a liberal party the Democratic Union should have been more confronta-tional on the Church-State question: 'The people have rejected the level of Church interference. Our mistake was that we didn't recognize it. We should have clearly criticized some of the tendencies. But we were afraid of attacks from right-wing elements within the Church. We tried to have good relations with them because we wanted them to leave the rest of the reforms alone. It was a mistake.'

The last four years have been difficult for both Church and state in Poland. The shadow boxing and muscle flexing have perhaps come to an end. Ironically with the big moral battles already fought it is probable that a chastened hierarchy will be able to sustain far happier relations with a left-wing government anxious to keep contentious firecrackers well and truly dampened.

11

LECH WALESA

THE NOT SO RELUCTANT HERO?

It is no surprise that Lech Walesa has proved to be a controversial president. Long before television pictures of the moustachioed figure rallying workers outside the Gdansk shipyard gates became the cliched image of Solidarity throughout the world, Walesa aroused intense feelings of both admiration and contempt. During the presidential campaign in 1990, allegations that Walesa behaved like a dictator were voiced in the foreign media. There was nothing new in the charges that Walesa 'loved himself', that he liked being compared with Marshal Pilsudski, that he bullied people and that he was often out of his depth intellectually: all Poland knew the allegations.

The first time that I heard the name Lech Walesa was in discussion with Jan Litynski just before I visited Gdansk in early August 1980. I remember the smile on Jan's lips describing Walesa. It was clear that the intellectual dissident end of the opposition movement regarded him as a useful but somewhat comic figure. What I found interesting, then, was that this attitude did not reveal any dismissive attitude to the Free Trades Union movement as a whole, but what it does indicate is that from very early on prominent members of the opposition had reservations about Walesa's ability.

Armed with Jan's reservations I should have been able to adopt a more critical view of Walesa when I met him. But like many others after me I enjoyed his potent mixture of humour, charm and arrogant pomposity. Meeting him on the eve of the Gdansk shipyard strike in Anna Walentynowicz's flat, I was struck by his habit of injecting humour into serious business, his ability to take the floor and most of all by his lively, twinkling and definitely mischievous eyes. I had been allowed sit in on what was a private and conspiratorial meeting of the Coastal Free Trades Union movement. Looking back, I am still not quite clear why the committee tolerated my presence at such an important time. Neither can I understand why people who were as busy as they were, in the days before the strike, bothered giving interviews to an unknown journalist from the remotest outpost of Europe. But they were confused and in some respects trusting times. Years later, Alina Pienkowska, then a shipyard nurse and committee member, told me that her future husband, Bogdan Borusewicz, a founding member of the Free Trades Union movement, was furious that the committee had talked about the strike plan to a foreign journalist. Walesa displayed no such fury. Even though I had been followed by secret police, on my arrival in Gdansk, Walesa offered to travel home with me by tram from Anna's flat. It was a kind gesture from a man who must have been preoccupied on that sunny evening in mid-August.

Seven months later, in early March 1981, I interviewed Walesa at Solidarity's Gdansk headquarters. The atmosphere was chaotic. Journalists from all over the world wanted interviews. Remembering me from our first meeting, Walesa told his aides that he had given his first foreign press interview to this 'girl from Ireland'. This important event was commemorated with a celebratory hug.

By that stage the Solidarity machine was a well oiled mechanism. Visiting journalists or dignatories were provided with a picture service by a resident photographer who produced photos of a smiling Walesa and guest, in a matter of hours. Commemorative books, badges, tee-shirts, ribbons and paraphernalia were all available at Solidarity's hive-like headquarters. Looking back at that picture of a smiling Walesa, the pipe as always in his mouth, the Madonna of Czestochowa dominating his chest, there is no apparent sign of the darker side that many observers believe now dominates the soul of Poland's President. It would be naive to expect Walesa to have stood still. High office was bound to change the feisty electrician. The President's palace cannot be compared with the headquarters of a trade union leader, albeit a leader of millions. Sadly, any meeting with Walesa nowadays is overshadowed by the behaviour of those who dominate what has become satirically known as 'King Lech's court'. Given the allegations of corruption and collaboration against Walesa and his associates, not to mention the boorish and crude attitude of some of his immediate aides, it is difficult to ascertain who the real Lech Walesa is. Following a series of interviews with the President at the Belweder Palace, I was left wondering whether 'Lech's court' danced to his tune or whether he was in fact the marionette depicted in so many caricatures?

In a long interview with Walesa for the *Irish Press* after our second meeting in March 1981, I wrote: 'Meeting Lech Walesa for the second time seven months after he was catapulted onto the international stage by his rousing anthem-singing in the Lenin Shipyard, one is struck by how little the man himself has changed. Though he has developed a method of dealing with the press that seems to come completely natural to him, the only obvious difference is that by now he is a very tired man. Detractors are inclined to say that "he loves himself", that he plays the hero just a little too much, but perhaps they miss that which was always an essential part of the man's personality and is now certainly essential to the tense situation in Poland.

'It was very obvious in the Solidarity headquarters in Gdansk that the staff worshipped this man. He has charm and a natural political strength which even the most vocal of his critics will not deny. To say he is a simple man is not to malign him but to state the truth and to emphasize his greatest strength and weakness all in one . . . In as complicated a society as Poland, however, with its many different intellectual outlooks and with its conflicting lobbies, Lech Walesa finds himself, as a simple man, advised by a large variety of diverse groups. There is no consensus in the information and opinions he is receiving, and therefore he sometimes seems to sway with the opinion of the last man to see him. Because of his strong religious impulse, this often means that Church advisers have an unfair advantage which, in terms of the calibre of these advisers, is not always a good thing.

'He claims not to be surprised by what happened in Poland after the strikes, but one detects a certain incredulity with his personal position.'[1]

Twelve years later the fundamental issues regarding Walesa's abilities are still the same as I outlined after that second meeting. Does he love himself so much that he confuses his own interest with that of the nation? Has his simplicity left him intellectually incapable of dealing with the complex issues which face the leader of a society undergoing a huge transition? Is he capable of choosing advisers or has he become the puppet of his entourage? In addition to all of this he now has to face down allegations from former advisers and colleagues who claim that he was a communist agent. People like Andrzej and Joanna Gwiazda, and Anna Walentynowicz have been claiming that Walesa was a spy and a traitor to Solidarity for some time now. Their claims are largely ignored because they're regarded as bitter, having been left behind in the shadow of Walesa's rise to international fame. Walesa laughs at the allegations of his former friends. It hasn't however been quite as easy for Walesa to laugh off the 'agent Bolek' allegations and as *The Times* correspondent in Warsaw, Roger Boys, has pointed out these allegations are very 'easy to make, and impossible to disprove. Any revisionist biographer can show that Walesa sometimes played into the hands of the authorities, and quite frequently they also played into his hands. So what? That was the political game of the 1980s, its very essence. There are not many "clean" politicians nowadays because to be politically active in the dissident years was to invite the attention of the secret police and to have a dossier in Rakowiecka Street.'[2]

One of the recurring themes in the various allegations made against Walesa is that he and his entourage have contemplated a *coup d'état*. This allegation was particularly in vogue just before the collapse of Jan Olszewski's government in April, May and June of 1992 at a time when it seemed that coup plots were being hatched in every quarter. At the end of April, *Gazetta Wyborcza* published a series of interviews with a number of Walesa's former aides. The picture painted was of a megalomaniac who is unable to work with competent politicians and experts. He was presented as someone incapable of taking difficult decisions, unable to think in strategic terms and inclined to spontaneous outbursts. Walesa's people at the Belweder are described as unprofessional toadies with little skill, training or ability. It is alleged that Mieczslaw Wachowski, the head of the chancellery, is corrupt, is either a former KGB or CIA agent, and is intent on undermining democracy. The article was written by Jaroslaw Kurski, who had at one time worked for Walesa and published in a newspaper edited by former dissident, Adam Michnik. The fact that people, once so close to Walesa, were prepared to publicly make very serious statements about their former hero is another example of the damage done to politics in Poland as a result of Walesa's 'War at the Top.' It is in fact a reasonable proposition that Walesa is merely reaping the harvest of the seed of discontent that he sowed when he set Solidarity against itself. The former head of Walesa's chancellery, Jaroslaw Kaczynski, told *Gazetta Wyborcza* that 'Walesa can be dangerous for the country. As has been proved by his recent statements about the necessity of suspending democracy. In my opinion, that whole group is having a destructive influence on the state. Walesa would like to have broad authority, and that authority will still last for a long time, although it will not be unlimited. I believe that he would be comfortable with the position of Pilsudski, who made all the decisions while at the same time being able to remain a little off to the side.' Krzysztof Wyszkowski, one of the founding members of the Free Trades Union movement in Gdansk and latterly one of Walesa's presidential campaign organizers was caustic in his comments: 'The persistence with which he is destroying the political scene stems from a radical lack of understanding of what constitutes a state. "The State and I", thinks Walesa, and for him, these two things are equally important, and maybe the "I" is more important than Poland . . . Walesa is personally too weak to become a dictator. A dictator is someone who accumulates power, who has an intellectual grasp of it and acts within the powers entrusted to him. Walesa isn't able to plan out a dictatorship. He can't, he's too lazy for that. What is possible, though, is dictatorship by decree. What Walesa would then need would be someone competent who would hold complete sway over him and a good team of economic experts. Slogans would become simple then. Enough of politics in the public arena. Now it's time to get to work. What's needed is order and results, a march in some direction.'

Arkadiusz Rybicki, a one-time political adviser to Walesa, describes him as an individual completely out of his depth: 'Not being able to get a grip on the subject which he was suddenly faced with, Walesa dismissed from his immediate surroundings all the people who had any political significance and who asked difficult questions while surveying his various moves with reproach. Walesa backed into a shell, surrounded himself with yes men, and adapted himself for survival. He isolated himself from his advisers because they forced him to make an effort which he couldn't bear. This is the loneliness that comes from the feeling of defeat. In such a situation, the easiest thing for him to say is that nobody understands his plans and that the elites are failing. He has forgotten that he himself is the elite of the elites.

'The spokesman's assurance that the President had ten solutions to every problem meant that he didn't have any. Everybody knows that Walesa is a man who doesn't wait when he has ideas, but implements them before he's had time to rethink them . . . The lack of specific objectives, the internal tension, then the identity crisis, were throwing Walesa off balance and turned an ordinary day into a nightmare. Walesa shouted, threw people out, didn't allow them to put a word into the conversation. He felt that the situation was too big for him. That is why, when he says that he would like to leave, that he is not happy being President, I believe him. When you read into his press statements, the nightmare shows through every sentence, these months have been the worst period of his life. "Nie chce ale musze" (I don't want to, but I must): those words reveal a real internal conflict.'

Both Jaroslaw Kaczynski and a former Secretary of State for National Security, Jacek Merkel, claim that Walesa went very close to recognizing the Soviet coup against Gorbachev. 'I know,' says Kaczynski, 'that during the coup, there was a letter written, in which Walesa recognized President Yanayev. Only seconds more, and he would have sent it. I assume that the author of the letter was among the President's closest circle.' According to Merkel, it was only after much persuasion that Prime Minister Bielecki managed to stop the letter.

Jaroslaw Kaczynski's twin brother Lech made a number of unsubstantiated allegations about Mieczyslaw Wachowski: 'Wachowski is a man with influence, and he plays an enormous role in the country. He is also dangerous and ready for anything. His presence in the Belweder is an insult to the country. He is trying to gain influence, to worm his way in, to weave a net of invisible contacts in those areas of public life which he considers to be significant, and he is not wrong in his assessment of their importance. This means the armed forces, special services, Eastern politics. Lately, also the banking system. There are certain things that are commonly known in the chancellery, but which would be extremely hard to prove.'

Krzysztof Wyszkowski's hatred for Wachowski is almost palpable in the following paragraph: 'Wachowski creates around the President an atmosphere of a contemptuous, cynical, and venomous joking at the expense of the national interest and institutions. This is a way of venting psychological tension. Some drink, others swear, still others lock themselves up in bathrooms and scream. Wachowski relaxes Walesa with huge doses of rudely expressed contempt for the world, tinted with humour and a feverish, even pathological gaiety. If Walesa was a more civilized person by nature, he would find all this completely unbearable. Wachowski is nothing else than the dark side of Walesa himself. He is not two-faced. His face is completely unknown.'

Of course, many politicians who were by no means pro-Walesa regarded the Kurski interviews as having gone over the top. Aleksander Hall, who was leader of the right-wing faction in the Democratic Union when the interviews were published, dismissed the notion of an alleged coup: 'The presidency is not faring well. The mistakes are evident. But the vision of a coup, of an ongoing conspiracy: all this is completely absurd. The accusations put forward are not supported by any solid proof or logical arguments.' Others saw a more simple explanation for the inclusion of people such as Wachowski in Walesa's entourage: Walesa is overwhelmingly lonely. One Liberal Democratic Congress politician, Lech Mazewski, commented that 'it would be the best solution if Wachowski returned to his profession as a cab driver. Certainly he is not the Belweder's demon nor Lech Walesa's dark side. But he is living proof of the Polish political system's weakness. If it were not for the flawed system, a man of such modest qualities would not have such a career.'

On the other hand, Marcin Krol, the respected editor of the monthly, *Res Publica*, thinks that there was no smoke without fire: 'Wachowski has been present in Walesa's circle for many years, and it seems quite dubious that only now his true demonic face is being discovered. He did not fall out of the sky.'³ It seems that most respected politicians and observers seem to agree that Wachowski would be better off going back to driving cabs.

Men like Janusz Onyszkiewicz have known Walesa from the beginning of the Solidarity movement. Unlike the individuals who took jobs in Walesa's chancellery, Onyszkiewicz has a more detached attitude to the former trade union boss. Though critical of his role in the period of the 'War at the Top', Onyszkiewicz argues that Walesa's contribution has become more positive: 'His role between 1990 and 1992 was very negative but it stabilized. He destroyed the political scene to an enormous extent. He has a tendency to fight the strongest, so if a political framework emerges out of this fragmentation which would be able to provide strong leadership, Walesa might turn against it. He has a knee-jerk reaction to power. He is afraid always for his own position. His formal prerogatives as President are small – so he tries to secure his influence. He wants to call the shots – in simple terms. He'll be happy if two or three strong political groups emerge but he'll try to suppress one strong group – were it to emerge. One big problem is the people around Walesa. Their quality is debatable. There's the geographic factor. In the Belweder, he's away from his base in Gdansk, so he has his people, mainly from there, working with him. Walesa stays with his "court". There's definitely a "court" atmosphere in Belweder.'

In the four-year period during which I gathered material for this book I was repeatedly struck by the deterioration of Walesa's reputation among former colleagues from Solidarity times. As a key member of the original Gdansk strike committee Bogdan Lis knows Lech Walesa well. The following extract from an interview was recorded in the spring of 1992: 'Walesa has an ability to use others' knowledge: he has good political intuition. If he has wise people around him, then his activity is positive. But I don't think that he is himself capable of carrying out his presidential functions. He is not sure what to do. He looks to blame others around him – if there are problems. The situation gets worse when there are bad advisers around him. But it is very difficult to get good people to work with him. It's a self-perpetuating problem. In the spring of 1991 he asked me to become a minister in his chancellery. But I refused because of the environment and the people around him – they're completely incompetent. Walesa is a pawn. He allowed himself to be used as a pawn in the war with Mazowiecki and Geremek. He was the pawn of the two Kaczynski brothers. Now look at them. Unfortunately Walesa's behaviour now is very important for the future. The behaviour of the current Polish President will have an effect on how the presidential functions will be defined in the new Constitution. Parliament could back away from giving the President too much power because of the way Walesa has behaved. On the other hand, if it's decided that Walesa has been wise, then perhaps the new Constitution will define wide powers. That's why what he does is so important. But he has failed so many times.' Bogdan Lis thought it was still a little early to say whether Walesa had outlived his usefulness to Poland, but he was sure that, in what he calls Poland's 'New Era', a great name, the mythology of the hero is no longer enough. 'Possibly his time is over. At the next election it would be a sign of social maturity were the people to choose someone else.'

I talked to Alina Pienkowska, the nurse who stopped Walesa from prematurely ending the strike, about her assessment of Walesa in early 1992 and in the autumn of 1993. Quoting from both interviews highlights the massive deterioration in her regard for her former colleague. In the first interview, while she agrees that Walesa has made many mistakes she argues that he is a positive force in Polish politics: 'One must differentiate between the behaviour of the leader of a union and the President of the country. During the presidential campaign I was definitely for Walesa. All those warnings about his dictatorial ways, all the allegations from the Democratic Union – none have been proven.' Alina, then a Solidarity Club Senator, was firmly in favour of widening Walesa's powers as President: 'I don't think that in the situation of so much change and splits that Walesa should have his powers restricted in any new Constitution. I don't think it would be safe. Look at the political parties. They are not responsible. The Centrum Alliance was meant to be a presidential party; instead it became something else. Various parties try to use Walesa for their own aims. Take the issue of control over the military. Given the splits I think that Walesa should retain control. It would be dangerous to give control to parliament. The political elites want to restrict his power but he won't agree to be a puppet.' Alina Pienkowska very obviously still admired Walesa but recognizsed the danger for constructive politics were he to be ever again politically sidelined. While acknowledging that Walesa was always a controversial figure Alina felt that the bottom line in relation to any evaluation of his role was that he led Poland out from behind the 'Iron Curtain' and towards free elections: 'I know him well. I do believe that he puts Poland first. I don't think that he has his own private interest. There are many who disagree in my party – but I like him and political differences wouldn't colour my personal affection.'

A year and a half later the warmth is completely gone. She now says that it is not appropriate to discuss whether she 'likes' Walesa or not: 'During this recent period he has not used his position to solve Poland's problems. I don't believe that he has used his position properly. I treat all these allegations about "Bolek" lightly. It is not essential. What's important is how he uses the last remaining two years of his Presidency. Whether he uses the period for Poland or for Walesa. When my husband Bogdan [Borusewicz] met Walesa to discuss whether he would join the BBWR [Nonpartisan Reform Support Bloc] just before the election, Walesa put all his cards on the table. He talked of going down the Yeltsin road. Sometimes he says very dangerous things. One has to be very careful about what Lechu says and then watch what he does.'

Alina now thinks that the presidency was beyond Walesa's abilities, but she cautions that it would have been too big a job, given the traumatic times, no matter who the incumbent was.

Poland's second prime minister, Jan Krzyzstof Bielecki, had many opportunities to assess Walesa's abilities: 'Sometimes I had the impression that he couldn't manage the complex problems of these new times. I thought that the challenge was too strong for him: then suddenly he shows great political skill. That happens all the time.' Bielecki sees Walesa as a mixture of good and bad, as someone capable of greatness on the one hand and capable of appalling blunders on the other: 'When things are okay and the good side is dominant, then he often says or does something great. But if the situation is difficult or if he feels under pressure he tries to invent unique solutions and this is often very dangerous. He likes to play the role of the boss. I am of the opinion that playing the role of the coach is a better idea in politics. The coach is able to stay outside the field and keep the spirit of the team high.. But Walesa finds it hard now to manage the team, he can't play between the sides, because he has no team. He has no personal team any more. He's surrounded by his former driver, a priest and a journalist. It's very bad; he has lost contact with the outside world.'

The September '93 election result was proof, if any was needed, that the Walesa legend had waned. Walesa's BBWR managed only 16 seats in the Sejm. Bielecki says he tried to dissauade the President from supporting a party built around himself: 'I told him it was a bad move. I tried to convince him to stay with the government coalition. I asked him not to go ahead and form this new so called non-party party. I think Walesa was sure that he would win. The result diminished his position. But he's lucky now; because he's a loser, he's popular again. In many ways he's still the only one who has the ability to have a fast impact on events here. He's still a successful politician. Even when he says daft things he survives. He's still in the game. He has a certain way of getting the smell of the street. He has this political intuition. I think he can still be elected President next time. That is, if the Constitution still retains a President.'

Jacek Majiarski was once part of Walesa's kitchen cabinet in the days when the two Kaczynski brothers ruled the roost at the Belweder. Majiarski says that he ceased to admire Walesa after he became President: 'I realized that he wasn't interested in anything but strengthening his own position. He built structures around him to control political life. He used the worst elements of the Intelligence Service, the Army, pureblood communists from the old banking system. He just wanted power and money. In the last two years he simply attempted to destroy the democratic order. He stopped the introduction of a new constitution and impeded parliament at every turn. He was trying to keep everybody and everything weak so that he couldn't be opposed. He was trying to take power peacefully. He was constantly undermining the Suchocka government. The ministers under his influence were destroying her cabinet.'

During the presidential campaign I followed Walesa's entourage, interviewed him and watched him perform in halls and stadia around the country. Again and again I realized that my interpreter's commentary wasn't adding up to a coherent sentence. What was wrong? Certainly the interpreter was excellent and the crowds were normally roaring approval. Walesa talks in metaphors. He draws on symbolism and anecdote to enthuse his audience. It's normally earthy and gutsy stuff full of threats of dire remedy peppered with lots of bluff. In the past Walesa's charismatic style and macho delivery worked. It worked when there was but one issue. It didn't work when Walesa spoke to European Community representatives in Strasbourg and it didn't work when he addressed German parliamentarians in the spring of 1992. It doesn't work when journalists ask questions which require straight answers. Despite listening to many speeches, observing him being interviewed and talking to Walesa myself both during and after the presidential campaign, I always come away thinking, Words, words, words – but what does it all mean? Professor Wnuk-Lipinski describes Walesa as having 'a rare virtue. He has instinct. He knows by looking into his heart – not into his mind – what's happening. Some people think that he's authoritarian. But in fact it's a question of his competence with language. The superficial interpretation of his behaviour is that he is authoritarian. But in Walesa's case, I believe it is misleading. Walesa has played an enormous role in Poland, but now there are some disadvantages. Democratic transformation is difficult under a charismatic leader. The Solidarity revolution was self-limiting because the Party was still in power. I think Walesa has to learn to limit his charisma.' Walesa is amused by the fact that people often find it difficult to know what he is talking about: 'I think it's a good thing that I am ambiguous, they write their theses and get their diplomas. A lot of people earn a lot of money because I am ambiguous.'

President Walesa's press spokesman, Andrzej Drzycimski, decides which journalists see the President. Any deviation from the agreed list of questions can bring banishment. According to the grey and hooded-eyed Drzycimski, Walesa does not wish to speak about the past. Only questions relating to the future are tolerated. Present at all presidential interviews are Drzycimski, normally sitting beside the President, and Mieczyslaw Wachowski, pacing and exchanging knowing smiles and secrets with the rest of the Belweder flunkeys. There is most definitely a slight air of menace in the demeanour of Walesa's immediate entourage. The Belweder Palace is not a place where courtesy is valued. One is never quite sure whether Walesa encourages this style or whether he is its unwilling victim.

On my first visit to the Belweder in early 1992 I decided to risk Drzycimski's wrath and asked Walesa about the 'War at the Top'. I wanted to know if he felt he had wasted a golden opportunity to remain a unifying symbol by initiating the internal struggle in Solidarity. 'You can't build pluralism out of the kind of unity that existed,' he replied. 'That kind of unity used to be called communism. I knew that my task after the victory was to change the order, to bring pluralism into our society. How can you make pluralism without division? I had no choice but to make a division. I couldn't leave Solidarity as a monopoly group because how could that be pluralist? I am criticized as the author of the split, but I predicted that. The split was to reach down, to the unemployed, and together with everybody we were to create political parties. But after my split the elites settled in Warsaw and they look after their sofas; they don't get down with the people, they don't build and they don't seek alliances.'

Democratic Union leader Bronislaw Geremek was one of Walesa's earliest advisers. Their relationship was badly damaged by the "War at the Top" and the subsequent parting of the ways during the presidential campaign in which Geremek supported another former Walesa adviser, Prime Minister Tadeusz Mazowiecki: 'It is difficult for me to assess Walesa because it involves my personal relationship with him. We spent ten years of our lives together. It was a privileged and special relationship between us. I don't think that one year of the so-called "War at the Top" has destroyed this relationship. Not from my side and I hope not from his. I have a feeling that Walesa understood that the first year of his Presidency was lost for both himself and Poland. The role of the President can be that of an arbiter in social and political conflict. He was unable to play a role because he was one of the partners in this conflict. Now I can see that he is trying to change this situation. It was a negative experience for him. And from my point of view I am interested to see what Mr Walesa does with the rest of his period as President. The experience of the first year was very disappointing. It wasn't useful for Poland, for him or for the reforms.' Geremek acknowledges that the transition from trade union boss to President was a traumatic one for Walesa: 'There were two difficult problems for Walesa. The first was personal. It is not an easy passage from charismatic trade union boss to head of state. It is not possible to lead the nation as President in the same way that he led Solidarity. It was painful for both him and difficult for the office. Then there was the problem of the constitutional framework in which he found himself. Because of the fact that he was directly elected by the people, we were not able to define what his powers were and what controls should be placed on his activity. We had no experience of this office. I do think that we have a long tradition in Poland of the relationship between the king and his ministers. In the eighteenth century, under the Polish Constitution all decisions by the king had to be approved by the ministers. Now our Constitution gives an unclear framework for the President's powers I think that the counter signature of ministers is important if the President has executive powers. This authoritarianism that is alleged against Mr Walesa is a common problem in the post-communist situation. In all post-communist countries there is this authoritarian temptation, a weakness of the state apparatus and of the democratic mentality. This direct election of the President by the people is a symptom of this problem. Such Presidents are not on the French or American model – it's simply a continuation of the Secretary-General of the Communist Party. That's the real problem. At the beginning of this transformation process we were unable to form the political culture of a democratic society in which the government can be strong, but under the control of parliament. The relationship between the executive and the legislature has yet to be defined in democratic terms.'

Until the post-communist victory Lech Walesa hoped that Poland's new Constitution would create an American- or French-style President. Geremek argues that Walesa's mistake was not just the 'War at the Top' but also his 'decision to reject the proposal for defining his powers in the first constitutional reform proposal presented to him in late 1991. I think it gave both the government and Walesa a clear constitutional framework. But he wasn't satisfied. He thought it didn't give him enough power.'

The whole issue of the role of the President is controversial, and not just because of Walesa. The establishment of the office, which was at first elected by the National Assembly, was agreed at the Round Table as a means of retaining communist influence in the new order. 'We never accepted this presidential role at the Round Table,' says Geremek. 'But it was a guarantee that the whole process would continue. You must remember that the Communist Party had to disappear or be transformed and the only man who could do it was Mr Jaruzelski as long as he had presidential power. That's the reason for the introduction of this office. In a sense they proposed to change the peculiar role of the Party in the one-party system by the introduction of presidential power. It was in fact the continuation of the monopoly of power for the Communists but without the Party.'

While it was in the old Party's interest to enhance the role of the President during the period of transition, the post–communists are now committed to a parliamentary, cabinet-based system. How the SLD–PSL coalition government deal with the Presidency depends on a number of factors. Undoubtedly an important one is how useful Walesa can make himself to the new government. Bogdan Borusewicz says the situation is very clear: 'Walesa either gets a relationship going with Pawlak and Kwasniewski – with the new government – or he gets wiped off the political map because they'll make a new Constitution, redefine everything and then there'll be an election in two years. But he's clever and he can be useful to them right now.'

Over and over again politicians and political commentators, when asked for an assessment of Walesa, remarked that there was a massive difference between what he says and what he does. There seems to be a consensus that his oratory is a potential danger to democracy but that his deeds are generally of a moderate disposition. It appears that most Poles take Walesa's talk of going down the Yeltsin road with a pinch of salt.

Despite the many controversies, the allegations and the personal struggles, Bronislaw Geremek is convinced of the importance of Lech Walesa's historical role: 'I am absolutely sure that Walesa is an historical figure. His role in the creation of Solidarity and in the survival of Solidarity during the repression and after martial law was tremendous and fundamental. Also he played an important symbolic role during the process of liberation from Communist rule in Eastern Europe. Lech Walesa's role was enormous, it was emblematic in the sense that the worker which was the whole basis of the communist regime was, in the end, the very killer of this regime. I have the feeling that the collapse of Communist rule was inevitable for many reasons. There was the economic collapse and the interantional situation in which the Soviet Union was no longer able to play its superpower role. But the crucial role was played by the revival of the civil society in our country. That means the independent activity of the people, their awareness of the possibility of activity which was separate from communist society. Lech Walesa was a man who saw the importance of such independent activity. He had enough courage and imagination to start a strike in 1980, to begin Solidarity and finally in 1989 to ask for

Round Table talks. On the one hand Lech Walesa can be treated as a symbolic person of this process. On the other hand, he played a crucial role because of his personal qualities. In my opinion his individual role was tremendous. And behind him there were thousands of workers and intellectuals who were doing the same thing. It was the conjunction of the role of Walesa and the leaders of other resistance movements in various communist countries with the social situation and economic and military collapse in the Soviet Union which was the origin of this process. But now the *anciens combattants* cannot be considered seriously. The Solidarity times are over.We have a normal political situation in which we cannot play with the merits of the past. We have to build a modern state apparatus, a market economy. The merits gained in the struggle against Communism is now only a chapter in our history. But Mr Walesa is different. There is the question of charisma. Can a charismatic leader become President? Can he lead the country? I don't know. But what of his role now after this post-communist victory and in this new Presidential campaign. What will he do? He knows that his popularity is over and now he must build up a new image if he is to get support. What way will he do this: nobody knows.'

12

THE PEOPLE'S VERDICT

The 19 September 1993 election returns 303 post-communist deputies to the Sejm.

On the night after the announcement of the new cabinet, Marek Balicki, the outgoing Deputy-Minister of Health, sipped Jameson in Jan and Krystyna's flat. That afternoon the new Minister of Health, Jacek Zochowski, a former communist and onetime physician to General Jaruzelski, had made a courtesy visit to the Health Ministry. His message to an expectant staff was somewhat terse: 'Do nothing until I come back on Thursday.' It is difficult to describe the atmosphere in that small flat, because nobody felt sure whether they were at a wake for the remains of all that Solidarity had fought for or whether Solidarity in defeat had nurtured a natural democratic process which had on this particular occasion brought victory to the former enemy. In reality there was but one question on everyone's mind: could the leopard be trusted to change his spots? It wasn't long before the balance of opinion began to shift towards a negative view after Jan heard by telephone that the new head of the Council of Ministers' office, Michal Strak (from the Peasants Party) had written to all the voivedships (local councils) telling them to stop the process of decentralization and administrative reform. 'And so it starts,' mused Krystyna as she pummelled the pastry for our *pieroggi* supper.

So why is it that four years after the world celebrated the fall of communism in Eastern Europe and the peaceful victory of Solidarity post-communist parties hold 303 in the 460-seat parliament. In victory the deputy leader of the SdRP in Warsaw, Professor Jerzy Wiatr, is scathing in his analysis of four years of Solidarity-bred government: 'The electorate voted against Solidarity for many reasons. Obviously the state of the economy was a powerful factor in the mass frustration felt here. But there's more. The type of social structures that are emerging because of the government's policies are also a factor. There is an uneven distribution of the social cost of the transformation process. People voted not only against austerity but against the fact that forty per cent live below the poverty line and eighty per cent are worse off than they were four years ago. That's happening while a small minority enrich themselves in

a fabulous way. Decommunization is another factor. It backfired. Now
the rightwingers say that they lost the election because decommunization
was not completed. I think they lost because they damaged themselves
by trying to divide the whole nation into three categories – the good,
the worse, and the worst. The good are those who positively opposed
communism. The worse are those who did nothing and the worst are
those who supported it. The majority of the country are in the latter two
categories. So now the majority who weren't in the underground in the
eighties or political *émigrés* feel like second-class citizens. And remember
people were fired all over the place to make room for Solidarity supporters. Then there is the historical factor. They [Solidarity] presented
the post-war period as nothing but a sham, as some sort of crime which
defies the way in which ordinary Poles think about it. The ordinary Pole
does not glorify this period, nor does he villify it. The truth is somewhere in between, but by departing from the truth they lost touch with
the majority of the people. The fourth factor was of course the way
Poland was on its way to becoming a Catholic version of an Islamic
republic. Abortion was the hottest issue, but there were many other
things. Family planning, contraceptives were never as easily available
here as they were in the West, but in the last four years they became
even less available. The attack on sex education in school made its teaching a sham. We [SdRP] did write a proviso into the abortion law that
schools should teach family planning. But the Department of Education
got around that. They instructed schools to teach that chastity was the
best form of family planning. Altogether it explains why public approval
of the Church fell so dramatically and why the Catholic parties lost the
election. The fifth factor was the disarray of the post-Solidarity political
elites. And here I'm not just talking about the technical side of the new
electoral law and the fact they failed to understand how to operate it so
that they would not fall foul of the five per cent threshold. Their
disarray was much deeper. They presented an image of quarrelling factions who could not agree on anything between themselves. That's not a
very good credential for governing the country. They reduced the right-
wing slice of the cake by such quarrelling. The continuous "War at the
Top" carried a very heavy price for the post-Solidarity parties. The
essence of my analysis is that the social cost of the transformation process is only one of the components in the electorate's reaction.'

Wiatr argues that Poles did not vote for a return to communism but
for a a third way which is an alternative to both central planning and

the post-Solidarity reform recipe: 'Both the SdRP and the PSL articulated their opposition during the election and before in terms of this third road. The Liberals kept rejecting the idea and the Suchocka cabinet all said, whoever is against us is against reform. They honestly believed that there is only one pro-reform or anti-reform road. I don't believe it. I do believe in a different road and not necessarily the middle one. And there is a growing body of research in the West to support this view. If the economic transition from command to market economy is to succeed, the condition is that it is combined with an effective social policy that would protect the poor. Governments during this transition must make a choice between protecting basic income and fighting unemployment. If the minimum income (from social security) is protected, then unemployment can be tolerated.'

Poland's last communist prime minister, Mieczyslaw Rakowski, echoes Wiatr's analysis: 'Solidarity lost because it tried to build up capitalism too quickly. People here are not ready for Madame Thatcher or Reagonomics. For two generations they have lived under a completely different system. The material situation of the people dropped for the first since the War. People saw that only a few benefited from the Solidarity changes and they saw their behaviour in parliament. They saw that they were a political gang and they noted the arrogance of the new political elites. And they saw that the Church has replaced the Communist Party. In every town now the priest is the real power. An anti-clerical feeling is growing year by year. In 1989 they voted against us, but they didn't vote for the priest to replace the first secretary. The episcopate has shown a huge appetite. There has been a wave of claims for former property, buildings etc. and they have shown a huge appetite for controlling society.'

Democratic Union MP and Minister of Defence Janusz Onyszkiewicz takes a more philosophical view of the election result. He sees it in terms of a clash between expectation and reality: 'If you embark on an action which results in the change of an entire political system, it can only be achieved with the mobilization of tremendous support from the people. That support only comes when there is huge expectation. The crunch comes when the harsh reality hits home. In Poland there was a simplistic concept that democracy meant automatically prosperity. The people didn't vote for communism. That's a dead ideology. It was a combination of a protest vote and nostalgia. They voted for a myth, a myth that was cherished by the communists – the myth of security. It was the main plank of communism. There should be no crime, no unemployment. But this is the security of prison, where everyone gets three meals a day. The clash between security and freedom is inevitable. Now the people have shown that they are not prepared to accept the risks that freedom brings.'

In a somewhat more bitter analysis of Solidarity's defeat, Bronislaw Geremek acknowledges the vagaries of the new election law and the right's inability to operate it effectively: 'The new electoral law introduced a threshold of five per cent which parties must reach in order to get into the Sejm. The Democratic Union proposed another version of the system which would have introduced a half proportional representation and half majority system. But the Sejm voted for PR and the five per cent threshold. It was a tremendous change and unfortunately almost immediately the Sejm was dissolved. The parties were not prepared for this new situation. There was no realization of the importance of coalition in the new circumstances and no culture of consensus which is at the heart of coalition politics. That's the technical reason, but the most important reason was people's disappointment with the Solidarity government's policies. Peasants, pensioners and workers were all disappointed. And the big thing was the lack of a feeling of security. Three million unemployed is a tremendous phenomenon but more important was the fact that the majority of workers, some sixty-five per cent, told opinion pollsters that they could be touched by unemployment. It means that the feeling of insecurity was huge and our government was unable to convince the public that we were on the right path for future prosperity. The irony of history is that Poland is now the leading country in the process of transformation in Eastern Europe. We are the only country where the rate of growth is not only positive but is more than four per cent. But the social perception of our economic situation is still bad and we could not convince the people otherwise.'

The laconic Liberal leader Jan Krzysztof Bielecki headed the Ministry of European Integration in the Suchocka government. His party failed to cross the five per cent barrier. 'This period of the division of Polish politics into two post-communist or post-Solidarity camps is over. The people have spoken. They have shown that they want more social justice, an egalitarian approach and a better standard of living. They want politicans to stop searching for secret agents and they would like more distance between the Church and the state. We made a

tremendous number of mistakes. We showed the public a completely
fragmented political scene. All they got was tension and battles,
whereas the Democratic Left Alliance (SLD), a coalition of some
twenty-eight groups, presented a united front. Of course the price of
transition was a new stratification of society. In the old Poland the coal-
miner was the vehicle of the economy. He had a privileged position.
So how do we explain the market economy to him? As he sees it, he
has lost out.' Bielecki, like Bronislaw Geremek, bitterly regrets the
inability of the Liberals and the Democratic Union to reach an election
pact and coalition agreement: 'I think that the Polish political elites are
too proud sometimes to be rational. It was not only a political error not
to coalesce with the Democratic Union: it has been a loss for Poland.
We were in a fantastic position before the election as the country leading the transformation process in Eastern Europe. We could have had
between 120 and 130 seats in the Sejm, almost a third. It's a catas-
trophe. And it is not the fault of the electoral law. I didn't envisage
this level of shortsightedness from Polish politicians.'

The *anciens combattants* know that the age of Solidarity is over. The
single goal the unifying battle against communism has been won but
the democratic path has many roads. Bronislaw Geremek sees the election result as more the defeat of Solidarity rather than the victory of
the post-communist parties. 'What is new is not only that the Solidarity
period is over but that both post-communist parties obtained a legitimacy in the democratic context. Before the election we perceived them
as the continuation of an authoritarian regime, this one-party system.
Now they have won a free and fair election and we have to wait and
see the result. Even though my party was defeated we got more votes
than in the presidential election. We have more seats. But we are
unable to find partners in this parliament because with the exception
of KPN and the BBWR the other parties are our enemies. The absence
of the right, centre right or extreme right from the Sejm changes the
situation. The SLD and the Peasants [PSL] got between them thirty-
five per cent of the fifty-two per cent of the electorate who voted. That
is not mass support but with the new election law they can take more
than sixty per cent of the seats in parliament with thirty-five per cent
of the vote.'

Mieczyslaw Rakowski accepts that the new left coalition faces the
possibility of the same kind of fragmentation that tore Solidarity

asunder. He argues that in opposition and while under attack from the right the left managed to retain a homogeneous front. For him there is no question but that the SdRP (the main party of the SLD coalition) is a social democratic party that has left its communist roots far behind: 'The new party is made up of former reformers. They were and are now social democrats and in the Polish Communist Party there was always this social democratic tradition. In simple terms this means that we accept the market economy and believe in parliamentary democracy. The leading role of the Party is gone. Now the real, pure left in Polish politics is not in our party but in the Labour Union run by Ryszard Bugaj and Zbigniew Bujak. There you will find the new edition of the old dogma.' Professor Jerzy Wiatr rejects the view that there are many unreconstructed communists in the new SdRP and dismisses suggestions that they have found cabinet places in the new coalition government. He says that the proof of the pudding is in the eating and cites the controlled response of Western governments to the Polish elections. He also argues that the initial downward move on the Polish Stock Exchange was shortlived in the days following the election and that confidence was quickly restored: 'We did a clever thing when we dissolved the PZPR [the old Communist Party] in 1990. The Bulgarians kept the old party going and they're now split. We made a surgical cut and put reformers in control. The hardliners were never able to build their own party. Now the SdRP is riding high so the hardliners are weak. We don't have a problem with control in the party. The social democrats are on top. Our real problem is that there are huge expectations from below. But the question of the trade union element of the coalition is a different story. The OPZZ [All Poland Trade Union Alliance, formed after Solidarity was banned after martial law] is the second biggest group in the coalition. They will have to live up to the expectations of their members and of course they will make demands on the government which it might be impossible to satisfy. In that situation they might form a separate parliamentary caucus in the future. But that doesn't necessarily mean that they will vote against the government. Even if they do, the PSL and the SdRP still have an overall majority. The happy outcome of the election, however, is that neither the Peasants [PSL] or the SdRP can go it alone. This means compromise. Left alone, either party would come under huge pressure from our supporters but without a controlling majority we can talk back to our supporters. So that means compromise – and not just in the economic area. The Peasants are committed to Christian values. So that means that we can't make the changes to the last government's abortion law and sex education policy as fast or as radically as we would like to. This is probably going to be good for the country. By having to compromise we will have to find a middle road. We will change the abortion law and liberalize it but being in this coalition with the PSL gives us a perfect alibi. It would have been more difficult to be moderate if we'd been in full control.'

In the run up to the formation of the new government SdRP leader Aleksander Kwasniewski looked every bit the new post-communist fully reformed and reconstucted social democrat. Following Boris Yeltsin's move against the Russian parliament, Kwasniewski withdrew any previous prevarication over Poland's entry into the NATO alliance and came out backing membership a hundred per cent. He presents a pragmatic, no nonsense image. He's young, clean cut, has been compared to actor Kevin Costner and says he keeps himself together by eschewing meat, bread and alcohol. Publicly he never fails to repeat that the SdRP voted for the Balcerowicz plan, that the reform process is not in jeopardy and that no old diehards lurk behind the nice-guy faces of the new Social Democracy of Poland. Kwasniewski certainly proved his pragmatism by stepping back and allowing PSL leader Waldemar Pawlak become prime minister. Regarded by many as a clever move it leaves Kwasniewski as the prime minister-in-waiting when and if the public become disenchanted with the government's inability to deliver on all of its election promises.

Jan Krzysztof Bielecki describes Kwasniewski as a clever politician, 'a man with a global view. Under him I could see a government lasting. But with Pawlak as PM, I'm not so sure. The PSL were able to force the issue because they knew that the SLD had to form a government and that Kwasniewski would have to compromise to get the PSL in. But the Peasants are a one-issue party. And that interest, the interest of farmers, is at odds with the interest of the rest of Poland and the people that Kwasniewski represents. The SLD faces huge problems, it's a combination of so many groups. The OPZZ trade union has seventy votes. How can they accept a tough economy or a failure to increase the standard of living?' It's hardly surprising that in the immediate post-election period the SdRP have all sung the same tune: there will be no problem delivering their election promise to give people back their security. In public Kwasniewski argues that the money to finance increased state spending will come from improved collection of customs duties and border taxes and an assault on the black or grey market. He is banking on the idea that economic growth will carry the poor segments of society along on its coat tails. However, the SdRP's new young liberal economists[1] are not so sure. Men such as Deputy Prime Minister Marek Borowski and Josef Oleksy argue that more taxes and a bigger budget deficit would be disasterous. But Professor Wiatr is convinced that the government can pull off its' election promises: 'Polish inflation is high but only high by comparison with Western countries. It is modest when compared with underdeveloped countries. A certain degree of inflation is inevitable. But if the government is making the choice between lowering inflation and maintaining its present level and improving the standard of living, social services and reducing unemployment, then from the economic and political point of view the second policy is far more preferable. There will be more money for education, medicare, pensions and indexation of the salaries of state employees. That of course means a bigger burden on the budget. And where will we get the money? First, there is a predicted increase in domestic product and that should produce more revenue. Secondly, we propose a more aggressive policy of collecting unpaid taxes and customs fees. Thirdly, our government has a new programme to improve Polish exports and, fourthly, we will change the taxation system to increase the yield from the richer categories and reduce the tax burden of the less well off. And we will introduce new exemptions for investment money.' Mieczyslaw Rakowski relies on democracy for his argument: 'The government has to change some of the economic policies introduced under the Solidarity governments because the people have voted against it. But there is no way back. Now we must find a different kind of market economy. Balcerowicz chose one way. There is no Keynesian aspect to this economic philosophy. The God now is Milton Friedman. The invisible hand of the market has been allowed to regulate everything. But in a period of massive transition from a command to a market economy the government must be seen. It must intervene. Eastern Europe will find its own place midway between capitalism and the socialist system.'

Janusz Onyszkiewicz sees the whole issue from the perspective of a laboratory where new options and formulas are being tested: 'We have already tested one formula for Polish society. That was the right wing-nationalist option of Mr Olszewski's government. That failed and was not an issue in this last election. Now we must test the view that it is possible to keep certain social programmes and security measures at the level we experienced during communist times. This, I believe, is a myth which I hope will be disproved. I hope that there won't be much damage during the testing process. I do hope that this new government will realize that their election promises, if delivered, will ruin the economy. I do have a certain conviction that they'll behave rationally. Already one can see their attitude. I hope they'll see that the reforms of the last four years must be carried on, that the basic line must be kept.' Onyszkiewicz points out that every government since Mazowiecki's has claimed that it 'would be the government of the breakthrough. But in fact each successive government has turned out to be one of continuity. So I hope that this government will also be one of continuity.'

One potential area for the exhibition of consensus politics is in the atitude the coalition takes to the drafting of the new constitution. Though the SdRP is firmly committed to a parliamentary and cabinet-led system of government and therefore favours a reduction in the current level of powers of the office of the President, the SdRP is likely to modify its stance given its need for President Lech Walesa's support. Jan Litynski guesses that 'they'll be careful about doing anything too quickly with the constitution. I think they might trade the issue for Walesa's support.' Jerzy Wiatr appears to hint at a deal: 'It will be dealt with slowly. Of course there are legal mechanisms which specify certain time periods in between each change to the constitution. But there are also political reasons for not changing the constitutional role of the President too early. We don't want to change the terms under which President Walesa completes the last two years of his term of office. It would be wrong and politically stupid to change the terms before his term is over. The ideal time would be to have it changed and adopted coming near the end of the current term so that he and anyone who runs for the Presidency knows what it is they are running for. What we want is a strong parliamentary cabinet style system where the President is a moderator but not a co-equal partner. The Democratic Union and the Labour Union agree on this so it will be changed.'

Bronislaw Geremek says it is unfortunate that the new constitution was not adopted much earlier: 'This new government can vote a con-stitution with no problem. Will they propose changes that accept democratic principles and respect human rights and political pluralism? We don't know. They are proposing to hold a referendum on concrete

constitutional issues and we are against this. We favour a general referendum asking the people to accept a complete constitution. I don't
believe that individual constitutional issues can be dealt with separately
in such a political climate. I hope that there will be pressure on the
new government to put a constitution to the people. I have the feeling
that the SLD and PSL are ready to accept a consensus on this issue.

'However, I think that the issue of the constitutional role of the
President is still open. The campaign for the presidential elections will
begin very soon; in some ways it has already begun. I don't think that
the SLD know what their strategy is yet – whether they will propose a
candidate or not. It is possible that they are still thinking of a return to
the old system whereby the National Assembly elects the President.
My own feeling is that it's difficult to take back a right once it has been
given to the people.'

It is ironic that Poland's first social democratic government probably
faces the same kind of identity seeking struggle from which the post-
Solidarity parties are gradually emerging. Both sides originating with
a strong sense of what they were against must in victory embrace
diversity and political and philosophical clarification. When the post-
communists pass through their inevitable period of flux it is possible
that Poland's political parties will be closer to a comprehensible clas-
sification based on political, economic and programmatic criteria.

Casting a cold but by no means malevolent eye on the new government's future, Janusz Onyszkiewicz points out the many comparisons
between Solidarity in 1989 and the post-communists in 1993: 'This
government will have to face what we experienced. The SLD is a
coalition of more than twenty groups. I think that it will undergo a
process which we know from our Solidarity days. This is the process of
fragmentation and of diversification. Until now they were kept together
by a certain external pressure. They were isolated and ostracized and so
the only way to survive was to keep together. Within that coalition they
have groups that represent orthodox communists and people who are
modern social democrats. This process of fragmentation is most obvious if you look at their trade union element. The OPZZ have made
it quite clear that they are giving the government half a year and then
they'll see what their attitude will be. That's exactly the attitude
adopted by the Solidarity Trade union to the Democratic Union and
other political parties. The result might be a reshuffle in the political
scene because if the process of diversification within the SLD goes on

there could be a situation where groups that we [Democratic Union] find it very difficult to accept will be dropped out of the coalition altogether and then groups who do look like potential partners for us may emerge.' So while not prepared to state it directly, there is an inherent acceptance in what Onyszkiewicz is saying of the possibility of the coming together of the liberal wing of the post-communists and elements of the Democratic Union: 'Our parties are still in the process of finding their identities. The Polish political scene has not yet reached a stable political shape.'

Journalist Jacek Majiarski describes himself as a Christian Democrat. Formerly a Centrum Alliance MP and close ally of the Kaczynski brothers, he too predicts a narrowing of the gap between the Democratic Union and the SLD: 'I think that the SLD will adopt policies quite close to that of Unia [DU]. But the Peasants won't. They are not rational and their view of the world is anti-European and anti-progressive and agrarian. A marriage between the PSL and the SLD won't last long. In the last Sejm, Unia and the SLD were very close. The privatization programme was the deciding moment. If the last parliament was still going there could well have been an SLD-Unia coalition. All the cards are being shuffled.'

With only six parties surviving the September '93 election, it is obvious that much political activity will be extra-parliamentary. Though the Centrum Alliance failed to make the threshold as did the Christian National Union (ZChN) there's no doubt that there is a Christian Democratic constituency awaiting consolidation. Because of the personality-based nature of the divisions within political parties it is likely that the tendency for politicians to slip between this or that wing of opposing parties will continue for some time. Bronislaw Geremek sees it as the golden opportunity for his party to take the centre ground: 'Unia must transform itself into a big centre party. It should be open to the left and the right. At the moment we are limited to the intelligentsia and to the small middle class. In order to become a big party we should organize and mobilize some big social milieu. But what kind of milieu: that's the question.' Looking at the wider political scene Geremek is somewhat pessimistic: 'I don't see an easy evolution away from fragmented politics. I'm afraid I see a very fragile democracy and political culture. It is much easier to attain freedom and easier to build the first democratic institution than to form a democratic mentality. I feel that political parties are still badly needed here. This image of quarrelling parties and a quarrelling parliament is used against democracy and against democratic institutions. I think that the new election law will put pressure on the parties to form coalitions and bigger parties. But each group must begin to think in terms of projects and programmes for the future and not just slogans. We must forget our personal biographies. In this sense then we are on the path to the rationalization of Polish politics but it will take time.'

As I have argued earlier, much of the Polish public's response to the huge process of transformation has been coloured by an expectation that would contrast starkly with reality. That expectation was encouraged by an applauding West awakened out of its cynicism by images such as the fall of the Berlin Wall and the figure of the moustachioed and feisty electrician who climbed another wall and reclaimed his nation's democratic heritage. But then the images died away and the story became more complex and the West left the heroes it had feted to fulfil the people's expectation alone. Piotr Nowina Konopka was chairman of the European Community Commission in the last parliament. He argues that the lack of Western and European support was a key factor in the political collapse of Solidarity: 'The West has not understood what happened in Eastern Europe. It is my deep conviction that it has not been understood that the changes in Lithuania, Russia, Czechoslovakia required an adequate response, and it has not yet come. In Poland there'll be no revival of communism. We've gone too far for that. But that is not the case in Lithuania, Ukraine and Russia. The military powers within Russia are a potential danger for a united Europe. The great chance for Europe was if Western Europe made an effort to engage itself in the process of change here in Poland, in the Czech Republic, in Slovakia and in Hungary in order that other Eastern European countries would be encouraged to follow the route of reform. It hasn't happened.' Jan Krzysztof Bielecki states the issue baldly: 'The psychological opinion of the people is that they've been betrayed by the West.' For Janusz Onyszkiewicz it is a simple conflict between rhetoric and action: 'I think we had a lot of verbal support but as for practical support we do blame the West for keeping the markets closed to us. After all we lost the markets in the East and now there is a huge deficit in our trade with the EC. We have to compensate for that somewhere. The barriers that were raised against our exports to the European Community are very painful for us. It doesn't fit in with the rhetoric of openness which sees us as future members of the Community.'

For an *ancien combattant* such as Bronislaw Geremek, imbued with a sense of Poland's place as a nation firmly ensconced in European culture, the West's failure to embrace his country has been a bitter blow: 'I feel that the West's response to the challenge of 1989 was always unclear and weak. Now there are some governments and politicians trying to propose a strategy towards Eastern Europe. It's four years too late. And now when I see projects, talk of a kind of Marshall Plan for Central Europe, I feel that four years ago it could have been a vision for the future of our countries. But now not only Poles but Czechs, Hungarians, Slovaks and Bulgarians are disappointed and angry, and now they don't trust the West. And that's a big change in the situation when you think of the enthusiasm in which in 1989 we all celebrated our return to Europe and European civilization. We invested our hopes in this European integration. Now political parties here can use anti-European feelings and slogans in our society.'

NOTES

CHAPTER 1

1 Norman Davies, *God's Playground*, (Clarendon Press, Oxford, 1981), p. 509.
2 Ibid., pp. 544–5.
3 The sixteen had been invited to Moscow for talks and were then abducted and put on trial.
4 Czeslaw Milosz, *The Captive Mind*, (Penguin, London, 1980), pp. 235–6.
5 Teresa Toranska, *Oni* (Collins Harvill, London 1987), p. 129.
6 Edward Ochab quoted in *Oni*, op. cit., p. 80.
7 Ibid., p. 196.
8 Czeslaw Milosz, *The Captive Mind*, op. cit., p. 54.

CHAPTER 2

1 Daniel Singer, *The Road to Gdansk*, (Monthly Review Press, New York 1981), p. 233.
2 *Irish Times*, 2 September, 1980
3 Timothy Garton Ash, *The Polish Revolution* (Granta Books, London 1991).
4 Coup of May 1926.
5 Edward Gierek went to Gdansk in January 1971 during the workers' revolt and won them over with his promise of change.

CHAPTER 3

1 For more on how the underground worked, see Chapter 4.
2 *Sunday Tribune* (Dublin), 2 July 1989.

CHAPTER 4

1 Neal Acherson, *The Struggles for Poland* (Pan Books, London, 1988), p. 217.
2 It is not normal to have an open fire in a Polish flat.

3 See Chapter 10, which is primarily based on interviews with the Polish primate Josef Glemp and theologian Josef Tischner.

CHAPTER 5

1 The Round Table was split up into various specialist committees dealing with political, economic, constitutional and other areas.
2 The theory that allowed one socialist country to interfere to protect the socialist interest of another country.
3 Influential KOR leader, editor of *Gazetta Wyborcza* and then a newly elected MP.
4 Timothy Garton Ash, *The Polish Revolution*, op. cit., p. 366.
5 I have not altered the above pen-picture in the light of the post-communist victory because I believe it is an accurate view of Rakowski's own analysis of the Party's defeat at the time.

CHAPTER 6

1 Known as 'kingmakers', the twin brothers were, until the end of 1991, two of Walesa's key advisers. As Centrum Alliance leader, Jaroslaw Kaczynski led the anti-Walesa camp. His party failed to make the five per cent threshold and has no seats in the Sejm following the September '93 post-communist election victory.
2 ZChN, quoted in *Warsaw Voice*, 10 May 1992.
3 Minister for EC Integration in Suchocka's government.

CHAPTER 7

1 *Warsaw Voice*, 2 February 1992.
2 Ibid., 31 May 1992.

3 Ibid., 14 June 1992.
4 Ibid.
5 Ibid
6 Lech Walesa, *Path of Hope*, first published in Britain by Collins Harvill in 1987.
7 Jerzy Ciemniewski, Professor of Constitutional Law at the Institute of Legal Sciences of the Polish Academy of Sciences and also a Democratic Union Deputy.
8 *Warsaw Voice*, 28 June 1992.
9 Ibid., 26 July 1992.
10 Ibid., 24 January 1993.
11 Ibid., 7 February 1993.
12 Ibid., 9 August 1992.

CHAPTER 8
1 *Warsaw Voice*, 24 May 1992.
2 Quoted from *The Times* of 22 February 1982 in T. Garton Ash, *The Polish Revolution*, op. cit., p. 257.
3 Polls published in *Prawo i Zycie*, 14 December 1991. Fifty-six per cent said introduction of martial law legitimate. Fifty per cent thought that Jaruzelski acted to avoid Soviet intervention, while sixteen per cent thought he acted to prevent the disintegration of the state.
4 All quotations from General Jaruzelski's books taken from *Warsaw Voice* of 24 May 1992.

5 Norman Davies, *God's Playground*, op. cit., p. 29.
6 *Warsaw Voice*, 24 May 1992.

CHAPTER 9
1 Marshall Dmitri Yazov, Soviet Minister of Defence.

CHAPTER 10
1 Timothy Garton Ash, *The Polish Revolution*, op. cit., p. 213.
2 Ibid., p. 280.
3 Quoted in *Warsaw Voice*, 10 May 1992.
4 Ibid.
5 Interview with Bishop Adam Lepa in *Warsaw Voice*, 10 May 1992.
6 Quoted in *Warsaw Voice*, 29 November 1992.
7 Ibid., 3 January 1993.
8 Ibid., 13 December 1992.
9 Ibid., 10 May 1992.
10 Ibid., 10 January 1993.

CHAPTER 11
1 *Irish Press*, 14 March 1981.
2 Roger Boys in an article in *Warsaw Voice*, 21 June 1992. See Chapter 7 for details on Bolek.
3 *Warsaw Voice*, 3 May 1992.

CHAPTER 12
1 Marek Borowski resigned his post in February 1994.

CHRONOLOGY

1939	23 August	Nazi-Soviet Union Non-Aggression Pact
	1 September	Germany invades Poland
	17 September	Soviet Union invades Poland. Poland divided for the fourth time.
1940		Murder of Polish officers in Katyn Forest
1943	April	Warsaw Ghetto Uprising
1944	August–October	Warsaw Uprising
1944–5		Liberation and occupation by Soviet and Polish armies. Provisional Government installed after February 1945 Yalta Agreement is signed.
1945–7		Civil war between pro and anti-Soviet-Communists.
1948		Polish United Workers' Party (PZPR) established.
1949–55		Stalinism dominates PZPR.
1956	June	Poznan Workers' Uprising.
	October	The 'Polish October.' Wladislaw Gomulka reappointed Party leader. Soviets invade Hungary.
1968	March	Violent repression of student protests and anti-Semitic campaign and purge.
	August	Warsaw Pact forces invade Czechoslovakia.
1970	December	Food price rises lead to workers' protests which are suppressed violently on the Baltic Coast.
1971	February	Edward Gierek replaces Gomulka as Party leader.
1976	June	Workers' protests precipitated by food price rises lead to strikes and violence in Radom and Ursus.
	September	Workers' Defence Committee—KOR is formed.
1978	October	Cardinal Karol Wojtyla, Archbishop of Cracow, is elected Pope John Paul II.
1979		Pope John Paul II visits Poland.
1980	July	Workers' protests across Poland.
	14 August	Beginning of strike at Lenin Shipyard in Gdansk.
1981	19 March	Three Solidarity activists are beaten in Bydgoszcz. Bydgoszcz Crisis begins.
	28 May	Cardinal Wyszynski dies.
	7 July	Bishop Josef Glemp named as new Primate.

	4 November	Meeting between General Jaruzelski, Archbishop Glemp and Lech Walesa.
	1 December	Warsaw Pact Defence Ministers meet in Moscow.
	3 December	Radom meeting of Solidarity's Presidium and regional chairman.
	11–12 December	Solidarity's National Commission meeting in Gdansk.
	13 December	General Jarulzelski declares martial war.
1982	22 April	Solidarity's underground Temporary Co-ordinating Commission (TKK) is formed.
	October	Solidarity is legally dissolved.
1984	19 October	Father Jerzy Popieluszko abducted and killed by secret police associates.
1985	11 March	Gorbachev becomes general secretary of the Communist Party of the Soviet Union.
	May–June	Trial begins in Gdansk of Wladislaw Frasyniuk, Adam Michnik and Bogdan Lis.
1986	11 September	General Amnesty of political prisoners.
	29 September	Lech Walesa forms Temporary Council of Independent Self-Governing Trades Union 'Solidarity.'
	6 December	General Jarulzelski forms Consultative Council.
1988	April–May	Wave of strikes in Solidarity strongholds.
	August	Another round of strikes.
	31 August	Meeting between Lech Walesa and General Kiszczak. First discussion of possibility of Round Table talks with Solidarity.
	29 September	Mieczyslaw Rakowski becomes prime minister.
	18 December	Walesa establishes Citizens' Committee.
1989	10 January	Plenum of Central Committee of Communist Party agrees in principle to relegalization of Solidarity.
1989	6 February	Round Table begins
	17 April	Solidarity reregistered as a trade union.
	4 June	Election gives Solidarity 99 out of 100 seats in the senate and 35% of the seats in the Sejm, the 35% being the agreed maximum figure at Round Table.
	24 August	Veteran Solidarity adviser, Tadeusz Mazowiecki appointed prime minister.
	12 September	Grand Coalition formed with four communist ministers.
	December	Parliament agrees to the passage of the 'Balcerowicz plan'. The economic transformation begins.
1990	24 June	Break-up of the Citizens' Committee.
	9 December	Lech Walesa elected President of the Republic of Poland.
1991	4 January	Liberal Leader Jan Krzysztof Bielecki becomes Poland's second post-communist prime minister.

	27 October	57% of Polish electorate abstain in election. Of the 120 parties active, 29 gain seats in the Sejm. Democratic Union 51 seats, Democratic Left Alliance (post-communists) 49 seats, Centre Alliance (PC) 44 seats, ZChN 49 seats, KPN 51 seats, Polish Peasant Party 48 seats.
	6 December	After long delay Jan Olszewski, a member of the Christian Democratic faction of PC (Centre Alliance) and a former Solidarity lawyer critical of of the free market reforms is named prime minister.
	17 December	Olszewski resigns but following a vote of confidence he forms a centre-right coalition government which includes The Centre Alliance, ZChN, Polish Peasant's Party, and the Christian Democrats.
	December	This month also sees the conclusion of negotiations for Poland's associate membership of the EC.
1992	4 June	Jan Olszewski's government ousted amid rumours of military coups and accusations of secret police links that reached as high as President Walesa.
	5 June	Polish Peasant Party leader Waldemar Pawlak is named prime minister by President Walesa. Faced with the prospect of losing power various post-Solidarity parties bury their differences and support the candidacy of the Democratic Union's Hanna Suchocka.
1992	8 July	Hanna Suchocka forms a coalition government with the support of seven parties. The participating parties are: Democratic Union, Liberal Democratic Congress, Polish Economic Programme, Christian National Union, Peasant Alliance, Peasant Christian Party and the Christian Democrat's Party.
1993	31 May	Poland's first democratically elected parliament is dissolved after vote of no confidence orchestrated by Solidarity's Sejm representatives.
1993	19 September	Election victory for post-communists— SLD Democratic Left Alliance 171 seats; PSL Polish Peasants' Party 132 seats; Democratic Union 74 seats; Unia Pracy Labour Union (post-Solidarity social democrats) 41 seats; KPN Confederation for an Independent Poland 22 seats; BBWR Nonpartisan Reform Support Bloc 16 seats. German minority organization 4 seats.
	25 October	PSL leader and Prime Minister Waldemar Pawlak names his SLD-PSL coalition cabinet.

ABBREVIATIONS

AK	Armia Krajowa: Home Army. Underground resistance formed in 1941 under the command of the Polish government in exile in London.
AP	Polish Army, subordiante to Soviet Command.
BBWR	Nonpartisan Reform Support Bloc (pro-Walesa group set up prior to 1993 election).
KIK	Kluby Inteligencji Katolickiej: Clubs of the Catholic Intelligentsia
KLD	Kongres Liberalno-Demokratyczny: Liberal Democratic Congress.
KOR	Komitet Obrony Robotnikow: Workers' Defence Committee
KPN	Confederacja Polski Niepodlegtej: Confederation for an Independent Poland.
MKS	Miedzyzakladowy Komitet Strajkowy: Interfactory Strike Committee
MO	Milicja Obywatelska: Civil Militia(police)
NSZZ	Niezalezny Samorzadny Zwiazek Zawadowy: Independent Self-Governing Trades Union.
OPZZ	All Poland Trade Union Alliance (set up after Solidarity was made illegal – now part of SLD coalition)
PC	Porozumienie Centrum: Centre Alliance.
PPS	Polska Partia Socjalistyczna:Polish Socialist Party (1892–48)
PSL	Polish Peasant Party formed after dissolution of ZSL:United Peasant Party which from 1949 was the 'Party's' coalition partner.
PZPR	Polska Zjednoczona Partia Robotnicza: Polish United Workers' Party (1948–1990 – the 'Party')
ROPCiO	Ruch Obrony Praw Czlowieka Obywatela: Movement for the Defence of Human and Civil Rights.
SB	Sluzba Bezpieczenstwa: Security Service, known as UB, the pre-1956 acronym, and popularly called Ubeks.
SdRP	Socjaldemokracja Rzeczypospolitej Polskiej: Social Democratic Party of the Republic of Poland (post-communist party formed after the dissolution of the PZPR – the 'Party')
SLD	Democratic Left Alliance – coalition of post-communist groups.
UD	Unia Demokratyczna: Democratic Union or Unia for short.
UP	Unia Pracy: Labour Union
ZChN	Zjednoczenie Chrzescijansko-Narodowe: Christian National Union.
ZOMO	Zmotoryzowane Oddzialy Milicji Obywatelskiej: Motorised Units of Civil Militia (riot police)

BIBLIOGRAPHY

Amalrik, A. *Will the Soviet Union Survive until 1984?* (Allen Lane, London, 1970).

Ascherson, Neal. *The Polish August: The Self-Limiting Revolution* (Allen Lane, London, 1981).

Ascherson, Neal. *The Struggles for Poland* (Michael Joseph, London 1987).

Blazuca, George and Rapacki, Ryszard. *Poland into the 1990s* (Pinter Publishers, London, 1991).

Brogan, Patrick. *Eastern Europe 1939–1989: The Fifty Years War* (Bloomsbury, London, 1990).

Carter, Stephen. *Russian Nationalism* (Pinter Publishers, London, 1990).

Davies, Norman. *God's Playground. A History of Poland*, 2 vols. (Clarendon Press, Oxford, 1981).

Dobbs, Michael, and others. *Poland, Solidarity, Walesa* (Pergamon Press, Oxford, 1981).

Garton Ash, Timothy. *The Polish Revolution* (Jonathan Cape, London, 1983).

Gwertzman, Bernard and Kaufman, Michael T. *The Collapse of Communism* (New York Times Company, New York, 1990).

Jones, Lynn. *States of Change: A Central European Diary. Autumn 1989* (Merlin Press, London, 1990).

Kaufman, Michael T. *Mad Dreams, Saving Graces. Poland: A Nation in Conspiracy* (Random House, New York, 1989).

Lewis, Jonathan and Whitehead, Phillip. *Stalin: A Time for Judgement* (Methuen, London, 1990).

McShane, Denis. *Solidarity: Poland's Independent Trade Union* (Spokesman, Nottingham, 1981).

Milosz, Czeslaw. *The Captive Mind* (Martin Secker & Warburg, London, 1953).

Morrison, John. *Boris Yeltsin* (Penguin, London 1991).

Ruane, Kevin. *The Polish Challenge* (BBC, London, 1982).

Singer, Daniel. *The Road to Gdansk* (Monthly Review Press, New York, 1981).

Sword, Keith, *The Times Guide to Eastern Europe: The Changing Face of the Warsaw Pact* (Times Books, London, 1990).

Toranska, Teresa. *ONI: Stalin's Polish Puppets* (Collins Harvill, London, 1987).

Walesa, Lech. *A Path of Hope: An Autobiography by Lech Walesa* (Collins Harvill, London, 1987).

Weschler, Lawrence. *The Passion of Poland* (Pantheon Books, New York, 1982).

Zamoyski, Adam. *The Polish Way* (John Murray, London 1987).

INDEX